Consciences

—— and the Legends of The Big Game

WRITTEN AND ILLUSTRATED BY:

SUNA FLORES

Copyright © 2023 Suna Flores.

All rights reserved. No part of this book may be reproduced, stored, or transmitted by any means—whether auditory, graphic, mechanical, or electronic—without written permission of both publisher and author, except in the case of brief excerpts used in critical articles and reviews. Unauthorized reproduction of any part of this work is illegal and is punishable by law.

This is a work of fiction. Names, characters, places and incidents either are the product of the author's imagination or are used fictitiously, and any resemblance to any actual persons, living or dead, events, or locales is entirely coincidental.

ISBN: 979-8-89031-631-8 (sc)
ISBN: 979-8-89031-632-5 (hc)
ISBN: 979-8-89031-633-2 (e)

Library of Congress Control Number: 2023904684

Because of the dynamic nature of the Internet, any web addresses or links contained in this book may have changed since publication and may no longer be valid. The views expressed in this work are solely those of the author and do not necessarily reflect the views of the publisher, and the publisher hereby disclaims any responsibility for them.

One Galleria Blvd., Suite 1900, Metairie, LA 70001
(504) 702-6708

Contents

An Introduction v

Legend I

The Book of Amos 3
    The Early Game Record 6
    Special Clay 14
    Spirit Fans 17
    The Drop 22
    The Pledge 24
    The Rescue 27
    The Discovery 31
The Cavemen 35
A Civilized Game? 43
The Others 45
Small Players 53
Game Royalty 58
Afternoon Delight 60
Royal Judgment 63
Miserable Monarchs 68
The Rodent Rally 76
Lemonade Plans 92

Legend II

The 2nd Quarter 105
More About the Scraps 105
The Fireflies and the Queen 118
The Rescue 128
Remorse and Inspiration 131
The Great Fire 136

The Morning After 141
The Royal Yesmen 151
After the Yesmen 160
After The Great Fire 164
The Book of Moses 174
The Gift 183
The New Prince 191

Legend III

The 3rd Quarter Begins 196
Abandoned Scraps 198
The Search for Scrap Real Estate 202
The Sew 206
More Solutions Needed 209
Prince Sol, the early days 211
The Safety Issue 216
The Pain of Small 217
The Change 218
Freedom 220
The Reveal 223
Figuring it Out 225
The New Wave 229
Lessons 230
Breaking Rules 243
Training, Mouse Style 244
The Game Heats Up 250
Fighter's Stance 254
Pining for Goodness 256
The Wretcheds 259
After King Heart 269
Enter Awake 276
The Book Hunter 284
The Brothers 286
Fighter's Coaching Scores 300
Brood Returns 305

Legend IV

The Heroes Arrive 311
Success! 318
Confrontation 322
The Plot Thickens 327
The Drawer 331
The Glory Story 333
The Big Sell 335
Where is Spirit? 342
Meanwhile, Back at the Castle 343
Stranded 347
Roots and Revelation 353
Trouble at the Gate 359
Back in Town 368
Prince Sol and the Hall 371
Confronting Misery 376
The Conscience Army 379
The New Plan 381
Frustration 383
Where are They? 385
The Big Game is On—or is it War? 391
Insurrection- the Final Play 395
Doomsday Begins 407
The Goal Line Stand 408
The Handshake 412

An Introduction

What is a Conscience? Before you decide to read four Legends about Consciences, it is probably a good idea to think about what Consciences are and whether or not they are real.

According to the dictionary, "a Conscience is an **inner voice** acting as a guide to the rightness or wrongness of one's behavior." That is pretty easy to understand and probably even important.

Throughout time, some very famous people have recorded that they did "the right thing" because their Conscience told them to do it... or *not* to do it. History relates that Lincoln freed the slaves because his Conscience dictated that he must.

His *Conscience told him?* ....*Yes.*

That *real* history indicated to me that Consciences are both real *and* important, but the dictionary definition of Consciences was inadequate. It spoke of an "inner voice acting as a guide" but it never indicated **whose** voice it was or **how** that voice got in contact with a human.

When I was a child, my parents told me 'let your Conscience be your guide'. I just assumed that there had to be someone inside me or at least nearby, someone who was smarter than I was and could help me figure out what was right or wrong to do.

When I saw the movie, "Pinocchio", I loved it, but I was confused. Pinocchio's Conscience was a *bug*. I had never seen my Conscience, but I was sure that *my* Conscience wasn't a bug. I envisioned someone more like myself but smaller and able to change position so quickly that he or she couldn't be seen. As I grew up, however, I stopped giving that much thought.

Lately, as people around the world seem to be losing track of the ability to tell right from wrong, I decided to think about it again. It might be easier for all of us humans to talk to our Consciences and make good decisions with their help if we knew more about them and how they came to be.

Fortunately, after some research, I discovered the Legends. That discovery is the reason for this book. The following 'fantasy' relates their complete history of the origin of Consciences and the way they came to be part of our lives.

Even though *I* believe in Consciences, the Legends presented here are called 'a fantasy'. That is probably because some chapters were written by mice. Others were written by Scraps, a wonderful species that will be introduced within Legend I. The reason to read works from these authors is simple: both mice and Scraps are very intelligent and these Legends are *their* history.

Suna Flores

PS: Mice think and write in rhyme for some reason. Scraps don't.

LEGEND I

𝔗𝔥𝔢 𝔅𝔬𝔬𝔨 𝔬𝔣 𝔄𝔪𝔬𝔰

- by Amos Mouse

Time: before the world began   **Location: an empty universe**

Imagine a universe, time before time—
no beginning or ending, no rhythm or rhyme . . .
All that exists is space upon space—
no up and no down, no location, no place . . .
In this nowhere and nothing, two spirits existed.
Through black, empty space, they floated and twisted.
Nothing was happening...nothing at all...
two spirits free floating, with no rise or fall.

But an idea showed up in the mind of one.
"Something that's better than this should be done.
We should do *something useful*. We're just wasting time,
even though the air's clean and the view is sublime,"
said this lonely spirit, a grin on his face.
We could sprinkle some stars. That would spruce up this place."

"That's stupid, you moron. Who'd be here to see?
I'll just blow things up. That sounds 'useful' to me."
It was very plain that these spirits, indeed,
were not much alike, but for sure, they *did* need
a hobby or pastime or something brand new.
Their lives were just boring with nothing to do.
"Here's a thought," said the first while he drifted in space.
"We've got lots of room. How 'bout a race?
We do nothing at all with the powers we claim.
We are just useless spirits. We both share that blame.
Why don't the two of us start up a game?

"What's 'a game'?" yawned the second from his boring run.
"It's my brand new idea that has never been done.

And we could do good while we're just having fun.
We can play in the cosmos a game that would test
which one of us spirits is really the best
at improving the cosmos as a matter of pride.
'Improving the cosmos' has never been tried."

"That is a game that I know I can win,"
the second said, smirking. Let this *"Big Game"* begin.
I'll crush all the planets. They clutter the dark
just waiting to light up with only one spark.
I'll blow up all space junk to win this contest.
My explosions and chaos will show I'm the best!"

"No way!" the first shuddered. "That sounds like your style.
Brimstone and fire might be fun for a while.
But our game should *make* something that's peaceful and good
and happy, the way that all good spirits should."

"How lame," growled the second. I knew what you'd say.
I'll play your stupid game with you but if you want me to play,
whoever wins this Big Game, should get to claim a prize.
It should be something awesome so that all will realize
who is the strongest spirit, whose ideas should rule.

"I call for **"The Fate of The Cosmos!"** for the winner of this duel
and I, of course, will win this game. I will make *my* Cosmos, cool!
Useless Goodness won't have a chance when the cosmos goes my way.
Only the fires of destruction will rule each cosmic day.
And here is another cool idea in which I'll have my say:
If *I* win, *peace and 'Goodness' will* be quickly blown away!"

The first Spirit thought it over... *This should be 'just a game.*
But **this** *spirit's game plan is serious. His game is not the same*
gentle game that I thought of. I only seek something Good
to brighten life in the cosmos. At least, I thought that we could.
Goodness could bring us both happiness. I thought he understood.

*Maybe I can change his mind and make his prize more tame.
Goodness makes everyone happier. That's the prize I'd claim.*
"Yours is too big a prize," he said quietly.
Maybe we should think through this."
"This was your idea," the second scoffed. "Come on, let's just do this!
You sound like you're afraid of me. You're just afraid you'll lose.
Take my idea or I won't play. Which option will you choose?"

Spirit one wanted to appear brave and show he was not afraid
so reluctantly he said 'okay' to the game plan that was made.
The two had now decided to begin this frightening 'Game',
not for honor or pleasure, not even money or fame
but, instead, for 'The Fate of the Cosmos'. How bad could that be?
That prize would come due at the end of the
Game that neither one could see.

But . . .
as the contest began, each side took its place.
They staked out their goals in the endzones of space.
Both spirits were Players. No one would give in.
Each fought for the future they thought they could win.

Huge comets streaked by, leaving flames hot and bright
while others lit stars, spreading soft rays of light.
In the black, endless nothing, both sides rose and fell.
Which side was winning? Who knows? Who could tell?

This was the Game's start, so it needed a name.
Just for the record, it was dubbed 'The Big Game."
These spirits were haughty. Each thought he knew best.
If their prize was the cosmos, they were up to that test!
There were no snacks or bleachers, no cheerleaders there,
no scores on a scoreboard. There was no one to care
There wasn't an umpire. There was no one to say
who was cheating or not in this first field of play.
(Note from Amos)

*Only spirits were there then, so nobody knows
how the early times went or if they came to blows.
But both spirits vouch for this story I tell.
Both spirits were there, so they know the truth well.
And I've spoken with Fireflies. (You, of course, realize
the trustworthy nature of all Fireflies.)
And the teams needed names. They asked me to provide
the names that were needed to keep score for each side.
I required names because two sides were there
and I needed to keep this first Game Record fair.*

*So the Fireflies spoke up with two names that would show
the intent of each side so that history would know.
"Spirit of Good" played for Goodness to score.
"Fighter for Chaos" played for Chaos... and more.
Shorter names worked better for reporting a Game.
I used 'Spirit' and 'Fighter'. They meant just the same.
A spirit named 'Spirit' seems a bit odd to some,
but these names showed clearly where both sides came from.)*

The Early Game Record

The score was a seesaw, no winner to call.
First Fighter would light up a massive fire wall.
Then Spirit would spray the fire down with a twist
of milky white stars in a heavenly mist.

The cosmos was neutral. It chose to ignore
the Game taking place on its dark, endless floor.
But suddenly, the balance changed. What happened, isn't clear.
Fire began raining through the skies. Spirit shrunk with fear.
Fighter's Game got stronger, churning to extend
a bigger clash of cosmic fire than Spirit could defend.

Spirit's peace was fading, a very frightening trend.
Spirit must do something or his Goodness goal would end.
I need an awesome strategy to turn this Game around,
Spirit thought to himself alone, without uttering sound.
Fighter has found more Chaos. That, I see is true.
I must discover a counter move... so that's just what I'll do.
I'll change up my strategy for a Game Plan that's brand new!
This plan will show the cosmos what Spirit of Good can do!

Spirit flew into a churning hole between the light and dark.
Whirling beyond the universe, he harnessed a passing spark
and worked with greater focus than he had shown before,
making a *peaceful game ball*. "This will raise my score."

"There," said Spirit to himself. "With this ball, I'll rule.
Let's see what Fighter thinks of this. It's "Universally Cool".
I know this move will win the Game. That's what its peace is worth.
I think I'll give my ball a name. I think I'll call it 'earth'."
He fastened the ball in the cosmos to make sure it wouldn't fall

and waited for Fighter to notice his beautiful, *peaceful* ball.
Now Fighter spotted the ball.

Around the new and peaceful globe, Fighter for Chaos spun.
"This ball is useless garbage. It isn't even fun.
It clutters up the universe. Space junk isn't cool.
If Spirit thinks this wins our Game, he's just a rookie fool.
I'll blow it up in a minute while he sails off all proud.
My firestorms are worth *ten* of these. He makes me laugh out loud."

Fighter had built planets before on his own.
All *his* globes had exploded and shattered and blown.
They were built for destruction. Each one was pre-fated
to flame out in a fireball when it was created.

They didn't last long and no longer existed.
But Spirit's ball swayed where a gentle breeze misted
and quietly floated. It hung in the air
with a warm glow of promise and Goodness to share.
Fighter tried to destroy it, but it didn't destroy.
It just floated and shone like a beautiful toy.
He struck it again. Fighter grumbled and waited
for his blows to wipe out the ball Spirit created.

Fighter crept up on Spirit. *His* Game rose and fell
on tricks he could pull. He now hid himself well
and lurked close to Spirit, determined to see
just what the secret of this ball might be.
He scouted and scanned for the smallest detail
that could blow up this game ball and cause it to fail.

But, as Fighter watched, he grew grimly alarmed.
Drifting there in the mist, Spirit's peaceful earth warmed.
What Spirit had made seemed quite different and rare.
It was not blowing up. It was still shining there.
Could this 'Fighter Proof' ball change the balance of power?
Fighter got nervous, more so by the hour.

Spirit sat back. He knew he had scored.
He was no longer nervous and no longer bored.
He next made a sun and then made a moon,
then crafted the seas, sky and plants and soon,
he felt more than successful. His creations were good
and they looked cool together as he hoped they would.
The sun, moon, and earth glowed from morning through night,
lighting the skies with a Game-winning light.

"This is just what I wanted! I can finally see
a place where real Goodness can shine and be free.
With these moves, I've won!" Spirit laughed long and loud.
"I am Spirit of Good! This is righteous! I'm proud!

"And there's no Chaos on this ball. Fighter can no longer try
to replace this Good with Chaos. That move didn't fly.
Goodness, itself, has guarded this ball that I *with Goodness* made.
With this 'Good Earth' I've won the Game with the Goodness
Game I played!"

As The Big Game's first winner, Spirit thought he should
shake hands with the loser. "Sportsmanship is Good."
Besides, there was no one nearby with whom he could share
his awesome new creations. No one else was there.

So Spirit stuck out a friendly hand and waved it in the air.
"I've won this Game, Fighter. Let's hang out together.
We don't need more violence. Help me decide whether
to throw a big party! We can be friends
and invite other spirits. That's how victories should end!"
The ball *was* a beauty. Spirit *was* proud
but there was no party and there was no crowd.
Spirit felt lonely so he said so out loud.

"I now see one problem. There's no need to create this
when there's no one around to appreciate this.
Goodness is great, a fact I've always known,

but Good is not good by itself, all alone.
Good is not good if no one can see
just why Good is good. It can't be only 'me'.
"Come over here, Fighter. We can catch us some sun.
I need someone here to cheer what I have done.
If no one applauds, I won't feel like I've won.
My Good is not good by itself. It's not fun!"

Fighter couldn't believe it! What Spirit had confessed
was that his earth *wasn't Good by itself!* It had flunked the 'Winner!' test!
Fighter laughed in the darkness and growled with a sneer.
"Poor Spirit...You're lonely? Let's all shed a tear.
That means you're a loser! Don't feed me your line.
You don't get the prize 'cause it soon will be mine.

"You thought you'd be happy when your game ball was done,
but you're still sad and lonely. Is that "happiness", son?
Your earth is not Good enough. *You* haven't *won*.
We may not have rules written down...we may just be beginners,
but I can see that your ball, alone, does not make you a winner.

Fighter sailed through darkness. His counterplan was brewing.
What did stupid Spirit of Good think that he was doing?
"Spirit's "win" was premature. Why did he think that I
thought his earth was a winner?" Spirit pummeled Spirit's sky
with violent, new explosions. He would not give in.
"That's why I'm called Fighter! *That's* why *I will* win!"

With the energy of anger, he spun the earth around.
He bombed it now with meteors that tore its fertile ground.
He froze it hard and hammered it with storms from outer space,
But when, at last, the smoke had cleared, the earth still held its place.

Spirit looked at his game ball and waited all alone.
Hus earth still had its beauty that had not been undone.
"My earth is still floating peacefully. I still think I've won."

CONSCIENCES—AND THE LEGENDS OF THE BIG GAME

Now Fighter checked his options so that Spirit wouldn't know
how he still plotted to win the Game. His new plan wouldn't show.
That ball was now his target. This was now more than a Game.
Fighter became determined to earn his "Fighter" name.

Now this Game was personal. He decided here that he
would ruin *that ball* with Chaos that the universe could see.
He drew up plans for his next drive, for Chaos built on hate.
Sparing Spirit's peaceful ball was not in the debate.
The Game he had been playing was now a full-on war.
Fighter's need for victory was greater than before.

"Spirit is naive," he smirked. "He *will* know the shame,
the shame that he tried to lay on me when he said *he'd* won the Game.
Ha! One way or another, Spirit will realize
that Chaos will always conquer Good and *his* earth will be *my* prize.
Spirit can't fix his problem. He doesn't have a clue
about why he's not a winner yet or what else he should do.
I'll soon claim my victory! I'm sneaky and discreet.
My new plan is simple. I'll just use force...and cheat."

Spirit walked on his new earth with beauty on every side.
Spirit of Good looked for Goodness there that couldn't be denied.
Instead, he found a loneliness he couldn't seem to hide.
Spirit knew he hadn't won yet. A new plan must be tried.

"I don't get it!" he griped to himself. "I don't understand.
The success of my peaceful earth ball is just what I have planned.
Everything that I have made has completely gone my way.
Why is my earth not Good enough? Is there more Game yet to play?

Spirit went to a river on his earth and sat on the river's bank.
He was lonely. He wasn't happy. His creative mind went blank.

Note from Amos:
(The Fireflies, with due respect, have related
that here the young Spirit hesitated.

With this new earth, he was still perplexed,
With no clue at all of what to do next.
And the Fireflies will tell you, even up to this day,
that Spirit, not thinking, picked up some clay and,
without thought or focus, just started to play,
turning and forming it, very unplanned,
....'til a creature was there in the palm of his hand.
Fireflies observed that this live addition
in Spirit's hand was a heavenly mission
and knew that it was meant to be
that **life** *was what the earth needed to see.)*

The creature that Spirit first created,
though tiny, thin, and understated,
at once became a trial run
to show how life forms could be done.
Spirit gathered up his breath and blew it
into his hand, and before he knew it,
a living creature began to kick!
It had come alive! It was just that quick!
Spirit shouted in jubilation.
"A mouse...my very first *live* creation."

Yes, it is true that a mouse was first
and was placed near the water to quench his thirst.
Spirit watched him drinking there
and knew right away that it wasn't fair
to leave just one mouse there all alone,
a tiny bit of fur and bone.
There should be at least two.
There really ought to be two,
the lonely spirit thought.
A lady mouse for company
will help this mouse live happily.

The Fireflies sang both loud and clear
while he made a girl mouse and placed her near.
Spirit watched as the mice united

for the first time, and he was delighted.
The mice came together, side by side,
and before long, the pair had multiplied.
The 'multiplying', which then began,
became a new part of Spirit's plan.

"At last, I see what has been the need
to make my peaceful earth succeed.
It needed life! This fact seems true.
What a wonderful thing to find out! Who knew?

"Everything's different. I see now that I can
create what I need for my Goodness Plan.
Goodness and happiness now begin.
More life is the play that will bring my win!"
So Spirit made two fish to swim,
a girl fish first and then 'a him'.
He shaped birds to sing as they flew and then
a rooster and a laying hen
to lay some eggs and reveal the trick
that turns an egg into a chick.
Then he made dogs and pigs and cats
and mice that could fly—he called them bats.

Fighter churned high to view the scene
and watched his rival below, unseen
from the gray horizon, in between
what had now become the sea and sky.
What other moves would his rival try?
He scouted this flurry of 'life creating'
but found the new creatures irritating.

Fighter for Chaos now paced earth's ground.
These tactics confused him. He made no sound
but Team Good was scoring and gaining ground.
Counter measures to *'creatures'* must now be found.
As Fighter for Chaos, his defenses were frayed
by this globe filled with life that Spirit now made.

If something miraculous wasn't done,
Spirit of Good might discover he'd won.

When he finished the creatures that he'd created,
Spirit of Good still hesitated.
He looked around and what he saw
was fur and fin and wing and claw.
Animals of each kind and size
roamed freely there before his eyes.
But Spirit, strangely, could not yet to see
what his winning creation needed to be.

He had scored but, somehow, he hadn't won.
"The Big Game's not over. My work's not done.
I've made some awesome things," said he.
"But, they're not the answer I thought they'd be.
They're all good creatures, so I don't understand
why they don't spell out Goodness the way I planned."

"What I've made so far hasn't finished this war
or delivered the Goodness I'm looking for.
What final play do I need to do
to make my Goodness goal come true?
There's a missing move in this cosmic Game
and if I don't find it, I'll deserve the name,
'The Spirit of Good who can't win The Big Game'.
I must create one last creation."
He looked around for some inspiration.

Special Clay

And there they were! Fireflies in a swarm!
The sun shone down. The day grew warm.
What had the Fireflies come to show?
Why were they here now? What did they know?

Spirit noticed *something*. Was this his play?
On the shore, he spotted some Special Clay.
Just why it was special, he couldn't say,
but it beckoned in a most mysterious way.

As Fireflies hovered, Spirit thought he knew
that this Clay had his answer. Could this be true?
Would he need to make something he'd not yet made,
a masterpiece with *this Clay* displayed?

Spirit rose slowly to his feet
and studied the Clay, so smooth and sweet.
He had to think this problem through
to understand what the Fireflies knew.

At last a message sifted through:
"Good" calls for the 'judgement' of what is true.
What anyone does can be good or bad.
'Which is which' is the knowledge you've never had.
With the help of this Clay, one can judge what's good
and make good decisions the way they should.
One creature must have that understanding.
This is what your new earth will be demanding.
Create a species with this one skill.
It is in this Clay and it will fulfill
the knowledge that your earth will need
to allow Goodness and happiness to succeed.

At last poor Spirit understood
that this Clay held the answer—the **"knowledge of 'Good'!**
Without that knowledge, no one could say
what was good or bad. There was just no way.

Spirit rejoiced with this revelation
that he needed to form his last creation.
"I know now what earth's Goodness has been demanding.

I was looking for 'Good' without understanding
what made something 'Good' or 'Bad'.
This was a knowledge I never had.

"When looking for "Good", one needs to know
what is really "Good" and that knowledge must go
in the head and heart of one special creature
who will have the blessing of this great feature.

"With this Clay I will form both heads and hearts
so this creature will realize from the start
the true meaning of "Good". That will set them apart
so that they can live lives that are kind and Good.
as someone with knowledge of Goodness should.

"I will form this new creature to stand up strong
and be filled with this knowledge of right and wrong
in head and heart where such knowledge belongs.
I think I'll call this new creature Man.
Man will fulfil my Goodness Plan."

Fighter eased in between earth and sea
and crept onto the land. He geared up to see
what kind of damage he could turn loose
to wreck what Spirit might next produce.

Fighter was shrewd. Fighter was smart.
He could sense that Spirit was about to start
something new for a bold, new score
that might lead to a win in this cosmic war.

Where was *his* Chaos in this new mix?
Shrewdly, he watched for his chance to fix
and *silence* Spirit's happy tune
with a counter-offensive to quash it... *soon.*

"Fighter for Chaos is no one's fool.
'Know your enemy!' That's my rule.
If Goodness fails, Chaos will grow
and take over the universe high and low.
So I'll spy to find out what I need to know!"

Spirit Fans

However,
neither spirit could have suspected...
Spirit Fans were watching, undetected.
Behind rough rocks that were on the shore
was *the first mouse made and now many more.*
The mice fans chattered with fascination
as Spirit began his new creation.
The first mouse created and quick to grow
was a mouse named Michael Angelo.
Among all mice, he was the one
who watched more closely than anyone.

This mouse, the first mouse ever made,
was proud of his role and the part he'd played
to be the 'firstborn'. It was clear that he
took his position seriously.
Michael watched Spirit every day
and took note of his labors in every way.
He watched Spirit mold each feature
on every new and amazing creature.
With great respect, he wanted to learn
how to create like Spirit, to shape and turn.
Michael knew of the Game and wanted to be
a part of The Big Game's history.
Maybe I should ask, thought he,
if this spirit would like some help from me.

This is why I came first, I know,"
thought the mouse named Michael Angelo.
"To be *in* The Big Game—that's the reason that I
must watch and think and learn and try
to be his best and most loyal fan
until I can help him with his Game Plan."

So Michael kept watching without even a squeak.
He wanted to learn Spirit's best technique.
Maybe someday he could try it.
Until then, he would watch and be very quiet.

Spirit reached down with a careful hand
and pulled from the river some mud and sand.
With a look intense, so clear and bright
that it seemed to shine with its own bright light,
he shaped two legs to be long and straight
then a handsome body to give it weight.
He pulled it erect. He pulled it tall
to stand on two feet, not swim or crawl.

Michael watched with particular care
for this new creation seemed new and rare.

Now Spirit was building before his eyes
a unique life form reaching toward the skies!
Tall and slim the new creature stood,
though stiff, much like a stick of wood.
And just when he was almost done,
Spirit created another one.
The first humans arose beneath the sun!
Now The Big Game would *surely* be won!
Proud on the bank these creatures were,
sleek and smooth and without much fur,
smooth and clean, but it must be said
that neither creature had heart nor head.

Spirit of Good now looked around
for the Special Clay that he had found.
There it was. It was near his feet,
that Special Clay, so pure and sweet.
Spirit smiled because he knew
what this Special Clay was meant to do.
"My new creatures," Spirit said,
"will have a *special* heart and head.
Their heads must think and their hearts must love.
Of all my creatures, below or above,
their heads and hearts must do even more
than any creatures I've made before."
He held the Special Clay up high
and promised these creatures beneath the sky,

"With this Special Clay, I will give to you
the care of this world with a task that's new.
You must care for all of my new-formed earth
with minds and hearts that display your worth.
You must care for this earth as you know you should
And confront what's bad on this earth with Good.

"Into your head, I will place with care
that knowledge that makes you smart, aware.
With Special Clay, I will form your mind
with all the intelligence I can find
so that you can learn, understand, and grow
and discover the answers you need to know.

"The gift that Special Clay gives your heart
is the **knowledge**, the most important part
that discerns real Goodness from the start
and the understanding of right and wrong.
You must seek that truth and you must be strong.
This Clay is the key to your understanding
what Goodness on earth will be demanding.

No others have I made this way,
with heads and hearts of Special Clay."

Spirit picked up some of the Special Clay
and began to sculpt in a focused way.
Concentration showed upon his face
as he worked at a strong and steady pace
to complete what we now call "The Human Race."

Though some of the *Clay* that he had found
was falling unnoticed to the ground,
he just reached down to the river floor
and felt until he found some more.

Gently, gently, he formed a brow,
a brain, a chin, two eyes, and now,
a handsome face all sweet and clear
began like magic to appear.
Michael Angelo strained to see
what final touches there would be.

As Spirit worked, more Clay would drop,
but Spirit kept working. He didn't stop.
So focused on his goal was he
there was nothing else that he could see.
But Fighter heard from horizon's edge
as Spirit made his creative pledge.
Hovering, Fighter picked up the clue
and heard of the Good Spirit's plan might do.

"*This Clay is his secret!*" Fighter suddenly knew
just how he could win and what he could do.
He won't succeed when this is tried.
I'll see to that." Fighter grimly cried.
"Spirit thinks this Clay has special skills
that will correct his creatures' future ills

and steer them away from hate and wrath
to walk on his boring Goodness Path. Ha!

"Such boring Goodness will be denied.
I won't stand by in useless silence
while Spirit plans to avoid my violence.
I have heard enough. I understand.
Right now, I'll make my goal line stand."

"I see that he has found this Clay
to make heads and hearts in a special way.
My new plan will defeat this play.
With that Clay he's planning to use today,
Spirit is making a special face
with his Special Clay from its special place.
It's a simple solution! That's why it's so great.
Sabotage his Clay, and he'll lose! That's fate."

Fighter grew strong with the strength of hate.
Fighter no longer feared what was on his plate.
He knew exactly what to do.
Special Clay's promise would not come true.
Fighter's plan would work perfectly.

"This stupid creature will never be
a challenge to my Chaos curse,
bringing peace on earth or, even worse,
bringing Good to all the universe."

"Never!" he boasted. "I'll rule this day.
I'll just get rid of that stupid Clay.
I'll force a fumble and steal it away."
"Lost Clay will cause Spirit's scoring to stop.
This will go down in history. I'll call it *'The Drop'*."

The Drop

Fighter's powers caused daylight to fade.
He expected the Game to be delayed
and the Clay, in the dark, to be 'mislaid'
so the creature's heads could *not* be made.

Spirit dropped some Clay but he didn't regret it.
Fighter snuck down to the shore to get it.
"I'll pick it all up. Spirit can forget it!
But . . .

What? Oh no!

Now Fighter saw in the setting sun.
Spirit's faces and heads were already done.
Spirit had continued to create
while Fighter was boasting. He was irate.

"Drat! Don't tell me that I'm too late."

Fighter squinted to see Spirit's creatures more clear.
They were awesome creatures and standing near.
Spirit was working hard and fast, still forming the final parts.
But Fighter saw what was missing. The creatures had no hearts.

Fighter flew above Spirit and hissed a silent vow,
"Give up! *Your creations both are doomed!* You'll feel *my Chaos now!*"
He summoned all the fury that the cosmos would allow.

Fighter created a huge storm with a force unknown and new.
He called this storm 'Tornado'. It twisted, crushed, and blew!
Earth's trees were torn up from their roots. Rocks tumbled from the skies.
Spirit held his creatures tight, to shield from this surprise.

Then Fighter invented a 'Hurricane', as his cruel offensive grew.

CONSCIENCES—AND THE LEGENDS OF THE BIG GAME

The animals couldn't hold their ground as through the air they flew!
Spirit guarded his creatures. These were Fighter's tricks he knew.

But Spirit *was determined to finish* what he'd planned.
This Special Clay held the knowledge of Good that his earth would demand.
The Goodness that Spirit was working for was *dependent on this Clay*.
He *had* to keep on working. *He could not give up today!*

But Fighter wasn't finished. He forced an eclipse of the sun
that blocked the earth in blackness. *"My Chaos must be won.*
Spirit can't see how his precious Clay is melting before his eyes.
He's completely blindsided! He won't realize
that I'm taking control of The Big Game with my offense from the skies."

Fighter's vicious tactics were full-force underway.
On both sides of Spirit's worksite, there were piles of Special Clay,
but Fighter sent a storm surge, causing all to slosh away.

Spirit pushed his offense. He reached down to the land,
searching the ground that he couldn't see to find Clay in the sand.
Against a wave, Spirit doubled down and battled his mighty best.
He *must* find the Special Clay that defined each human's chest.
He wiped the wave's thrust from his face and frantically searched the ground,
braving the wind and the driving rain for the Clay that must be found.

Finally, he found it! He could feel it soft and warm.
He pulled some closer to his chest to protect it from the storm.
Ground washed away beneath him, but still he wouldn't stop.
He fell to the ground but stood again. Then it happened. It was—*The Drop!*

Into the water it tumbled, the Clay he had been holding.
Frantic, Spirit searched the ground. A nightmare was unfolding.
He rose and fell against Fighter' storms, clutching bits of Clay in his hand.
Now, Spirit finally finished the hearts...but not as he had planned.
Most of the Clay he had gathered before had *dropped* down from his hand!
The hearts he made on that fateful night were *mostly made of sand!*

The Pledge

In the storms, the tortured sun went down,
but two handsome humans now stood their ground.
They were fine to look at, a lovely sight,
though the moon was swallowed by storms that night.
Spirit felt with pride, even in that light,
that what he had made was Good and right.

But, sadly, he didn't understand
that his humans' hearts held too much sand.
He knew their heads were of Special Clay,
now ready for thinking in every way,
but neither one had a perfect heart.
Human hearts were too sandy right from the start.

Spirit thought the human hearts were good, but he couldn't see the flaw.
His humans both looked perfect. He was proud of what he saw.
Too much sand was in their hearts, but he could hear them beat,
so he had no way of knowing, that the hearts were incomplete.

Although the hearts could feel love, there was not enough to share.
The crucial knowledge of right and wrong just simply was not there
but Spirit didn't know this as he looked on with pride.
Sadly, he had no knowledge of what *was not* inside.

What a triumph it was for Fighter! *His* plan was coming true.
He had struck a blow for Chaos. He was thrilled with what he knew.

Had he ruined Spirit's creatures? Soon results would show
the imperfections of the hearts but Spirit wouldn't know
that sandy-hearted humans were his unknowing blunder.
Fighter cheered his tremendous Play with a mighty clap of thunder.

Spirit was still working. He had no way of knowing
what had happened to the hearts and Fighter's storm was blowing

his new humans in all directions. They were needing shelter
as Fighter's storm continued, raging, helter-skelter.

Spirit studied his humans. Should he find them a place to nest?
No. These humans were very smart. They'd find their own place to rest.
But first, a prideful Spirit filled his mighty chest
and blew out a joyful gust of life, his very personal best.

Into the air he happily blew
and covered them both with a life-giving dew.
He made sure his magical breath would surround
each human, (though some of it fell to the ground
and landed unnoticed where the Clay scraps lay.
(Not just any scraps. *They were all Special Clay.*)

Now the humans awakened and moved from their place.
They hugged each other, their first embrace.
Spirit smiled. He didn't know

that he'd made a mistake. It just didn't show.
So he spoke to his humans with love and pride
and a trust in the Goodness he *thought* was inside.

"The life I have given you on this day
is for humans to use in a most special way.
I pledge to you that the life I give
will be *yours and yours alone to live.*
I will watch from the cosmos and not interfere
but I expect Goodness. That's why you're here.

"You must make decisions by your own choice
between right and wrong but without my voice.
I've already given you what is best,
the Special Clay in your heads and chests.
The Goodness you show will be my real test.
You have the tools. *You* must now do the rest.
You must fight hard for Good! First develop that skill!
With these heads and hearts, I know that you will
live a life that is smart, kind and loving and true
on the wonderful earth that I've made for you.

"I'm sure Fighter knows now that he's lost the Game.
It's too bad he won't say so. That's really a shame."
Spirit's creations began to breathe. Their new lives had begun.
Spirit was smug and full of pride, content with what he'd done.
Though Fighter's storm still pounded, blocking both moon and sun,
Spirit was proud of these humans. Now his work was truly done.
He flew out into the cosmos, knowing he'd finally won.

Fighter watched from above the world.
From far overhead, he zoomed and whirled
as more celebrational storms unfurled.
"Spirit has lost!" Fighter cheered through his clouds.
"But he hasn't a clue as he sails off all proud.
There won't be much Goodness or love he can see.
Just meanness and hate, and it's all *thanks to me!*

CONSCIENCES—AND THE LEGENDS OF THE BIG GAME

"As his new world fills with hate my Chaos will be displayed,
Spirit won't guess why man is flawed or know the mistake he's made.
And though he won't know of the damage he's done,
he will have to admit what is true: I have won!"
Fighter stormed off. This wild storm was his way
to enjoy The Big Game and his triumph today.

The Rescue

Fighter's storm continued its fitful stewing.
The mice fans had stopped what they were doing
to run from the riverbank helter-skelter,
scampering off to find some shelter.

The human creatures began to stir
to escape from the riverbank. Now they were
in search of a spot that was dry and warm,
protected from Fighter's pounding storm.

Michael Angelo was a 'Spirit Fan'.
He had watched Spirit's making of Woman and Man.
He was amazed at what he saw
in Spirit's work. He found no flaw.

Sadly, he thought, *I could never do
the artistic creations that Spirit can do.
Why in the world did I ever believe
that this was a talent I had up my sleeve?*

Michael Angelo, alone, remained
on the field of the Game as the cold rain rained.
The black clouds had darkened both moon and sun
on destructive damage that had been done.

But a bolt of lightning split the night
and flushed the riverbank with light.
Michael Angelo saw clearly then
just where the human pair had been,
and he also saw with great dismay
where scraps of the Special Clay still lay.
In the storm, those pieces of Special Clay
were washing steadily away.

Spirit was gone, but he'd dropped some Clay.
His Game Plan might need to use more someday,
Maybe make something more? Who knew? Who could say?
This mouse couldn't let that good Clay wash away.

Fighter had seen the mouse but paid no attention,
mice being too small in his Game Plan to mention.

So Michael began to gather the scraps.
He wasn't quite sure, but he thought perhaps
this could be his mission, *this* could be his duty—
to protect all this Clay of such great beauty.
He would gather the pieces of Special Clay
to keep safe for Spirit to use the next day.

This was not the 'creating' he wished it could be,
but Michael was humble as a good mouse should be.
He knew, at last, just what he must do.
He was not in the Game, but he could be *ground crew*.
Michael was loyal. This new job was right.
He must rescue the Special Clay scraps now...tonight!

With his little arms full of the wet, precious stuff,
he scrambled the river rocks, jagged and rough,
slipping and sliding and stumbling his way
to find a safe spot to preserve Special Clay.

At long last, he found it, an overhung rock,
a good place to shelter his quick-melting stock.
Beneath that big rock was a place safe and dry,
a spot also hidden from those who passed by.

As the Game's only ground crew, he returned to the shore
to search for the Clay and to rescue some more.
Under its weight, he returned to his climb.
His way lit by lightning, he struggled each time.
And at last, when the Clay scraps had all been preserved,
Michael Angelo slept, a deep sleep well-deserved.

While he was sleeping, Michael Angelo dreamed
he was no longer rescuing scraps, so it seemed.
He himself was creating with the found Special Clay
and in Michael's dream, he heard himself say,
"Maybe, if I really try,
I can make some creatures too, and I
can help my cool hero with his Goodness Plan.
If I work very hard, I think maybe I can!"

From the dark of the cave, soft lights now occurred.
Fireflies were entering without a word
and swarming the spot of the cave's dampened ground
where all of the rare Special Clay could be found.

Now there was singing, mist drifting and soft,
as the Fireflies all circled and hovered aloft,
over the spot where the sleeping mouse lay
as though guarding the stash of the rare Special Clay.

In Michael's dream, it was clear to see
that the Fireflies knew instinctively
how important this Special Clay might be.
Michael dreamed of Spirit once again.
He pictured his way of creating, and then

Michael picked up some of the Special Clay
to imitate in his own way
what Spirit himself had done that day.

What was this? What was taking shape?
With molding and smoothing, with carving and scrape,
Michael was making something more,
something better than he had dreamed before.
It was a tiny human!
In Michael's dream, most real and clear,
a tiny creature began to appear.
Michael could see right before his eyes
what looked like a person but less than mouse's size!
As Michael dreamed, he first made one,
then formed one more as Spirit had done.

In his dream, Michael did pretty well,
(at least as far as a dream can tell.)
In his dream, he knew just what to do,
molding the Special Clay through and through.
Though they looked like humans in every way,
what he made was 'as small as a mouse', you could say,
and formed completely of Special Clay!
Michael Angelo checked out his creatures.
They were pretty and handsome with people-like features.
And the Fireflies swarmed overhead in the night,
bathing the two with their twinkling light,
a wondrous event of dreamed creation!
Was it real or Michael's imagination?

"What awesomeness I will someday feel
if you two turn out to be really real,"
murmured Michael, drooling beneath the rock.
He was not prepared for the next day's shock.

The Discovery

At dawn, the sun shone through the trees,
glistening and sparkling in the breeze,
revealing a day that could leave no doubt
that the bright joy of Goodness was round-about.

Michael Angelo stretched and opened his eyes.
It was only then that he realized
that the Clay he had rescued last night was gone,
stolen away before the dawn!

That Clay had been his to guard and keep.
How could he have possibly fallen asleep?
In one movement, Michael leapt
from the rocky ledge under which he slept.
He was mad at himself! Extremely mad!
How could he have slept the way he had?
He had lost that which he should have been protecting,
now ripped off without him even suspecting.

Michael stumbled down to the river and then
slumped down to think things over again.
Two other mice were sitting there too.
Maybe they could tell him what to do.

He turned to speak and then rubbed his eyes.
His little jaw dropped in complete surprise.
He was looking at people who were just his size!

They moved and yawned and then, wouldn't you know,
began smiling at Michael Angelo.
Michael squinted closely. They looked, it seems,
like the creatures that he had made in his dreams.

"No!" Michael whispered. "You can't be real!"
He reached over and pinched them. They laughed and squealed.
And suddenly, in a flash, he knew
what he had dreamed last night was true.
If his eyes could be believed,
from the scraps of Clay he had retrieved
with Spirit's breath upon them warmed,
small "scrap people" had been formed.

And here they sat in the morning sun.
Michael couldn't believe what he had done.
That Clay was for Spirit's heads and hearts,
but now it would never become a part
of anything else Spirit might have planned.
Spirit's humans would always have hearts of sand!

"Good grief!" Michael Angelo cried.
"It appears that, in my dreams I tried
to use Special Clay, making my own creatures
to imitate Spirit's humans' features.
I'm just the ground crew. It wasn't right
for me to make creatures myself last night!

"Special Clay hearts would know right from wrong,
but where do these Special Clay People belong?"

No answer came, but the river shone.
Michael stood on the riverbank all alone
and wondered with the morning sun
just what would become of what he'd done.

But there was one thing he instinctively knew.
Like Spirit, he needed to make a pledge now too.
So, to the cosmos and Spirit, he declared aloud,
"I pledge that these creatures will make you proud.
Because they were made of your Special Clay,

they are destined to do special things someday.
I know, as well as any mouse can,
that Goodness in Mankind was always the plan.
There are reasons for everything far and near,
but the use for my creatures is not yet clear.
If the time becomes right, mice will help with their mission.
Until then, we mice will await your cosmic decision."

PS—They're too small to be humans, but they're special. Perhaps, because of their makeup, can we just call them Scraps?

Sincerely,
Michael Angelo Mouse

(Keeping watch over all below,
Fireflies flew, as if to show
that there might be a plan Michael didn't know.
Had 'The Drop' been the key to a destiny
that Michael Angelo couldn't see?)

Sincerely, Amos Mouse
—faithful recorder of The Big Game History

The Cavemen

Note: The following narrative was compiled from Scrap archives

The Big Game was now continuing. Spirit and Fighter decided that they were still in the 1st Quarter of their Big Game that would have four, full quarters. The field of play had moved permanently from the cosmos to the game ball (hereafter known as earth or world).

There was a bit of discussion about this at first. Fighter didn't trust the field of play completely. "We're going to fall off. I know we're going to fall off. This thing is round, you know."

"You won't fall off, Fighter." Spirit smiled patiently. "Don't be a chicken. Look at all the animals running around on this ball. They're not falling off. Just jump on or I'll penalize you for delay of game."

"Is that a new rule?"

"Yep, I just made it up."

"Okay, I'll play the Game on your stupid game ball, but no cheating just because you made the thing."

Action was already happening among all the living things, so both spirits could see that this move from the cosmos was a good idea. The humans now became the main players in the Game just as Spirit had thought they would. Did both of the spirits approve of the way things were going on their side? Sure. They both thought they were winning.

Fighter now loved this whole 'earth idea'. He knew what he had done to the creation of human hearts. He knew Spirit's whole Game Plan depended on the humans learning to use the Special Clay in their hearts for his elusive "Goodness". He was just waiting to see Spirit's face when he discovered that he had dropped the Special Clay and Goodness just wasn't in human hearts at all. His secret was delicious.

From Fighter's point of view, this game ball was a good place to watch Spirit's Game fall apart. The results of 'The Drop' began taking their toll on Spirit's precious humans immediately. People were not developing the kindness skills that Spirit expected at all. They were vicious! Fighter couldn't wait for the humans to destroy themselves with their own natural meanness.

Spirit, although not seeing much to be happy about, was not worried, however. He was willing to allow human hearts time to mature slowly and gradually produce the kind, happy humans he was expecting. He talked about patience day after day, but mostly to himself. The only thing he was proud of was the continued use of his beautiful earth as the playing field.

To help the cause of friendly competition, Spirit even accepted Fighter's suggestion that they both become Coaches, in spite of the fact that he had pledged to not interfere with his Players. He had faith in his humans. They didn't really need a Coach. They would develop their skills by themselves in time. This was only the 1st Quarter and both coaches had decided that the Game would be played in four quarters. Fighter suspected that Spirit already knew he was going to need a lot of time...if he was going to score at all.

The first quarter of this *first* game was proceeding slowly but it was soon discovered that these Game-playing spirits had no way of scoring what was happening in their Game. Neither Spirit nor Fighter accepted that the other side had a chance of winning, of course, but ongoing success was really hard to measure. Because of the newness of the whole Game idea, they both decided that any observable 'progress' on *their* side meant that *they* were scoring. The fact that the humans and animals continued to live on the game ball without falling off was considered a success on both sides but gave no one an additional score.

Spirit was sure of his eventual victory so he didn't worry about a slow first quarter. He knew that the Players on his side would have to practice the skills he had given them. If he got the kinks out in this Game though, there might be more spirits who would check out The Big Game and make more game balls. There could be numerous 'Goodness Games' in the universe. That would be outstanding. They could start a league.

On the other hand, Fighter knew what he had done on the sly to damage the Goodness Game Plan, and he was sure that the Chaos side of the Game would soon take over this game ball and everyone on it. Fire and fury—he was looking for that, and he was ready to make a run for a quick win of the Game with it. Unfortunately, the new humans hadn't invented fire yet. They were cavemen. Fighter had to settle for fury, alone. Meanwhile, he would just have fun watching the Goodness Team that was missing their dropped 'heart equipment'. He was sure they would continue to fail probably to the point of extinction.

As both spirits watched, humans and all other creatures began to bunch up according to species—humans with humans, mice with mice, and so forth. The grasslands next to the river was where all creatures were created and so this area became prime real estate. Water was necessary for everybody for everything. All creatures claimed parts of the riverbank and fought over their space regularly. Fighting for turf was a practice that every living creature learned early

...Generosity?...no. Sharing?...no. *Score for Fighter.*

Fighter was now Coach Fighter. He had no trouble teaching all species, human and otherwise, the training activities for his side. And he was a talented coach. Animals fought animals and, sometimes, humans. Humans fought humans and, sometimes, animals. Often in the caveman days, everybody fought everybody and dined on the leftovers. Perfect.

Peace and friendship?...no. *Score, Fighter.*

Spirit was true to his hands-off pledge, but the humans that were supposed to have superior skills, really *were* cavemen. Spirit thought that was an okay way to start. Their Special Clay brains were obviously learning

some things that were helpful but loving and caring for one another was a concept that didn't do well in caves. Spirit continued to be patient.

Time had little meaning for either spirit, so the early teams of Good and Chaos duked it out for centuries. Year after year, century after century, all the world's creatures battled one another while both spirits just watched and did their own thing. Fighter loved these early times. He coached humans in hair-pulling, food stealing, and major brawls over territory. *Why not score when it was easy?*

But this was a worrisome time for Spirit, and there was no Game Clock. This part of the Game was bloody and seemed to go on and on, forever.

"Come on, People," Spirit would whisper under his breath. But obviously, he couldn't actually coach. A pledge was a pledge.

At last, the first humans' began learning many survival skills which were a real tribute to their superior brains, but the thing they learned best, unfortunately, was survival of the fittest—"Grab, take, big over small, I win. you lose."

Observing the scoring this produced for Spirit, Fighter was still sure that Team Chaos was the team of the future. He could see that no humans knew anything at all about Goodness. They just growled and fought a lot. To Fighter, progress in The Big Game was working out totally as he expected, but, after several hundred years, Spirit of Good began to be a bit concerned.

Spirit could see that the Special Clay brains of human intelligence were doing fine. Humans finally discovered fire and learned to cook with it. That was a good thing. Then they invented the wheel, which was almost as big a thing as fire. *Score for Spirit.*

But the feelings of love and goodness that should be showing up in humans' hearts were just not happening at the same rate. Early People discovered clubs and beat one another with them. They invented hatchets but chased one another with their new invention but there was no kindness or love at all. Why was this happening? Spirit began pacing the sidelines.

Fighter just kicked back and ate popcorn, only dropping a hint to his players now and then. The violence in the world seemed to be happening without too much coaching from him. Humans were naturals at Chaos.

Both spirits were happy, however, with the fact that the number of Players in their first Game continued to increase. Humanity was multiplying, in spite of their tough lives in the caves. Spirit thought that the Game in the caves needed rules. The Game needed referees. Spirit made these suggestions to Fighter. Rules would improve the Game. Fighter just ate more popcorn and laughed. No rules meant that there were no ways to judge between Right and Wrong, so *Wrong* was common and Fighter liked that.

In fact, 'wrong' and 'force' were making their own rules. There were times when the poor human players of the game (now called the Game) threatened to wipe themselves out with their own greed, selfishness, and violence. Pestilence, war and famine. The Special Clay in their hearts was just not kicking in. Goodness seemed to have no energy, no drive toward the goal.

"What the heck is wrong with my team? They're supposed to be fighting for Goodness here, not fighting one another," said Spirit to himself. "I used Special Clay. I know that was the right stuff. Why isn't it working?"

Fighter looked down on the raw and ruthless humanity with pride. "That's because *your* team's players are all joining *my* team, big guy. They are selfish, hateful and violent," he boasted to Spirit with a grin. "You made 'em, but they're my kind of People now."

Spirit was silent.

"I've won the Game, Spirit. You've got to see that. Are you ready to surrender?" Fighter taunted. "Have you thrown in the towel? Looks like your precious People love Chaos so much they are willing to die with it. They're not too good at Goodness in the world you made for them, and they love *my* style. Goodness is obviously a losing idea. And like I said before, it's boring. Too bad. So sad."

"It's still early in the Game," Spirit responded.

"Dream on. We're only in the 1st Quarter, but your team is already down for the count!" Fighter smirked.

"We're getting ready for a comeback," Spirit shot back.

Spirit didn't want to admit it, but what Fighter said was pretty true. He tried to get hold of some other spirits for a consult, but he couldn't find any that were ready to get down to earth. He *did* talk to Fireflies from time to time, but they were like all loyal fans. They just kept advising "wait until next year."

Fireflies had been around the universe forever, but Spirit did not depend on their advice. They seemed to be on his side but maybe too much so. They were always around. They were almost too hopeful. They always told him that things would work out in the future.

But this was *already* the future. Spirit needed to talk more about the reality of what was going on *right now*. It never occurred to him that Fireflies might actually know something that he didn't know. They were 'old school'. Oh well. At least they liked him.

Spirit's ego was huge, and it still told him that he could win this Game. A small ego was not his problem. He was smug. *He* had made all the players. *He* had given them all the Special Clay equipment. *He* had made the earth they were standing on. He would remember this someday and laugh. He was determined to see some scoring but the name of the Game right now was patience and *more* patience.

Spirit decided to focus on some different positive gains his players were making in the Game. These gains of a practical sort. They were using their brains. At least this part of his humans was doing something that could be called 'good'. Cavemen deserted their caves and scratched out wretched hovels, homes of sorts. Family compounds grew into groups of huts, the beginnings of small villages. Civilization. Things were looking up. *Score, Spirit.*

And new children were being born to the humans every day. New children were a source of hope for Spirit. Every new generation of babies might have a more developed use of the Special Clay in their hearts than their parents or grandparents. That kind of evolution was working for human brains. People were getting smarter. The Goodness in their hearts was worth the wait. Spirit was not giving up.

Fighter chuckled darkly at Spirit's optimism. Some spirits never learned. And Spirit was now looking for *happiness* among his humans. He had a new Game theory. Happiness might help Goodness in hearts to grow, and today, a baby was being born. A new, living baby was a good place to check among humans for happiness. He was standing by to watch this new birth in person.

Fighter also squatted next to the hut of the parents. There was much groaning coming from inside. "Check this out, Spirit. Can't you see that new babies cause pain? New babies die a lot," sneered Fighter. "So do their mothers. Don't you get it? Haven't you been watching? They don't have doctors yet.

"You are such a loser, Spirit. This is no place to look for happiness. Humans don't hold up. Babies cause pain. Pain causes misery. Misery puts them on *my* team. This baby is doomed. *My* team is full of *your* People who can't keep happiness even if they find it. And, if the baby lives, the parents will have misery they don't even know about yet."

Spirit ignored Fighter and watched as a new child emerged healthy. The parents celebrated, showed off their newborn to their neighbors, and congratulated themselves. They were happy, very happy. They looked like they really loved this baby. *Score, Spirit.*

Happiness...love...real love! This was a small sign of Special Clay in human hearts. Maybe these feelings of love would stand up and turn into Good feelings toward others. Spirit turned with pride to Fighter, but he was gone.

Fighter always left these occasions of unnecessary happiness early. Happiness *was* related to Goodness. He could see it. Of what possible benefit to *his* Game Plan could a live human birth be? A cause for a party? Rubbish! Early death was more his style. Successful childbirth was only a feeble delay of human misery, a delay in the Game.

"Spirit still thinks he has created humans with Goodness and happiness potential. What a moron! Happiness is weak. It doesn't last. Chaos is the only thing with real juice." Fighter wished he had interrupted Spirit's stupid creative process earlier, however. There might still be a little bit of that ridiculous Clay left in some hearts. Not much, but some.

Much to Fighter's disgust, Spirit discovered another source of happiness for his beloved humans. Physical attraction between People began morphing into something that could also be called love. It was almost equal to the hope and joy of proud new parents. It seemed to be very intense. Spirit discovered that when young love was going strong, humans now seemed to be able to find real affection for a partner. They were happy. *Score.*

Eureka! More signs of hearts coming to life, at last.

Many lovers would happily live it up during these early romances. There was much hand-holding, hugging, kissing. Babies were produced. It was truly a happy time. For a while, the fresh love of romance, like the joy of childbirth, would create wonderful happiness for People. Sometimes these feelings of love would last for months or even a few years.

Spirit noticed, however, that the love in human hearts would wear out. His humans liked to *get love* but tired of putting themselves out to *give love*. What was that all about? Romance would fade, and partners would become bored and even be mean to each other.

"Do you want to go for a walk, dear?"
"Explain to me why I would want to do that."
"You used to like to do that."
"That was then, and now is now."
"That's true. Forget I ever said anything."
"I already did."

In this way, most love eventually died, leaving the poor couples with nothing ahead but a difficult life and bad dispositions. Spirit hoped that human intelligence might produce nice words that could start some romance back up again, but kind words were signs of weakness and were seldom spoken. No one saw the need for that kind of risk.

Spirit haunted the hovels of the River People, looking for more sparks of love and happiness. He felt that his patience was beginning to pay off, but he suspected that his Goodness Team did not have their hearts in the Game. Why, why, why?

The truth was, humans probably needed a coach, but Spirit knew he couldn't do that. He had made that pledge. Dumb! What an idiot! Why had he been so smug? Why had he made that stupid pledge? Overconfidence...a fatal flaw.

Fighter was not about to tell Spirit a thing. The Game was delivering Chaos for the universe, just the way he thought it would but he wasn't ready to quit, either. A long, losing Game would be torture for Spirit. Delightful! Fighter expected victory, but he was willing to let the Game run its course and just watch Spirit's loss of the universe become more miserably complete.

A Civilized Game?

The idea of leadership among humans began now to develop quickly but not exactly the way Spirit had hoped. Did intelligence start it? No.

How about creativity? No.

Kindness? No.

Force? Of course. Force became power. Power equaled leadership. That was all that was necessary. Obviously, force and power worked together. Early on, the strongest man on Fighter's Team drafted a gang of warrior types, men as strong as he was—*almost* as strong, but not quite. (There was a reason for that.)

One after another, the first strong man beat every other strong man to a pulp, murdered some, and looked around for more challengers. Not finding any, he declared himself King of River Kingdom, the first 'All-Star' in the Game!

The warriors that had lived through the 'draft process' became the King's personal henchmen, which was the best way of insuring themselves against being beaten again or killed. Power and force equaled leadership. This was another notch in Fighter's belt.

"I'll make a collection of these guys for my Dream Team," crowed Fighter. "These men definitely belong on my side. Spirit made a pledge against interfering with these humans, but *I* didn't. Stupid move, Spirit! Cool move on my part! These guys will wipe out anybody that disagrees with me. I must say, this was a smart recruit for my side of the Game."

The first king erected a huge rock fortress on a rise overlooking the rest of his kingdom. From here, he and his henchmen could see anybody who approached and decide what type of 'enemy blocking' they should deliver. Great strategy. Eventually, this impressive fortress became called the Castle.

The Castle frowned down on the nearby village and the Riverbank. Because size was important to all, the Castle added rooms and towers, columns and barricades, year after year, becoming a hulking show of ever-increasing power.

Being a king meant power, and power had its rewards—taxes, slavery, fear. Fighter spent a lot of time around the Castle. Castle Rule was a new core provider of talent for his team. *Score.*

The Castle was surrounded by a rock wall and closed off from any challengers. As the years went by, successive kings were completely isolated and hated by their subjects, so they needed all the protection they could get.

All kings ruled with fear. Dungeons were filled with slaves. Beheadings were common. This was expected and accepted. The skills of selfishness and cruelty grew well here. The Castle was fertile ground for new recruits. Life was so good that Fighter kept forgetting to keep track of his score.

Spirit did not spend much time with Royalty. Royalty was already too dedicated to Chaos. He had decided to continue to focus on the intelligence of the common folk, instead. At least the intelligence of the humans along the River was moving along pretty well. Hopefully, Goodness and happiness would catch up soon.

Intelligence might even be able to fight off some Chaos, Spirit thought. There was Special Clay in human brains. It was worth a try in this weird game, since human hearts weren't working up to their potential at all.

And intelligence on the Riverbank *did* continue to evolve even though the River People were selfish. No surprise.

After a while, they discovered that they could not exist by hoarding their own individual crops as had been their practice. What if they needed potatoes and they only grew carrots on their land? The People needed to trade with one another just to stay alive. Wasn't this sort of like sharing?

But there were few ways to trade without bloodshed. Who was getting more...less...rotten stuff? And there were so many more humans now crowded onto the Riverbank and cheating each other that the bloodshed was getting bloodier. Somebody needed to fix something!

"Come on, Special Clay," cheered Spirit quietly. "I gave you People some problem-solving skills. Get on with it!"

The Others

In early civilization, there was a pecking order. Farmers had scrounged land together and produced food. Everyone needed food. Farmers, for that reason, were important. They were top dog among the commoners.

Non-Farmers were not important and could be manipulated. Farmers, therefore, had the power among the commoners, so they were the ones who decided to "get on with it." It was in their own best interest (more leadership through power).

Those who were chosen by the Farmers to perform the new duties that the Farmers didn't want to do became known as '**The Others**', a lower but necessary class of People.

Farmers were People 'of quality' who actually grew things. So who was going to do these *other* things? The answer became "Let Others do it."

These Others soon became very necessary to life in the villages although they were not respected or appreciated by the Farmer landowners. Over time, however, the Others became important, themselves, in the young society.

The first group of Others was chosen due to the need for a place where Farmers could do this new thing called 'trading'. Fighter encouraged traders to get nastier with each other, and this part of the Game was full of scoring for his side.

"I'm telling you, Harvey, you need ta keep yer jackass down at the other end of the road. It's eatin' my turnips and rutabagas before I can sell 'em! How do you 'spect me to make a livin' and pay my taxes?"

(Oh! Did I forget to mention taxes? The kings figured out that part of the Game right from the get-go.)

"I don't *'spect* ya to make a livin'! I don't *care* if ya make a livin', neither! And I sure don't *give a hoot* about yer taxes! Jest keep *yer* turnips away from *my* donkey, you jackass! Did you ever see what comes *out* of a donkey that's been eatin' turnips? It ain't purty! I'm sending my donkey over to yer place to *give back* what he ate!"

After a fistfight and a messy roll in the dirt, Farmer Harvey lost a tooth but gained a new understanding.

"Maybe we should get somebody to set up some separate spots for each of us where we can put our stuff fer sellin'. See that guy over there? He doesn't grow nothin'. He's just watchin' us fight. Let's make that *other* guy do it."

"Good plan. Hey, you!"

Thus, the first **Other** was created.

The first Others were, of course, not volunteers. They weren't Farmers, after all. These Others were forced in large numbers by those that *were* Farmers to clear out a strip of land on which goods could be traded. This action created a Marketplace (and slavery) and the beginnings of a town center.

Although the Others who formed the Marketplace were originally slaves, Spirit's gift of intelligence took over, and some of these Others gradually began to profit from trading and reselling. It might not have been what they wanted to do at the beginning, but it was better than starving or being beaten. *Score for Spirit*

And because the Farmers began to depend on them, some Others learned to hold out for more of the Marketplace proceeds. These **Others** became Landlords and even Merchants. Amazing.

No one was being kind, but they *were* being smart! Spirit was pleased with this growing ingenuity. He just wished his People were as good natured as they were intelligent. The dealing among the Merchants, Landlords, and Farmers became known as bargaining, another new concept for the young world. It was a step in the right direction…*Score*…if they didn't cheat.

"Duh!" sneered Fighter." Let 'em cheat. Inside every cheater, you'll always find a fighter. I tell you, these are my People. Let 'em cheat and lie. They were made for it."

Fighter watched these developments with contentment for the most part but was a bit concerned about cooperation that showed up now and then in the Marketplace. *There might be at least a tiny amount of that stupid Special Clay left in the hearts of a few humans,* he thought.

The effects of a bit of that Clay surfaced every once in a while. Fighter would keep an eye on the whole thing. He was ready to step into the Game and yank any cooperative misfits if he had to. Unlike Spirit, he hadn't given anyone a pledge of anything.

Spirit now decided to focus on Game Plan B with his People. Plan B was all about the babies that had encouraged him before. He would not intervene, but babies and their parents still gave him hope for more human Happiness. Goodness was the goal of the Game, and Spirit now became sure that babies were at least one of the keys.

Fighter favored Plan P (for poverty). Poverty and overcrowding along the Riverbank were making parents work harder, steal more and feel meaner. Exhaustion and overwork were useful tools for Chaos.

Sadly, parents' affection for their babies was lasting a shorter amount of time as civilization increased. Both parents knew there was work to be done and a hard life to be lived. Children got in the way. Fighter planted these truths wherever he thought they might take root.

"Babies outgrow their cute baby ways and become annoying, messy children," he informed People constantly. "You parents have to focus on your own survival. You need to work just to keep up. Children just bog you down. Children are really a pain in the neck."

Survival of the fittest took over again. More like wild animals than children, the children of the working poor were increasingly neglected and became perceived as a problem instead of a reason to be happy.

Fighter pinched and prodded the impressionable children and added to their aggravating behaviors. He encouraged them to steal and bully one another and get in the way of adults. They became a community nuisance as soon as they could walk.

Unruly, ragtag gangs of children began running amok in the new markets. They stampeded through them. They climbed on them. They trampled the produce. They stole whatever they could grab, *and* they could run faster than the adults.

"Future fighters for the Game!" crowed Fighter. "New recruits! Marvelous! Early training for *my* team."

Spirit was horrified. "You love your babies! Take care of them," Spirit pleaded silently. "Children are your future!" No one was listening.

Farmers, Landlords, Merchants, and parents had clever brains, and, they all agreed that something must be done...by someone. Responsibility for these little beggars obviously belonged to... the **Others.** In order to solve this problem, the clever River People again resorted to their intelligence instead of their hearts.

A new group of **Others** was drafted to do *something* with the children. At first, these new Others were more jailers than anything else. Children who were caught at the markets were herded together and caged while the market was in session. Rude contraptions were built and supervised by the Others as one after another of the gangs of children were dragged into the cages, kicking and screaming.

"How did this happen?" mourned Spirit. "What happened to the idea of loving their babies? Do they have no love left for a growing child? Where did I go wrong?" The caged children screamed and yelled and shook their cages.

"Should I tell him?" whispered Fighter. "Should I let him know the reason that rotten parents are rotten? Nah! It's more fun to watch parents *and* children *and* Spirit suffer."

"You aren't using your hearts!" hollered Spirit in desperation.
"Right on! Maybe they don't have one!" yelled Fighter.

Oops! Fighter almost gave away the secret of his success in the Game. He would need to be more careful!

"What did you say?" questioned Spirit. "What did I hear you say?" But Fighter was gone.

The children did not take well to being jailed. The kids rocked and broke the cages. Their parents paid no attention. It wasn't a good time to be a kid *or* a parent.

Spirit's frustration grew. "They are just little children," Spirit moaned. How he wished he could speak to them. They were the promise of the future. He was sure that a word here or there would help parents understand this, but he had promised not to interfere.

Talk about stupid! What a stupid pledge. But he couldn't interfere, he thought. He was a spirit of honor.

Eventually, however, some of the smarter Others became more inventive and began to tell the children threatening stories (called "feary tales") designed to scare children, quiet them down and keep them in line. Surprisingly, the kids liked the stories, and as society grew, some of these creative Others began to teach the children a few things as well.

"This is how you count."

"This is how you read."

"This is how you find out about things."

In this way, the stories evolved and the cleverest of these **Others became Teachers,** another new concept. This was completely unanticipated! Score, score, score!

Spirit finally had a reason to smile. This was a good sign. Perhaps some of these Teaching Others understood kindness a bit. Maybe they had found some Special Clay in their hearts. Maybe these People were worth watching and encouraging. Maybe Plan B would work after all. He was sure this was a score.

Sadly, however, Teachers were seldom appreciated by the Farmers or Merchants or Landlords.

"Teachers read things and learn things that don't make no sense and are better off forgotten."

"Teachers spend most of their time squintin' and readin' and talkin' to the local brats. They don't farm nothin' or sell nothin', so they can't be too smart."

"They didn't learn me nothin' when I went ta school."

Learning by reading instead of doing was another new concept, but one that seemed to have little value for many. For this reason, Teachers were not universally liked, valued, or trusted.

"Teachers spend their days with children, so they never really work."

"Who wants to spend time with one of those Teacher types?"

"No way. Just 'cause they read stuff, they think they know everything. Who likes a know-it-all?"

There wasn't much appreciation for Teachers, but after a few more centuries, the King of that time decided "Education is important." He began to insist that all children go to school every day. Was this a sign of respect for teachers? Not really.

"We need to keep the little beggars quiet and out of my sight," announced the King. *"And* allow their parents to *work* enough to pay decent taxes!" These were the first reasons for education.

And so, mandatory education became one of the first laws of the new society. After that, all future kings insisted that children of the Kingdom attend school and be supervised (jailed?) by a Teacher. Neither the kings nor the children's parents cared if children learned much. That was not the point.

"A *few* of the children should learn a *few* things that will make them useful to royalty," declared the kings. "Writing about kingly glories would be nice. Have a few of them do that."

"Keep children out of sight until they can do some decent work for the household and are less of a bother," declared the parents. The kings and the parents were on the same page. The number of schools grew.

Now there were entire rooms in the Castle full of historical tablets, scrolls, and piles of parchment gathered in their stiff leather bindings.

Educated People spent their lives recording royal victories. This was, of course, an extremely important reason for schools to exist: Royal Manuscripts.

Most of the Royal Manuscripts told of bloody Royal battles and were, of course, the property of the Kings. According to these writings, Kings were brilliant, and they never lost a battle. Royalty was important to their subjects because of defeating the enemies who might want to destroy them—at least that's what most of these writings said. That's why Kings were important to Kingdoms. *Protection!* Kings had to fight enemies. That was a known (written-down) fact.

Some educated families and Teachers among the River People *did* have scrolls and parchments of their own, hidden away under straw mattresses or buried under floorboards. Intelligence was hard to keep down. Spirit was thrilled to see this. These writings of River People themselves were less complimentary to the kings than those that were stored in the Castle, so they stayed hidden. Many People read these books, however, and some children actually *did* enjoy school and learning something. That was a secret. For Spirit, these were small but important yardage gains in the Game. Learning showed promise.

After the Teachers, the most popular of the new **Others** were called Storytellers. They were the only members of the Kingdom who traveled regularly to villages up and down the Riverbank.

When absolutely nothing interesting was going on, they gathered information, true or not, from where ever they heard it, enhanced it and took it from village to village, telling it to anyone who would listen. If they were good Storytellers, their juicy gossip, true or not, was good for food or coin. This was how they made their living...*and* It was entertainment.

The villages along the Riverbank were several miles apart, so they hardly ever saw one another. For this reason, there was much suspicion and even fear between villages. But there was always curiosity and a large crowd ready to listen to the Storytellers' gossip wherever they went.

What was going on down there where they couldn't see it? It was probably terrible. (River People were just a bit paranoid.)

"Who knows what *those people* on the other side of the hill are thinking?"

"I'm sure they're up to no good."

"I heard that they don't have no women down that way!"

"How do they keep their villages alive then?"

"I heard tell that they steal other People's women! I bet that's what they do!

"They better not try to take mine! I'll fight 'em to the death!"

"They can take my woman if they wanna. I'll even help 'em!"

The Storytellers guaranteed crowd approval by telling each village that everyone in all the *other* villages was stupid, dishonest, and more miserable than they were. This made the hard-working River People feel a little bit better about their own situation. They loved to feel that they were the best—stronger, braver, and of course, smarter than everyone else. For this reason, Storytellers were very popular. Perfect.

Storytellers were highly valued by the Kings as well, and you can see why. Their stories of the misery in *other* villages definitely helped the *local* villagers feel more content. It took their minds off their local troubles. It slowed down the bloodshed. Entertainment was a brilliant solution to unhappiness and boredom.

Even though much of the "news" which the Storytellers delivered was bloody, exaggerated, or just plain wrong, River People loved it anyway. *It was the news!* Civilization was developing. What more could a new civilization need?

Spirit liked the imagination of the Storytellers. It showed that their minds were working. He just wished their stories would emphasize truth and Goodness more. Was their take on the news entertainment or just lies? Sometimes it was hard to tell the difference.

Fighter also had mixed emotions about these Others. He loved their lies but was not all that happy with the enjoyment that everyone got from being entertained. Enjoyment sometimes led to happiness. Happiness in The Big Game was to be avoided as the Game progressed.

Small Players

Did either spirit think of the animals or bugs that Spirit created as Players in the Game?

Of course, not. Both Coaches of The Big Game were watching human players only. To be honest, they were not even noticing any critters. That might not have been too smart a call for either spirit, but what did they know?

The animals knew a lot, however. All the creatures created along the Riverbank were developing and evolving fast on their own. They certainly weren't waiting for spirits to notice them or humans to lead the way, that's for sure. The reproducing that was necessary to keep each species alive was doing well, very well. That was their initial focus.

Champions at the skill of reproducing were Michael Angelo's descendants, the mice. They were definitely good at multiplying. As the first living creatures to be produced by Spirit, they realized early that this skill was important.

Humans thought that rodents were annoying but not worth much notice. They had no clue how smart all rodents were. Both rats and mice watched humans from among the grasses and through the cracks in floorboards. Humans would have been shocked to know what these animals *knew about them and* what they *thought* about them.

Rodents believed that they were smarter than humans. Rodents didn't fight with one another and were more productive than humans, pound for pound. *Smaller* did not mean "lesser than." Under the floor of the Castle lived a huge number of mice and rats that was as complex a society as that of humans. These were the descendants of Michael Angelo Mouse (the original mouse made) and Amos Mouse, the revered author of The Book of Amos.

There were thousands more rodents living in the fields along the Riverbank, but under the Castle floorboards was Mouse Hall, this was headquarters for all rodents. Rats lived in the lower parts of the Castle (the sewer). The Castle mice enjoyed living spaces within the walls or under the floors of the Castle rooms. They had higher status.

And what about Scraps? Glad you asked. Yes, Scraps survived from the time of their questionable creation in the cave as well and were still called Scraps, the name Michael Angelo had suggested on the morning they were discovered.

Scraps were as smart as the rodents. They had even carefully copied their own version of <u>The Book of Amos</u> from the original. They preferred to call their copy <u>The Scrap Book</u>, however, as it was the story of their own creation. (Both versions of this wonderful history were exactly the same. Mice and Scraps considered these books about creation to be truthful reporting of the beginning of The Big Game and important to its final outcome.)

The Special Clay from which Scraps were made had helped Scraps learn to survive peacefully and successfully after their creation. The reason for this was clear. Their entire being was created with the inbred knowledge of right and wrong. Although they looked like tiny humans, they didn't act like them. They hardly ever fought and never tried to destroy one another as humans did.

Scraps had a tiny Kingdom on roughly the same riverbank territory that was home to the humans. They built houses, planted and harvested crops, and even traded in tiny marketplaces. Come to think of it, they were almost exactly like River People but much smaller... and *much* nicer.

Full-grown Scraps were about the size of a pinky finger. Their tiny homes were scattered among the reeds and grasses near the River because Scraps needed the River water in much the same way that humans and other animals did. Scraps did take special care, however, to locate in areas less traveled by humans. They were small, but they weren't stupid.

Only the smallest creatures on the game ball knew about Scraps. Bugs and mice were the best friends of Scraps, but Scraps were so tiny that they had never been seen by humans who lived nearby.

Humans were not the only beings that did not know about Scraps. Neither Spirit nor Fighter knew that Scraps existed, either. Humans were the major players for both sides and Scraps were all around them, but neither Spirit nor Fighter had seen or heard of Scraps. Amazing.

Were Scraps any part of the Game? No, not really, although they *did* think of themselves as Spirit Fans since they, too, had read of their creation in *The Scrap Book.*

Both Fighter and Spirit were clueless. Fighter couldn't care less about anything smaller than his evil-behaving humans. Anything as small as a rodent was definitely not worth his attention.

It was more unexplainable for Spirit though. He *had* taken to watching some of the mice around him occasionally. He was impressed with what seemed to be their kind and generous ways. He was always searching for something on the game ball that showed the kind of behavior he wanted, and weird though it seemed, mice showed a lot of it. Mice were very small and sometimes hard to see, but they were amazingly intelligent *and* kind. They were actually pretty awesome. Why? How did mice learn so much about Goodness?

Spirit wandered along the Riverbank, thinking about Game Plans that he had tried so far. The mouse question kept popping up. He was curious and far from satisfied with any answers that came to mind. The nice mice had to be important to the Game somehow but how?

Spirit thought back over the days and nights of creation. He knew well what and how he had created—mice first, no Special Clay, and humans last, lots of Special Clay. He needed inspiration from somewhere. Mice might give him clues. He counseled himself to continue to watch mice for ideas and a possible new Game Plan with his humans. He must keep looking for answers.

Watching the mice for clues was not a bad idea. Mice and Scraps were best friends from the start, maybe because of the *The Book of Amos* and *The Scrap Book* or maybe just because of their similar size. Although neither had ever talked about it to each other, mice knew that their ancestor had participated in the creation of Scraps, and Scraps were grateful for that.

One particular strength of the Scraps was their uncanny sense of right and wrong. It was like built-in radar. And come to think of it, why not? They were made completely out of Special Clay, right? Goodness was a way of life that Scraps possessed naturally. It was clear that Scraps, even young ones, just had a knack for kindness, and mice spent a lot of time with Scraps. *Hmm . . .*

Oh, Scraps weren't perfect, especially the children. But the fact was that Scraps were sort of kind and forgiving by nature. They did not rush to judgment. They seemed to find good in everyone, even rats. Mice were fond of saying that Scraps were "just plain good-hearted".

Scrap parents, like People, had great love for their children from the first moment they snuggled them in their arms. Unlike the River People, however, this feeling didn't fade as Scrap babies grew older and more challenging. Scrap parents watched and educated their children carefully and even nagged them into the thoughtfulness and problem-solving abilities that they wanted to see in them as adults.

Scraps practiced and honed their problem-solving abilities through the centuries, trying to practice their understanding of right and wrong. They were also willing to share some of their practice with anyone around them, even though they didn't know they were doing it. For example, there was the 'Practice of Thoughtfulness':

When there was a problem, they would just ask, "Have you thought about this yet?"

And a mouse might answer, "No, not yet. Do you think I should?"

"Might be a good idea. There might be two sides."

"Okay, let me think about it."

"Great. I'll check with you later."

To share ideas more easily, Scraps developed more and more Scrap Practices that helped them get along better with one another. They were very inventive.

"Why are you crying? Did you skin a knee?"
"No. Owee! I skinned *two* knees!"
"Oh, that's too bad. Come here and let me take care of them for you."
"Okay."
This was the Practice of Kindness.
"I want this piece of rice. I've got it, and I'm going to eat it. "
"Who found it?"
"He did."
"Why are *you* going to eat it then?"
"Because I'm bigger, and I've got it!"
"Oh, I see. Because *you* are bigger, *you* get what *he* found, right?"
"That doesn't sound right, does it?. Here. I'll find another one."
That was the Practice of Truthfulness and Fairness.

"Thanks. Want a bite?"
That was the Practice of Sharing and Unselfishness.

These were only *some* Scrap Practices. And, during the earliest years, Scraps were learning and passing what they learned on to mice. That had been a great but unintentional learning process.

Without thinking too much about it, mice came to live their lives and solve their problems in a way that was very similar to that of the Scraps. They were best friends.

These results, of course, were what Spirit was seeing when he watched the nice mice, although he had no understanding of what was happening right under his nose.

There *was one* odd difference between mice and Scraps, though. Scraps took a long time to grow up. Mice babies who were born at the same time as Scrap babies were usually adults and having children of their own before Scraps were barely out of diapers. Mice friendships with Scraps became generational. The friendships would start when they were both the same age, but the mice would grow up so much faster that *the children of the first mouse* would take over as *playmates for the slow-growing Scraps!* Very weird, but true.

Both mice and Scraps noticed this, but neither seemed to mind. It was just the way it was. Scraps looked like tiny humans, and their growth rate was just like that of humans. That fact made sense to both mice and Scraps.

To boil it all down, Scraps evolved through the centuries like every other species. They learned, lived their lives, and made friends with most of the species of their size. They raised their families, made mistakes, tried to fix them, and also tried to practice their Practices.

It was really too bad that Spirit knew nothing of these tiny beings or their kindly ways. That was the bad news. The good news was that Fighter didn't know about Scraps either. Obviously, if neither spirit knew about Scraps, they were not Game Players for either side yet. Stay tuned.

Game Royalty

The fortress known as the Castle, now bigger than it had ever been, loomed darkly over the humans below it. It was very fancy on the inside, however. Every room was filled with gold and jewels. This was the home of the King, after all, and *should* appear both frightening and awesome. It did.

Because of Royal taxing and raiding and stealing, Royal riches stuffed the rooms up to the rafters and overflowed. The Castle continued to add more rooms, of course. River People needed to fear and envy Royalty. They did.

The current King (from now on known as the King or King Sol) was a thoughtless, and particularly heartless man. His formal name was King Sol the Selfish, a name that he proudly earned every day. What he owned was his alone, and he owned a lot. His talent for selfishness was inherited, handed down from earlier kings over the centuries, along with meanness, lack of caring, and a bad temper. Such qualities were signs of strength, and this King had no intention of ever appearing weak.

He was certainly the richest, most powerful man around, but his selfish heart was, according to Spirit's observation, not worth a penny.

"I do not share," declared the King. "*Getting* is the goal. Like my father before me, I am *great* at *getting*. I am also clever at *keeping* what I have *collected. Taxes* are *terrific! Mountains* of *monies* are *magnificent*. I am *marvelous at maintaining moolah*."

(This was the way the King usually talked. It's called alliteration. It is very impressive if you like that sort of thing, and he did.)

Above all, King Sol took pride in owning the best of everything, so when he wanted to possess a queen, he acquired the best female available. "She had better be better than the best and beautiful beyond belief," he declared. And that's what he got. She was, indeed, a beautiful woman and, of course, totally in love with her own beauty. She was known as Queen Luna the Loveless (from now on known as the Queen or Luna).

The King was said to have fallen madly in love with her the moment he saw her. (She **was** beautiful.) Strangely enough, Queen Luna had fallen in love with King Sol as well. (He **was** rich.) But, very strangely, this couple had *not* completely outgrown their ability to care for each other, at least not yet.

Queen Luna spent her days in front of her many mirrors, being combed and recombed, dressed and redressed. Although she was beautiful and the envy of all, she was never satisfied with the way she looked. She made sure that all who waited on her stayed near for touch-ups at all times. If she wanted them to make her *even more perfect,* they needed to be ready.

"The love of my King must never be taken for granted! Beauty is the main thing I have to offer him. Actually, it's the *only* thing. As yet, I am childless, so I must offer *outstanding* beauty to him at all times!"

She would remind herself of this day after day, gazing at her reflection in the shimmering walls, which were, at her insistence, lined with mirrors. "Mirrors are a wonderful thing! King Sol must have the most beautiful and most perfectly dressed woman in the Kingdom, and fortunately, here I am, as requested."

Queen Luna also enjoyed inviting favored subjects to the Castle to see her looking glorious in her robes and jewels. Grand entrances were her specialty. She *must* make sure that everyone knew that she had arrived. Spinning into the room with a flourish was her style. Having once arrived, Luna took even more pride in looking down her nose at others in the room and enjoying their jealousy without bothering to speak to them, of course. Charming, right?

"*Ooh! Ah!* Lovely!" her visitors would exclaim with great enthusiasm. Enthusiasm was required. Those persons who were not enthusiastic enough were dismissed immediately and never invited again. Envy, desire, and jealousy were the feelings that the Queen wished to inspire in her subjects, and she enjoyed inspiring all three. As the Queen, this was her passion.

As a result, however, the Queen had many admirers but no friends. Luna the Loveless was earning her name, but this lack of love was something she never really understood.

In truth, King Sol and Queen Luna wanted to be adored or, at the very least, appreciated by their subjects, but due to their thoughtless practices, this was never going to happen. No one ever just dropped by for a visit. No one sent them birthday cards. No one but the servants even spoke to them at all.

Maybe the Queen could have tried being nice, but it never occurred to her. She may have been perfect to look at, but her heart was simply not working well in terms of any kind thoughts for others. The King didn't know how to do anything but get more and more of what he already had and talk funny. These habits were certainly not a draw for friendship.

The lack of attention and love from their subjects caused the lonely Royals to feel more like animals in a cage than monarchs in a castle. More and more, they acted like animals, snarling and bullying anyone that came near. The idea of being friendly, fair, or even polite to their subjects or servants had never crossed their minds. Thinking of the feelings of others was unthinkable.

Afternoon Delight

Today, Fighter, skulking as he frequently did in the dark corners of the Castle, was ready to enjoy the Royals' terrible (wonderful from his point of view) behavior. He loved these particular Players on his team. Maybe they would hit a servant. Maybe they would put someone in a dungeon for no reason. They would probably throw things. (They usually did.) The King and Queen were a superior example of all the selfish, rotten ways that could and did produce misery. Fighter appreciated that kind of talent. He was a fan of the Royals. They were star Players.

Coach Fighter kept careful track of their skills. The Queen looked down her nose at her subjects and snubbed everyone who tried to speak with her. She was terrific. The King often punished People for no reason at all. Fighter underlined that observation in his notes. With these hateful behaviors in the Royal family, Fighter looked forward to a growing Chaotic future in the whole River Kingdom and the Game.

Spirit was only an occasional visitor to the Castle, but he also hovered today on a Castle rafter. This King and Queen, although frequently arguing, still loved each other, he had observed. Amazing! Just why, nobody knew; but to Spirit, that was a positive sign.

They had been married for over a year. Like Fighter, Spirit hoped they might set an example for their subjects, but in the love department, not fighting. Maybe the love they had in their hearts at the beginning of their romance would flare up again and become stronger. Such affection would be noticed and might encourage their subjects to more loving ways.

So, a hopeful Spirit also checked in at the Castle to see how things were going. *If only they had a child, Spirit thought* to himself. That would help. A child might prolong their love for each other at least *a bit* longer. Spirit was pretty sure that worked with some People. He was always hopeful, and he still thought babies were key. Maybe the Queen was pregnant.

But the King and Queen were particularly lonely today. The only thing that was interesting to them was who they should blame for their unhappiness.

"You must agree, Sol, that the reason we are not loved by our subjects is not our fault. It is obviously the fault of the original plan for this world," whined the Queen. "There must have been a flaw in the construction of most humanity.

(Spirit almost fell off his rafter. Did she know something that he didn't know about faulty creation?)

"I have no idea what spirit created us, but if the world were created correctly, *we* would be happy all the time, don't you think, Sol?" the Queen continued, strolling from her closets of satins and jewels.

"People of quality such as ourselves should have been created to be happy always. Our needs should be met, our faults should be excused, and lesser beings should adore us. That is the way the world should have been created, don't you agree?"

Fighter was too excited. This Queen was amazing. What a great attitude! Much better than he had even dreamed. Not only were these Royals miserable, but they blamed their unhappiness on Spirit himself. Fighter was so overjoyed he soared from the Castle in triumph. This was an excellent day. He needed to go celebrate.

Spirit threw up his hands. Score a point for Fighter.

"Faults? What faults?" the King responded indignantly. "*I* was created to be the King! *I* am fabulously faultless. And my Queen is equally qualified. The human hoard is fault-filled, a fact that is proven by their pitiful poverty. I find our sad subjects to be crude and classless. They are simple-minded and shiftless."

"Quite so, my dear!" the Queen agreed.

"Hulking and hairy!" the King added. "Dimwitted and disgusting! Sanction them *all* for the sin of stupidity."

"Oh dear." Spirit sank further into his corner.

"That's a fantastic idea," responded Queen Luna. "Let's do that. But wait, if everybody is thrown into the dungeons, who will be left to wait on me and tell me I'm gorgeous? Think about it, Sol. That would be so incorrect!"

"Good point, good point. That would present a problem."

"But we *do* have the power to do that if we want, don't we, dear? I mean, we *could* shove everybody into the dungeons to rot if we wanted, right?" The Queen needed reassurance.

"Indeed! We could *positively* punish and imprison all People! We have power aplenty! We have muscle and might! It could be marvelous! We could munch them, mutilate them and massacre them!" (King Sol was on a roll. Queen Luna the Loveless loved him when he was like this.)

"Well, at least they're getting along," mumbled Coach Spirit to himself as he disappeared. "But I definitely need to go back to the drawing board. The heart-based win that I'm waiting for in this Game is not going to be led by these two. I've got to figure out a new strategy before 2nd Quarter."

Royal Judgment

River People led unhappy lives, working hard, arguing, fighting, and dying early. They had no understanding of right and wrong, but they definitely understood getting mad. Today they were mad.

Why? Because of a Teacher who wouldn't teach. That's why. What nerve. Teaching was *the law*. Teachers could *not* refuse to teach. If the King said that school was mandatory, then teaching was mandatory too. This Teacher was not doing his duty.

All schools in the early times took place in the homes of the Teachers. Today, a burly farmer stopped by the home of his nearby Teacher to drop off his child. The Farmer was on his way to work in the fields, and he was in a hurry. The Teacher was not out in front of his hovel to accept children as usual. This Farmer was not going to stand for that.

"Homer, are you gonna teach our brats today, or am I gonna beat on you like I did before? My kid is right here, Homer, and my wife has ta be in the fields with me. Taxes are due. Our brat can't run loose, Homer. He's a terror. You know that. What's it gonna be? I can't stand here all day." More parents and children straggled up to the closed schoolhouse door.

"Yeah! Where are ya, Homer?" bellowed an arriving father, a screaming child at his side. "You Teachers don't have anything useful to do. Get out here and take care of my kid."

"I can't teach right now," the young Teacher pleaded from inside his cottage. "My wife is very sick, and I have no one to take care of my wife or our baby. Our baby is pretty young, you know."

The gathering crowd quieted down. River People liked babies, usually, so they thought for a minute. But this baby was not their problem. Why should they care? Being a parent took a lot of time away from work, and parenting didn't pay the taxes of the King. These parents were on their way to do *real* work. They didn't have time for a Teacher's stupid problem! This lazy Teacher needed to do his duty.

The crowd began to growl louder and took turns pounding on the Teacher's door. This Other was only a Teacher.

"Of course you can teach today, ya lowlife! Get out here!"

"What makes you think you have the right to say no?"

"Yer a Teacher! That's *all* ya do!"

"I have important stuff ta do today!" yelled a mother, pointing to her son who was busily kicking the child next to him. "I can't take time ta deal with this!"

Homer came to the door, an infant in his arms. "My wife is sickly since the baby. You all know that. I have to take care of my baby here as well as my poor wife."

"We don't care about yer wife or yer baby! They're not our problem!"

"This brat of mine needs watchin', and that's *yer* job. Do it!"

"I can't."

Suddenly, the obvious solution arose. This could be a matter for *Royal Judgment*. What a great idea! The King would surely do something about this lazy bum as soon as he heard about it. It was *his* law. "Teachers must teach."

Fierce fights that went unchecked in the Kingdom frequently ended in violent brawls. Too much violence kept folks away from work and reduced taxes for the King. No King liked that. Earlier Kings had decided on a solution. They called it 'Royal Judgment'.

The way it worked was easy: bring the problem to the King and let him decide how to solve it. The solution didn't need to be fair or just. There just needed to be a Royal Judgment. With a little luck, there would be some bloody whippings delivered by the Castle Guard to the losers of the Judgment. A little gore would be cool. Great even! These Royal Judgments usually solved the problem and provided a bit of entertainment. It was a win-win.

King Sol didn't care about being fair or just either, but he usually enjoyed these sessions. People dropped by and asked *him* for a Judgment. That made him feel wise and necessary.

Queen Luna liked Royal Judgments as well because she was not all alone in the Castle. In honor of such occasions, she could dress up in her latest gown and show off her beauty to a whole gaggle of People. Royal Judgments were more fun than a gala party.

"Alright, Teacher. If ya don't wanna do your job, we'll just take you to a Royal Judgment."

The crowd of parents loved the idea. This Teacher would be punished, and they could watch. Excellent. They surged forward and grabbed the Teacher, who was still clutching his baby.

The young man struggled to free himself and shield his baby from the angry mob, but both were now half carried, half dragged from their home.

The noisy parents were on their way to the Castle with their problem in hand. It was a social event. The crowd began howling with ghoulish anticipation, and the baby could be heard sobbing in terror

"Shut up, kid! Teachers must teach!"

"That's yer job, Teacher."

The crowd pushed through the heavy gates of the Castle. The Castle Guards didn't object. They liked these days too—a little yelling, a little violence. It was all good. The leaders of the People pounded confidently on the Castle door.

Queen Luna quickly ordered her maids to dress her in one of her fanciest gowns and dashed for the throne room to be appreciated. She arranged herself on her throne just so and waited. The Guards inside the Castle slowly opened the doors a crack but no more. The size of the crowd was impressive.

But the King was in a bad mood and impossibly angry already today. The Guards were being very careful. They didn't want any trouble from outside the Castle. They had enough to deal with *inside*.

Alone in his throne room except for servants, the King had screamed at everyone about everything all morning. He had even cussed out the Queen for no one knew what. The servants were pretty sure that the King would not appreciate ordinary People making noise at the door and care even less about their reason for being there. He already seemed to have a problem of his own. He didn't need anyone else's. King Sol glared at the growing noise.

The parents of the Kingdom were in a joyful mood and completely ready for the misery they hoped to cause with their judgement. They now focused on their wonderful moment of glory and took their places proudly before the Castle doorway, secure in the winning nature of their cause. The Teacher, trying to comfort his baby daughter, waited fearfully for the accusations against him to be laid before the King.

"Your Majesty! We come to you on a matter of the greatest urgency. We need a Royal Judgment," the loudest parent shouted boldly through the cracked door.

The Castle Guard, seeing that the King was not in danger and might really enjoy this, slowly opened the door wider. It was time for the parents to do their thing.

"In our village, we have an Other who considers himself a Teacher. This morning he refuses his duty to teach! We know *your* rule! We know *our* rights! A Teacher must teach! *We* won't stand for his refusal. We want *you* to issue a Royal Judgment."

King Sol slouched on his throne. He didn't care about the parents *or* their children today. Royal Judgments were usually entertaining, but not today. All he wanted today was to be left alone. He had made up his mind to be miserable, and he didn't need anybody to help him do that.

Why was he in such a bad mood? No one knew.

The King glared at the crowded doorway. "How dare you present such petty problems to me?" he snarled. "*This puny* problem is particularly unimpressive! Go away!"

The stunned crowd froze in place. This response was not expected.

They wanted a Judgment.

Queen Luna looked over the King's shoulder at the townspeople and whined to her husband quietly. "Maybe we could let them in for just a moment, dear. Look at me! I look great today! Everybody will be jealous, and we have not had company here to envy me in months. And check this out: they have a baby with them. You know how I love babies."

The King whirled to face his unsuspecting wife. "Quiet, Queen," the King hissed. "How would *I* know about how *you* feel about *babies*? *We don't have one.*"

The Queen did not see the significance of this fact.

"Please, dear. Look at my gown. I have dressed with particular care to receive visitors. You will be so proud of me. You *must* allow them entrance, if for no other reason than to appreciate this dress. Look how awesome it is."

The King stared at his Queen, his nose almost touching that of his shocked wife. With a withering look, he snarled at her, "Your wonderfulness is wasted. Blast your beauty!"

Queen Luna blinked and drew back. He had never put her *or* her beauty down like that before. The envy of the town was his favorite thing. And he was saying what he was saying in front of their subjects. How humiliating.

King Sol stomped to the door, pulled it wide, and addressed his cringing subjects in a frighteningly quiet tone. "*Your* confounded kids are of no concern to me. None, nothing, nada! *I* am a completely *kid-less King.*"

(The Queen shuddered. Now she knew what the King's bad temper was about.)

"Do you cluelessly conclude that I care about *your* kids? Foolish fantasy!" King Sol filled the doorway with anger. He scanned his subjects in the courtyard with a burning stare, one by one. The crowd retreated immediately to a quivering huddle farther out in the courtyard. They knew the look.

"Why do you present *this* problem to a person who has no progeny? Must you mock me? What do *I* care about *your* kids or their confounded caretaker? On the day that *my own* baby boy is born, then *you* can bother me about *yours!*"

The Queen silently backed farther away.

"Don't tell me *your* tiresome, trivial troubles today! *I* am oblivious to your obnoxious offspring! *I* ignore their ignorant instructor! Who among you is ready to relinquish their head as it is hacked for this ignorant interruption? Go away! Get out! *Go!*"

The huge Castle door slammed shut. The People stared at it, stunned. They had not thought before of their King as a person, with or without a child. They didn't care about the King's problem, but they *did* understand that their Royal Judgment was not going to happen. They were on their own. Disappointed, they turned back toward the village, keeping their mouths shut and their heads on their shoulders.

Miserable Monarchs

After the crowd of townsfolk left, King Sol and Queen Luna solemnly seated themselves in the gloomy throne room. At opposite ends of their enormous Royal Table, they awaited the service of their meal. They had no idea that they still had a visitor.

Spirit had followed the townsfolk to the Castle, hoping to see some kind of royal forgiveness for the young Teacher who cared so much for his wife and baby. Such caring was hugely important, and Spirit wanted to support it. Perhaps some Teachers had more Special Clay in their hearts. Maybe the King would honor that. Spirit lived in hope these days.

But Spirit's hopefulness had, as usual, not been rewarded. Neither the King nor the townsfolk had shown any feelings toward the poor Teacher. If anything, selfishness and anger were even more obvious. He looked around for Fighter, who usually appeared at angry gatherings. Fighter loved to gloat, but he wasn't here today. Good.

The Queen began arranging herself in her lovely gown, a gown she had been unable to display to the visitors. Such a waste. So unfair. She pouted.

Then another important thought occurred. Now she needed to distract the King from the baby issue. She wanted a baby, too, but that was no reason to not show off her beauty to her husband. He definitely was a fan of her beauty, and this tactic had worked many times before. She tried her most winning smile.

But King Sol didn't seem to notice her at all. The King's mood had not improved. He still had his own selfish worry on his mind, and this worry was much greater to him than those of his subjects or his Queen. He was King Sol the Selfish after all, and as King, selfishness was his right. But something else was even more important than getting his way.

The problem was major. King Sol was the son of a king. King Sol's father had been the son of the previous king as well and so on and so on. That was how Kingship was done. It was handed down from father to son. There was no other method. And King Sol had no son.

He had been brooding on this failure all day, looking for someone to blame. In fury now, he kicked his chair on its side, pounded the food-laden table with his fists, and finally turned the whole thing over with a thud. It was an amazing display of temper. The Queen covered her eyes and ducked. So did Spirit.

The Castle walls continued to echo with the clatter of thrown objects and the din of the King's shouting. The contents of wine pitchers, soup bowls, and platters of vegetables arrived together in a puddle of ooze on the throne room floor.

The Castle Cook ran screaming from the room. Guards and servants backed away. Serving wenches appeared from seven directions, complete with mops and rags, to slosh heroically at the mess.

"Why?" roared King Sol, pacing the throne room with fury. "Why does clueless incompetence constantly confound me? Can no one supply me successfully with sufficient spoons before my soup is served? These are spindly spoons! Can no one properly prepare for a powerful person?"

The King sent a nearby tray of soup spoons sailing, clattering, and clanking out the window. The women who were mopping the floor, the Castle Guards, and even Queen Luna, herself, ducked the hurtling hardware.

"Can you not care for a King? Were you People preparing for a peasant? Can no one see to my simplest supplies? Go at once and secure me a sufficient soup spoon and a great golden goblet. Do not delay! I *will* have what I want, and I *will* have it when I want it! You *will* properly please me or prepare for a particularly punishing punishment!"

King Sol gathered his robe about himself and plopped down again on his chair, which fortunately, a servant had set back on its legs behind him just in time. Now for some reason, he noticed the hungry, fearful stare of this servant and had a thought.

I see that my servants are looking slightly skinny. Maybe I should stop pounding and order them a portion of pot roast, he mused to himself.

Spirit perked up and listened to his thoughts closely. "I think I hear Special Clay at work! This shows a bit of kindness or thoughtfulness, even unselfishness, beginning to come to life! And I am here to see it!"

But the King shook his head, dismissing such an unusual passing thought.

"No! What an idiotic idea!" he hollered. "They just want me to weaken. Let the fools find their own food! I am positively the only important person present!"

Spirit drooped in the rafters.

Now Queen Luna tried her hand again at distracting the King. "Dear, you do yell majestically as any fine King should, but why don't you take just a moment to see how beautifully I am dressed? I know you love me in lavender, and I thought that this lavender outfit might really drive you wild today." Luna smiled sweetly and brushed her hair back into a golden set of curls. She posed elegantly. "What do you think, my kingly crumb cake? Don't you just love me in lavender?"

"The Queen still cares about what her husband thinks of her," Spirit observed. "Maybe she still loves this man."

Maids hovered over Queen Luna, lifting and smoothing her already perfect hair and holding up a mirror for her to see the results. The Queen smiled at the image of herself in the mirror. There was nothing she liked more than looking at her own reflection, and today, she knew she was even more beautiful than usual. She waited. King Sol said nothing.

"Oh, for Pete's sake!" Luna grumbled to herself. "I know *I* am beautiful. Obviously, this attire isn't fine enough to attract my husband's attention. That is just not right. If this gown was sufficient, he would have adored me instead of throwing things. It's the fault of this gown. That settles it. I *must* have an even more gorgeous dress made for me immediately. But what will attract his attention? This dress was just finished yesterday. It was already more than he deserved. He should be in awe of my beauty."

Again, Spirit was disappointed. The King was yelling about soup spoons, and the Queen was grumbling about more fancy clothes. Would they never understand each other enough to focus on what they both wanted the most? The child they both longed for was appearing more and more out of reach.

Yes, the King was thoughtless and selfish. The Queen was unsympathetic and vain. The sad truth was that their romance was pretty much history. In fact, the two of them were so unhappy that they had completely forgotten times, not too long ago, when they had actually loved each other very much. Spirit remembered those days fondly. He had enjoyed watching them then.

Only a little over a year ago, new romance had been in the air, and they had been full of joy. They had walked hand in hand, kissed under the willow tree, and whispered sweet nothings to each other by the hour.

"You are my most lovely lavender lilac! I love you endlessly, my own lovable Luna. I am so lucky to have captured you as my Queen."

Those tender word were no longer being spoken.

Spirit did understand, however, that the King, now in his second year of marriage, was consumed by his desire for an heir. For a King, an heir was crucial to his kingdom *and* his manhood.

Spirit could get that, but this passion for his kid and royal heir was now destroying thoughts of anything else. The Queen, who was completely convinced that her beauty was the key to the King's love, had fallen in love with her own good looks, but the truth was, she also wanted a child more than anything.

Real romance and caring for each other was now only a memory for both of them. Spirit could see that these poor Royals were beginning to treat each other the way they treated others, which was bad…really bad. Their deep love was a mere shadow of what it had been before, and Spirit feared it would soon be lost forever.

In the gloom of the throne room, the great golden goblet and superior soup spoons gleamed in front of the King. Queen Luna sat down again at the far end of the table and began picking at the soup placed in front of her while her servants hovered about her nervously. No one spoke.

Finally, the King glared down the long table at Queen Luna. "You show up here, my Queen, day after day, doing and undoing new hairdos and altering your attire. What use is all that creative combing and dreary dressing when you can't handle my most reasonable request? All I want is a son! Go tell the Queen what I say," King Sol commanded of a poor servant girl standing nearby.

The servant girl curtsied. "Yes, Your Majesty," she whispered in a trembling voice, dashing to the other end of the table.

Suddenly, from up in the rafters, Spirit noticed something else.

Oh wonderful! Fighter had arrived! He had probably heard the King turn over the table. That usually meant a good fight was coming. Fighter loved family feuds between the King and Queen. Times like these gave him bonus points in their Game. Spirit knew that Fighter was hoping for some big-time shouting and a mid-game display of his kind of talent. Fighter would be the cheering section.

The servant girl smiled at Queen Luna sweetly. "The King says that you look beautiful today," she lied.

The Queen stopped frowning and smiled demurely as she accepted the compliment she knew she deserved, but then she responded, "I am surprised that he can stop yelling long enough to even see me, the bellowing buffoon! Go tell the King what I said," commanded Queen Luna with a haughty glare from her end of the table.

The servant girl scampered back to King Sol.

"The Queen says to tell you that she is trying to look beautiful today, just for you," she informed him breathlessly. These little lies were one way that the servants kept a bit of peace in the Castle. Spirit smiled.

"That delay-of-game defense was nauseating," mumbled Fighter to himself. "When are these Royals going to get down to the good stuff? Why am I here? This fake chitchat is totally boring. Let's see a fight worth seeing. Let's move the ball!"

Spirit heard Fighter's noise from the cheering section. Fighter was, indeed, coaching from the sidelines, but King Sol did not appear to get the message. Good for him.

The King blushed and smiled. He was suddenly hopeful. Had he just heard something good from his Queen? The Queen appeared to be in a good mood. Could it be? Maybe she was finally going to tell him what he was waiting to hear. Slowly he rose and sidled hopefully down the table toward his wife.

"Has it happened?" he murmured, grinning hopefully. "Is today the day that you speak of the spectacular son for whom I have anxiously awaited? This is the best blessing that any Queen can bestow! Tell me this is true!" The King beamed in anticipation, caressing Luna's face tenderly.

The Queen stuck out her lower lip in a pout.

"Oh, Sol," she sniffed impatiently. "Is that the only thing you can talk to me about anymore? You *know* I would produce a son for you if I could. You *know* that I also want a child more than anything in the world. Can't you say something nice to *me* once in a while, without talking about a baby? Can't you just tell me that I am beautiful beyond bearing as you used to do, without asking me to *produce*? I can't have a baby if I can't. And I haven't had a baby, so . . . so . . . so . . . I haven't!" Tears welled up quickly.

"Harrumph!" growled the King, removing his hand and twisting his loving smile into a scowl.

"Here we go," sneered Fighter from his cheering section. "Now things ought to get good."

Sol stared coldly at the pleading Luna. "*No, no, no! Everyone* knows that the *real* reason, maybe the *only* reason for having a queen is *a son*, an heir to the throne. Queens must supply sons. You, my dear, are my Queen, but your production, in particular, is pitiful. All your ridiculous robes and hundreds of hairstyles do *me* no good! One of these days, no matter how many dresses you don, you will be too old to produce a proper son! *I* have a right to *reproduce!* It is *your* duty to do that! Do your duty, drat you!" King Sol glared at Queen Luna, his fist spearing the air to make his point.

Luna gasped and tried to defend herself. "You hurt my feelings when you talk like that, Sol. I can't do what I can't do, particularly when you are so mean and hateful," she whimpered. "When you yell and shout, I know I will never be able to give you the son you desire. Desire *me,* Sol. Desire *me* and perhaps *your* desire for a son will come true. What if I never have a baby? Does that mean you will never love me again, just for myself?"

Queen Luna was as miserable as her husband. She began to cry harder. She did not need to be told that she was a failure. She knew it. More than anything, she wanted to be a mother. Spirit's heart ached for both of them.

The King saw the Queen's tears and became even angrier. He hated it when she cried. He began to pace.

"Because I am the King, I can command that you stop crying and give me what I want," he announced, sounding more like a spoiled child than a king. "I don't care a fig for your feelings. Your blubbering doesn't bother me a bit. I have a Royal Right to a son."

The Queen started to wail. "You don't have a right to be so unfair," she sobbed. "You have no heart, Sol. Why should I give you a son anyway? I don't want to give birth to a son for a King with no heart."

Spirit jumped to his feet. "He has a heart! I made it with Special Clay! I know he has one! Why doesn't he use it like he should?"

Fighter started to laugh. "Maybe he doesn't use it because the heart inside him is no good," he snickered.

"I have a very healthy heart! A Royal heart! I am the King!" King Sol roared, and he pounded his fists on his chest where he thought his heart should be. "And my Royal Heart insists on its Royal Right to have a son!"

The Queen covered her face with her hands. "If you really do have a heart, then show it! Your miserable heart isn't working at all as far as I can see." She sobbed.

For a moment, the King felt sorry for his Queen, crying uncontrollably at the table. Spirit saw this. "Sympathy! Yes! Yes!" he whispered hopefully. "That means his heart is working."

"No, no! Don't give in. There's nothing where your heart should be but sand!" hissed Fighter from a few rafters down.

Spirit whirled around. "What?"

Fighter swallowed quickly. "Oh, nothing."

"Harrumph," the King muttered in frustration. Slowly Sol turned, and with shoulders drooping, he shuffled from the room without his meal.

The Queen continued to cry. Spirit, still in the rafters, shook his head. Fighter shook his head as well, though neither spirit looked at each other.

"That was almost a pretty good fight, but I've seen better down by the River," sighed Fighter. He left the throne room for the Riverbank, in search of more action. Spirit said nothing.

The Queen sat alone at the huge dining table with her maids. They immediately began trying to rearrange her hair. Queen Luna, however, was still crying, her shoulders shaking so hard that her ladies-in-waiting could do nothing but wait.

Spirit pitied the beautiful Queen. And what had she said? If the King really had a heart, "it isn't working at all." Could she possibly be right? Spirit recycled that question. If human hearts weren't working, had he done something wrong? Fighter's comment surfaced…something about sand. If Spirit had done something wrong back in the day, was there anything he could do about it now? Probably not. He had been the original producer, but now he was stuck. The Game was in progress. No in-game replacement allowed.

Forget about it! Spirit felt his failure. Whatever he had done or not done, he was responsible for an unfixable mess. He had made sad, unhappy People. Below him, a miserable Queen still sobbed. He could not pretend that she wasn't there. She was like all of her subjects. Spirit felt that he had to accept facts. Happy hearts may now just be his fantasy. Spirit's hope for winning the Game was fading.

Spirit was depressed. He needed relief. He decided to slip down below the floorboards of the throne room and watch the mice for a while. These gentle creatures would take his mind off things. Mice were *so Good*. Maybe today he would discover a clue as to why. If not, at least a visit to the mice was enjoyable.

The Rodent Rally

And what would Spirit find below the floorboards of the throne room today? As the King and Queen argued in the Castle above, beneath the floorboards, hundreds of mice were happily gathering for a Rodent Rally and Spirit Club in Mouse Hall. They were what? Yes. They were coming together for a Rodent Rally and Spirit Club.

Why? As ancestors of the famous author, Amos Mouse, and the world-famous creator, Michael Angelo Mouse, these rodents (mostly mice, actually) were proud members of a robust club that still cheered for Spirit's happy earth in the future and all the creative work he had done back in the day.

Unobserved by Spirit, this club had become and remained active as the Game with the humans progressed haltingly through the years. Mice were born 'loyal Spirit Fans' and their loyalty was still true blue. Today they were noisily awaiting their own Coach and mentor, Moses Mouse.

Spirit didn't even notice any of the Spirit posters that were up around Mouse Hall. He just slid into a dark corner to rest. He was good at blending in with the scenery, so nobody noticed. He was bummed by his humans. Mice seemed relatively problem-free. This was a good place to relax for a minute or two and maybe regroup.

Moses Mouse scurried fast on his way to Mouse Hall. He was the great-great-great-(etc., etc.) grandson of Amos Mouse, who was the great-great-grandson of Michael Angelo Mouse. Amos Mouse was, of course, the author of the books _The Book of Amos_ and _The Scrap Book_, the books of creation and heritage. That history made Moses very special.

Because Mouse Hall (hereafter known as the Hall) was the same size as the throne room above, the Hall was enormous, rough, sturdy, and ready for large crowds. Pictures of famous rodents from history had been placed along the walls beside the posters with such slogans as "Rodent Power!" and "Go, Spirit, Go!", which had been carefully reproduced by the clever paws of the Spirit Sister's Auxiliary. All in all, the room was a perfect place for Spirit Fans, and mice were definitely Spirit Fans. They were also potential players, or would be, if they were ever called upon to get into the Game.

Moses was carrying _The Book of Amos_ (hereafter referred to as _The Book_). It was a precious treasure, one of only two in existence. The Scraps had the other one, of course. Moses treasured this book, which had been entrusted to his care. He would guard it with his life.

Deep in thought, Moses passed Ramon and Reardon, twin rats who were leaning against a wall outside the Hall, looking bored. They had little respect for Moses or any mouse for that matter. They viewed mice as goody-goodies, uncomfortably tidy, and decidedly boring. Rats were sure that because of The Book, mice thought they were above other rodents. Unfortunately, this *was* pretty much what mice thought, too. To be honest, mice were snooty.

It was clear to Moses, as he noticed the rats' dingy fur and rumpled clothes, that these rats (like most of their brother rats) were *not* ready to contribute anything of value to the upcoming Rodent Rally. They had an annoying habit of lurking around activities in the Hall and looking down their long noses as though they were somehow superior. They didn't seem to have jobs or activities of their own that Moses could see but primarily got along by scavenging what others (including the mice) left behind. They weren't even signed up as players in the Game. *Not very loyal to Spirit,* Moses thought.

Moses, who didn't actually know any rats very well, thought of rats as lazy and basically untrustworthy, and he often grumbled that rats would stop living if the world stopped providing them with leftovers. Moses thought of his own use of the *same* leftovers as "obtaining provisions and supplies and reducing waste"—a different perspective on the same activity? *Hmm . . .*

"Gettin' set for another one of yer Rodent Rallies, are ya, Mose? Yer gonna read 'em that there fairy story 'bout The Big Game, ain't ya?" drawled one of the rat brothers.

The rats were not believers in Michael Angelo Mouse or The Book (most likely because they were not mentioned by name in the book anywhere *and* a mouse had written it).

"We are going to start our rally by reading from The Book, as usual, if that's what you mean, Reardon," said Moses, trying to appear cool and polite. "You are welcome to join us if you would like."

"Is that what ya have all wrapped up in that there shawl there?" Ramon poked a bony paw at the bundle Moses held protectively to his chest.

Instinctively, Moses shrank from Ramon's touch and turned away. It made him almost sick to think of these dirty, non-player, distant rodent cousins coming near his ancient treasure. His was the original, centuries-old volume after all.

Historians were sure that mice and rats were both rodents and created nearly at the same time, but Moses and the rest of the mice did not like to think about that. Rats, like People, seemed selfish, not hard working, and seemed to have no sense of right and wrong at all. Moses could see now, as The Book said, just what had been left out when Spirit had created humans *and* rats. Heart. What a shame.

A pang of guilt suddenly caused Moses to pause. Moses *did* have ideas of right and wrong that he had gathered from the Practices of the Scraps' generous nature. Moses was probably not right to think he was better than these rats, just because he didn't like the way they looked or lived. Scraps wouldn't treat rats badly. Moses knew he shouldn't. Subconsciously, he tried to imitate the Scraps and their ways. Moses turned back to the twins and smiled. He almost meant it.

"The Spirit Sister's Auxiliary will have cookies and lemonade at the snack bar during the break," he said with the closest thing to friendliness he could muster. "Feel free to stop by and have some, even if you don't want to listen to my presentation." Moses knew the Scraps would be proud of him for this gesture.

Reardon and Ramon appeared surprised by the offer from a mouse and were definitely speechless. They scratched themselves in an embarrassed fashion, mumbled something that vaguely sounded like 'okay', and shuffled off, looking sheepish.

Moses pulled open the curtains to the Hall, now full of hundreds of mice, chattering and mingling happily together in the huge space. Unlike River People, these mice were happy with their lives and honest and friendly with each other.

What a marvelous species, Moses thought proudly.

He entered the Hall and began weaving his way through the crowd toward a speaker's platform at the front. The Book was still securely wrapped in the soft purple cloth he used to protect it against moisture and mold, common problems for all those living near the River and under floorboards.

The mice began to quiet themselves, and the Rodent Rally respectfully parted to let Moses and his famous book pass. Moses was known to be a mentor for the younger members of the Spirit Club. He was a very smart mouse. As a direct descendant of Amos Mouse, he and his family had lived for many generations under the Castle right below the King. In his own way, Moses Mouse was almost "mouse royalty," but the humble Moses preferred to be called Mose.

Moses considered himself to be one of the decision makers for the Rodent Community, however, and he took his role seriously. He respected Spirit. He feared Fighter. He had never seen either one of them, but he tried to do what he thought Spirit would want him to do with the Spirit Team. The Big Game may have quieted down, but there was still a Game going on, after all. Goodness on the game ball was the goal, and all mice knew it was obvious that there was no winner yet. That fact was more than obvious for mice who were keeping score.

All mice knew what Fighter had done to try to wreck Goodness back in the day, and they could see how strong Fighter still was. The future on the game ball was what was important. Mice were waiting for Spirit to rework his Game Plan. They had been waiting for years and years and *years*. Mice were hoping that Spirit would step up positive action in the Game, but the mice were patient. When he got ready to make his move, mice would be part of the Goodness Comeback!

Moses believed in the Game, but he was painfully aware that Spirit knew nothing about Scraps and never had. This was weird. As a coach, Moses definitely thought that Scraps could and *should* be players on Spirit's side of the Game. He often wondered if somebody shouldn't at least tell Spirit about Scraps. Like his famous ancestor, Michael Angelo, Moses wanted to help. Scraps *should* be part of the Game, shouldn't they? Scraps were all about Goodness. But Moses also knew his place. He was just a Coach.

The purpose of Rodent Rallies was to remind mice of their role in The Big Game of the past and keep Spirit Club energy going for the Game that was still in progress. These mice were loyal.

But Moses had called this special Rodent Rally at an unusual time, in the fall. It was an emergency meeting. There was no time to wait. There was a crisis.

This day would be one of decision-making and planning for the Spirit Club. It was more than just important. Moses felt it was a matter of life or death for Scraps.

Spirit was dozing in a corner and awoke a bit to watch as more mice streamed into the Hall. He was ready to watch something happy and good. The mice kept coming, however. Hundreds of tiny creatures were peacefully gathering together, apparently for some sort of meeting. Spirit had watched mice in the fields before, but he had never attended a large gathering such as this. He didn't know they had such a thing. If these mice were People, fistfights would have broken out several times already. Spirit was fascinated. What was the occasion?

And what *was* the occasion? It was all about Scraps! Moses had suddenly realized that Scraps were in mortal danger! For years, Moses had made note of the growing numbers of the River People along the Riverbank. Fighter's mean and selfish humans were everywhere now. No big deal. Moses had faith that Spirit would come up with his new Game Plan to fight Fighter's Chaos sooner or later, but that was not what Moses was worried about now.

The behavior of all People was bad, but even more important was the fact that there were just *too many* of them. There were more and more evil humans every day, and they all still wanted to live along the River. *That* was the problem. Growing numbers of People were here *now*, and, almost daily, crushingly, they were *on top of Scraps*.

As their numbers increased along the Riverbank, the People had overflowed, spreading farther up and down stream into outlying grassy areas, areas which had been safe homes to the Scraps for centuries. The Scraps had tried to migrate away from the increasing hordes, but the growing ranks of large, human bodies were overtaking them. The People were a problem to one another, but even worse, they were now a threat to the very lives of Scraps who were more and more under their feet.

Scraps were smaller than most grown mice and decidedly slower. They could not escape trampling as easily as mice, and they lived in little communities above ground, just like People. Their homes, nestled among the grasses near the River, were increasingly in a very dangerous place. Some Scraps had already been killed by their huge neighbors. Moses had been told by Scraps of the unbelievable trampling of a whole Scrap family. And their killers, the giant River People, had no idea that the poor Scraps even existed.

In his bones, Moses felt the end of Scraps as a species coming. He could see it plain as day. If something didn't change soon, the Scrap Kingdom could be destroyed, wiped out, ground into extinction. The solution to this approaching doom needed to be discovered and implemented now before it was too late.

This was, of course, the reason for the special Rodent Rally. Moses had decided that he couldn't sit back and let destruction happen. Because of his position as leader of the Spirit Club and descendant of Michael Angelo, he felt responsible. Also, mice and Scraps were such close friends that he knew neither could picture life on the Riverbank without the other.

And there was the basic matter of Scrap Goodness. Goodness was the goal of the Game into which all Scraps had been born. The Spirit Club must do something to save that Goodness. Moses felt that *he*, as a mouse patriarch, must make it happen.

Today Moses was determined to pull together the great minds of the Rodent Rally and Spirit Club and find a way to help the Scraps. He had no idea what that way might be, but he was confident that the members of the Rodent Rally would come up with a solution. They were definitely ready to be players in Spirit's Game. It was time for them to take the field.

This is where The Book came in. Moses was hoping that his re-reading of their important history would stir up some inspiration in the creative mice minds of the Spirit Club. Moses concentrated on all this as he worked himself forward in the Hall, through the crowd of ears and tails and friendly paw-pats on the back. Preparation for inspiration of the Players—that's what it was all about. He was the Coach.

"Yo, Coach!"

"How's it goin'?"

"What's the good word?"

At last he reached the front of the Hall. With a serious Game face, he climbed to the speaker's platform, a small, once-discarded gift box, which was used as a stage or platform or whatever was necessary to raise a speaker above the crowd. Because the box was four or five inches taller than the floor, Moses could see and be seen.

Today, with an empowering sense of purpose, Moses surveyed his fellow players on the Goodness Team. Hundreds of mice gathered in front of him. There was an ocean of pink ears and twitching whiskers as far as his eyes could see. This was a group to be proud of.

Moses suddenly quivered with nervousness. If he could provide the right motivation, today might be the key to a rescue plan that was needed, but what if he couldn't? He had to do it right. The future of all Scraps might depend on it.

With great respect, Moses carefully removed the rich purple cloth in which The Book was wrapped. It was centuries old, but it was still a beautiful and priceless book. The cloth slid away and was given to a young Spirit Club member waiting nearby. Moses spoke.

"Yo, my fellow Spirit Club members and awesome Rodent Rally. I salute you. Many of you have traveled long distances to be here today in answer to my emergency request. When you show up to this moment, you demonstrate your respect for The Book and your commitment to the Game of Goodness. I appreciate that. *You* are the Rodents of the past, the present, and the future. *You* are the Players in the Game. *You* are the Spirit Club!"

The Spirit Club members energetically clicked their teeth and cheered for their own status. They were proud of their history... and Coach knew how to get his audience worked up.

"Most of you have heard from <u>The Book of Amos</u> many times before. You know its meaning, and you know the special part that a mouse played in The Big Game. It's all right here in <u>The Book</u>!"

All the mice shouted and yelled with a hearty, high-pitched "You can say that again, Coach! Michael Angelo was the best! Hall of Fame all the way!"

"Mice *were* Players!" the mice cheered.

"Mice *are* Players! Rah, rah, rah!"

"Right on, Team!" continued Moses. "We were there when Spirit made all the great creatures on the game ball. In fact, as <u>The Book</u> says, we were the first Players in <u>The Big Game</u>!"

"Hooray for mice!"

"<u>The Book</u> knows!"

"Let's hear it for <u>The Book</u>!"

Spirit, who had dozed off again in his shadowy corner of the Hall, perked up and listened. These marvelous mice had actually written down their own version of The Big Game in a book. They were even cheering for creation. Who knew what mice would do that?

Spirit was flabbergasted. He had always thought that mice were intelligent, but he had no idea that they had actually written their own history book and about The Big Game too! Spirit focused intently on this mouse with the large book. He seemed to be an authority of some kind.

"From our very first forefather, Michael Angelo Mouse, we mice have played our part in The Big Game!" Moses continued, the heavy book pressed against his chest. "This is the reason that we are here today, fellow Goodness Team members! To read once again from <u>The Book</u>, to read the story of The Big Game but also to think about what that first part of the Game means to the Game for Goodness that continues today. We must plan for the future. This future may be in crisis, and the future may also be *our* responsibility, and why? Because *we were the first Players on the Goodness Team, that's why!*"

Spirit stared...*and listened.*

"The Big Game!"

"The Game for Goodness!"

"We are Players!"

What else did the mice know? And the mice were cheering.

"All mice will pass the test!
From the beginning, mice were best!" squeaked the enthusiastic crowd.

Unbelievable.

The mouse called Coach joined in the cheer but waited for it to fade. Now he sat down on a bench that had been provided for him. He arranged his robes carefully and opened his book. Spirit watched carefully.

The cheering Spirit Club members settled back on their haunches to hear again the history story that made mice the first Players in The Big Game of creation. They glowed with pride. They never got tired of this old, first hand report, but what did Moses mean about future and crisis?

"Go, Coach, go!" the mice chanted. Now the Hall became hushed. Spirit eased forward to listen.

"Start reading now, Grandpa! You're taking too long!"

The mice gasped. Where did that voice come from? Who would dare to interrupt Coach? The mice strained to get a glimpse of the thoughtless creature who would dare to barge in at such a meaningful moment.

They didn't have long to wonder. Scrambling up on the speaker's platform was a tiny young mouse, no bigger than a piece of chewing gum. All watched in disbelief as the little fellow grabbed at the robes of Moses Mouse and scooted up to his lap, right next to <u>The Book.</u>

Moses smiled down at the little furry face looking up at him impatiently. "Soon, Max. Fellow rodents. Let me present my grandson, Maximilian, or Max, as we call him," Moses said.

The mice now chuckled. It was well known that Moses doted on this grandson, the youngest in the family, and some felt that the wild ways of this grandson reminded Moses of himself.

Moses placed little Max carefully on the floor at his feet and announced to the rally, "It is for the young players-to-be, *in particular*, that I have called you together today. I dedicate this reading to *their* future in the Game for Goodness. Max, can you sit still and listen?"

Max's large, pink ears bobbed up and down. Everyone doubted that Max could sit still for even one moment, but they understood why Moses let him stay close. The young ones needed to learn. Moses reopened <u>The Book.</u>

Suddenly, from the Castle far above them came a thundering crash, followed by loud voices and great thuds across the ceiling of the Hall. The King was throwing things again. The congregation of mice froze in place while the room shook. Max hid under his grandfather's robes.

"They should do something about that King's temper!" squeaked Max loudly.

"*Shh*, Max," hushed Moses.

"Well, they should," little Max muttered. "The King is a major Player for Fighter, I can tell. He should be thrown out of the Game. If we could just get up there in his face, I bet me and some Scraps could teach him a thing or two about not losing his temper so bad."

Spirit smiled at the suggestion of the young mouse. How smart he was for a little creature. This was the very thing Spirit wished he could do, but what was a Scrap? "Probably a small mouse," Spirit concluded.

Moses now brought the Rodent Rally back together and began to read again. Spirit strained to hear every word. It was about The Big Game, after all. How amazing was that? Moses read slowly and carefully, too slowly for grandson Max. Max fidgeted.

Moses began to read about Fighter for Chaos, but now Max pouted loudly. "I don't get it. Isn't Fighter a bad guy? Why is he in The Book?" asked Max with a scowl. "What did *he* make? Why do we need to hear about *him?*"

This was the most difficult part of The Book to explain to youngsters. Moses didn't want to scare them. "You've heard about Fighter before, Max. You're right. He didn't make anything at all. He just tried to destroy the good stuff Spirit made. But, the truth is, he still does that. His full name is Fighter for Chaos. We don't talk about him much. We hope that Spirit's River People will start practicing more Goodness soon so that they can tell Fighter to get lost. Fighter needs some strong positive offense on the game ball so that Spirit can win the Game. That's why we mention him, see?"

"Oh," responded Max. "You mean Fighter is real? I never thought Fighter was real. I thought he was just a bogeyman. But if Fighter *is* real, I bet I know where he hangs out these days," Max continued.

Moses was becoming a bit impatient. "Not now, Max," he corrected quietly.

"Okay, but I bet the *real* Fighter right now lives with humans. I bet that Fighter guy hangs out around the People all the time. That's why they are so mean."

"Smart kid," mused Spirit.

Moses thought for a minute. Max had a point, but Moses continued with his reading:

"Spirit had made beauty on every side, but he felt an emptiness inside."

"Wow!" exclaimed Max. "Spirit made the whole game ball, Grandpa? That's why we're all Spirit Fans, right? What did he do then?" Max's eyes were huge. Because he was very young, it was his first time to actually hear The Book of Amos, itself.

"He made a creature." Moses moved on with a smile. "That's what Spirit did."

"What was it, Grandpa?" Max's tail was curling with excitement. "Was it one of us? I've heard that! Was it a mouse?"

"Yes, Max," Moses admitted, smiling gently but proudly. "Yes, it is written in The Book that the first creature made by Spirit was a mouse."

Great cheering exploded throughout the Hall. Spirit smiled from his hiding place as the memory of his first creation efforts came back to him in a flash.

"But why a mouse, Grandpa?" questioned Max. "He should have made something big, like an elephant. When he could have made something really great, why did he start with a little old mouse?"

Spirit could not help but chuckle silently.

But the congregation buzzed. This was just wrong. How could this rude young mouse dare to question The Book, even if he *was* Coach's grandson?

Again, Moses seemed to be unruffled by Max's questions. Instead, he said simply, "Listen and learn," and patted Max's head.

Max backed off but grinned. "That is so cool! The first creature made was really a mouse! Awesome!" As Michael Angelo's great, great, great… grandson, he was now feeling pretty good.

The buzzing ceased. Moses continued to the rapt audience, until he read of the creation of cats.

"Okay, so Spirit made cats. That's still a good thing 'cause I love cats," squeaked Max cheerfully. The roomful of mice inhaled and frowned at this new interruption, then relaxed and chuckled.

At least Max was paying attention, Moses thought, *but The Book was a long book with a lot of details about The Big Game.* And Moses was a Coach. Maybe he should shorten the story for the young folks and reduce references to Fighter *and cats*. That might help everyone stay focused.

Moses placed The Book of Amos on a special stand made from a wooden spool that was polished to a very high gloss. This was The Book's place of honor. He pulled Max up to his lap.

"Do you mind," he asked his fellow mice, "if I just tell about some of our wonderful history in a way that is more understandable to our young people? I promise to do so carefully."

The congregation nodded and smiled in approval as there were many young listeners in the audience. Moses began from where he left off.

"Well, you see, in that time in the universe, it's possible that everything hadn't been thought through by any spirit, not even *our* Spirit of Goodness. It was only a game between two young spirits at that point. It appears that our Spirit had *some* basic ideas of the way he wanted the universe to be a good place and all. He knew he liked Goodness."

"Did Fighter like Goodness too?" chirped Max.

"Not so much," responded Moses. "Goodness was mostly Spirit's idea. But because the Game was a new thing and Spirit was only trying to win the Game against Fighter, much of his offense was, what shall I say, decided on the fly. (Spirit nodded, remembering.) And because he hadn't quite thought everything through ahead of time, he ended up calling an audible from time to time. Sometimes he made some very strange but awesome things. For example, he made some mammals that were designed to spend all their life *underwater* but could only breathe *air*."

"A whale, Grandfather! A whale!" squeaked Max.

"A whale! Good for you!" congratulated Moses. "And what do you think of a creature that barks like a dog and has fur like a dog but must *swim all day like a fish* because it has *fish flippers instead of legs*?"

Max thought about it.

"A seal?" That was a young lady mouse in the third row.

"Of course! Very good! And Spirit made a bird that *couldn't fly*. He called that a penguin. He even made a mouse that *could* fly!"

"You're kidding, Grandpa. There's a mouse that can fly?"

"Yes, Max. We call it a bat."

"Sounds like Spirit made some mistakes like I do sometimes!" blurted Max, obviously thrilled that someone else made mistakes. A slight chuckle went through the Spirit Club but quickly faded. They did not approve of making fun of Spirit.

"In a way, you might think that," agreed Moses. "The truth is, Spirit *did* make some odd creatures. Some of them have lasted on the game ball, and some of them haven't. But none of them were really mistakes, Max. They were just creatures that Spirit made because he was creative.

"Spirit was thinking about The Big Game, itself, more than any one particular creature. He was just trying to make a good, happy place, that's all. He figured that a lot of creatures and a lot of life would make a place happier and maybe provide the Goodness that would win the Game."

"The more the merrier! More animals, more Goodness!" chanted the Spirit Club.

Moses placed Max back on the floor and stepped forward toward the hundreds of eager mouse faces in front of him. They were doing the wave. The Spirit Club loved that, but upon seeing Moses's serious face, they quieted and leaned toward their leader to listen and to share the conclusion and their favorite part of <u>The Book.</u> It was *their* part.

As a mouse with a mission, Moses now cleared his throat to begin reading again from the closing chapter, working his way toward the finale with conviction.

Spirit leaned in as well, looking forward to the grand conclusion of Moses' presentation. This mouse's book had told about The Big Game exactly the way he remembered it so far. These mice had apparently written down *everything perfectly* in their book. It was wonderful. Why had he never known of this before? He was impressed.

Spirit was now completely focused on the mouse's reading. These final chapters of what they called '<u>The Book</u>' should be the most exciting. How well he remembered creating his wonderful humans in spite of Fighter's storm. He had been heroic! This was the part of the whole process that made 'just a game' into *The Big Game* in his mind. He was proud of the People he had created, and it sounded like the mice had captured every detail. Now he might actually find out about the final moments of that night, the ones that happened after he left. He wished he had stayed, but those storms had been so outrageous and he *had* completed his work.

Moses read carefully of the creation of humans. They were "tall and proud," he read. They had beautiful heads and faces and then what? The mouse read on about the hurricane and the tornado and the eclipse, all the negative moves of Fighter. Spirit remembered these too well. That's why he had left.

But now Moses read something else . . .something that he didn't remember. 'Something' was dropped. Something else was "too sandy, right from the start." This was new and Spirit didn't remember this part at all. He drew closer.

The mouse was reading that Spirit had dropped some of the Special Clay that he had been shaping into perfect hearts. Humans were the creations Spirit was most proud of, but this last part of his work *had* taken place in a storm.

Spirit was proud that he had stood up against Fighter. He remembered scooping up some of the dropped Special Clay. He remembered pushing it into the hearts of his beloved humans. Then he had breathed life into them and zoomed away. He had completed his mission against all odds, and he was proud.

But Moses kept reading <u>The Book.</u> It said more about 'sand'.

In his hurry, had he, a prideful spirit, made hearts with some sand in them instead of Special Clay? It had been raining and blowing. Fighter had been pouring on the bad weather.

Could it be? No! Never! I couldn't have! Spirit thought with a shudder. *My humans were perfect! I am sure of that!*

Spirit remembered taking off to get out of the pounding rain, but *after* making sure that Special Clay was in the hearts. His humans had been completed perfectly, hadn't they?

He remembered blowing life into them. They were alive and hugging when he left. Spirit was holding his breath now as he continued to listen.

Moses was, at last, at the part of <u>The Book</u> that detailed the creation of Scraps by the beloved ancestor of *all* the assembled mice. He read slowly and proudly of the struggles of Michael Angelo, dragging Special Clay to the overhanging rock.

"It was the Special Clay," Moses read, "that Spirit had dropped." The room was hushed.

Spirit couldn't move. Moses continued reading with solemn enthusiasm, but the story Spirit was hearing was completely unfamiliar... and frightening. This dignified mouse was reading about some sort of *additional* creation going on. There was a mention of Fireflies, but there was no more mention of him! None at all. Nothing.

The reading continued. Again there were Fireflies mentioned and a mouse having a dream, but there was absolutely nothing more about a spirit, either spirit. Something that Spirit knew nothing about had apparently been created by someone else *after* he left. Had that happened? If so, who had done such a thing?

As the reading droned on, <u>The Book</u> said that tiny people had been created—*tiny people!* Tiny People? There were tiny people somewhere? What tiny people? Where? And the book concluded that they might have even been created by a mouse! A mouse! Really? Spirit sat motionless.

Moses carefully closed the large book. Mouse Hall erupted with riotous cheers of self-congratulations. The lady mice blew their noses and wiped their eyes. This last chapter was always so moving.

"They were Scraps, huh, Grandpa? Those little people that great-great-grandpa Michael Angelo made were Scraps!" exploded Max. "They were real, live Scraps, weren't they, Grandpa? I bet they were! They were Scraps made from scraps of that stuff, that Special Clay, right? That's where the extra breath from Spirit went, I bet! Cool! Those were the first Scraps! That's what Michael Angelo did! He made the first Scraps, only he made them in his sleep!"

Little Max jumped off the platform and began sliding back and forth, occasionally spinning on his back. *That was a* mouse *that made those Scraps!* Max knew he was right, and he was proud! All thoughts of Fighter were forgotten.

Spirit drew back into his corner in amazement. Everything that the mice had written in their book up to this last chapter was absolutely true. Could this part of their book be true as well?

But The Book said that Scraps were tiny people that were made of Special Clay that *he had dropped in the Riverbed.* If so, could a mouse have made them? And if there *was* such a thing as Scraps, where were they? Why had he never seen any?

Spirit had never known that Scraps existed. It had never crossed his mind. These Scraps were, according to this book, made completely of the Special Clay that he thought he had shaped carefully into the human hearts. What if the mouse book was true?

Spirit's head was spinning. When the storm was most fierce, could he have picked up sand from the riverbed instead of Special Clay?

Suddenly everything became clear. Why had he not thought of this before? This was the reason that River People were so slow to use the Goodness in themselves. The understanding of right and wrong that Spirit thought he had placed in the hearts of Man was, possibly, not even there.

He couldn't believe it. Maybe his beloved humans continued to be miserable due to *his error, his* overreaction to a stupid storm brought on by Fighter. *He* had lost focus on that night so long ago! *He* had left behind the very ingredient that would have *created* the Goodness that he had always been after—kindness, knowledge of right and wrong, forgiveness. How could he have done such an unbelievably stupid thing?

The behavior that Spirit had watched in the lives of the River People all these years flashed before his eyes. It was horrible vision. Selfishness, cheating, greed, murder—many of these scenes could have been different for humans with the hearts that he had *intended* to give them.

Spirit was crushed. How could he have been so ignorant? He had given away The Big Game at the very beginning of time just because he was so sure of himself. Instead of a winner, he was a classic failure!

"No wonder Fighter has been such a smug SOB. Fighter has ruled with *his* advantage all these years, and my people haven't had enough of the good stuff in their hearts to fight him off. If there is any Special Clay in their hearts at all, it has never been enough. My People have been almost totally unarmed against Chaos, and it is all my fault!"

Spirit was stunned. Quietly, he left the joyous Rodent Rally and Spirit Club to its celebrating and snuck out, overcome with guilt. He knew for sure that *he* had lost the Game.

Lemonade Plans

Max was still celebrating and spinning around, but no one at the Rally was upset. This was their time to become proud as well. Everyone was on their feet, waving their paws in the air and cheering "Go, go, Michael Angelo!" and "Spirit, Spirit! We're with Spirit! How about you?"

There was no use in trying to pull the Spirit Club's attention back at this point, and Moses Mouse knew it. It was time for a break, so he announced one. The Spirit Club agreed and made their way to the lemonade and treats, still singing their fight song.

Moses placed *The Book* on its stand of honor and relaxed on his bench. He knew that this reading of his beloved book was only a preparation for the life-and-death questions that he would be discussing when his Rally members were full enough of lemonade and cookies.

Moses was concerned. There was Max's mention of Fighter. That was something that Moses didn't know exactly how to consider. He had never seen Fighter, but there was certainly enough Chaos among People to know that Fighter was still in the Game. Obviously, Max had been right. Fighter must be constantly hanging out with People. How could he combat that? It was warm in Mouse Hall. Moses began to nod.

"Grandpa! Grandpa! Are you dead? Wake up! Wake up!"

Max was at Moses's feet again, tugging on his robes. Moses opened a tired eye and looked down. Instead of one little face looking up at him, he saw two. The second one belonged to a tiny young Scrap.

"I don't think I am dead," responded Moses, yawning slowly. "But I am hungry!"

"I don't taste good, sir!" laughed the little Scrap, scooting back to an appropriate location. This was a favorite game.

"Come back," squeaked young Max. "My grandpa won't eat you. He doesn't like raw Scrap anyway!"

Inch by inch, the little boy edged his way playfully, back and forth in front of Moses, staying just beyond Moses's grasp. Moses was a grandfather figure to many young Scraps.

Max ran to his Scrap friend and dragged him back to his grandfather. The game was over. Everybody grinned. Moses shook the hand of the young Scrap, showing respect for the child that would someday be a Scrap man.

"Grandpa, you remember Shaver?" (*Shaver* was short for Little Shaver, a family nickname.) "I just told Shaver that you said that we mice *invented* his people," bragged Max. His chin jutted out with pride. "He doesn't believe it. He says I should tell the truth. But I *am* telling the truth. I'm not a liar, huh, Grandpa?" Max stood with his hands on his haunches and his chest pushed up, waiting to have his boast confirmed.

Moses looked carefully at Shaver. Moses knew his family. He knew most of the Scraps in Scrap Kingdom, including their King and Queen. He knew that many Scrap families did not begin teaching their children about <u>The Book</u> until they were several years older. Carefully, Moses responded. "I was reading from <u>The Book of Amos</u> about Spirit and Michael Angelo," Moses explained to Shaver. "That's like your <u>Scrap Book.</u> They are the same thing but with different titles. And the word is '*created*', not *invented*, Max. Have your mother and father ever told you the story of your creation, Shaver?"

Shaver dug his toe into the floor. "I think they might've told me and my sister a little bit," he said in a very small voice. "But I'm not sure we understood it."

Max pulled Shaver closer to his grandfather. "I brought Shaver to hear the rest of what you talk about today, Grandpa. Do you have some more of that book to read? Some of it might be about Scraps, right? Is it okay if he stays, Grandpa? We both promise to be real quiet." Max looked very sincere.

Shaver looked interested. "I'll be quiet as a mouse," he whispered with a grin.

Moses smiled. *This might be a good thing*, he thought. What he was about to talk about with the Spirit Club was important to everyone, both mice and Scraps. It might be good to have Shaver and Max hear this discussion together, along with everyone else. It was *their* future he was worried about.

"You both may stay," Moses said. "But this will be an adult discussion, so you must be still and listen." The boys nodded solemnly. "Now let's see what we can do to bring this noisy group of grown-ups back to order so we can begin our program again." Moses winked at them.

Moses climbed back up on the platform and tried to display some dignity. "Spirit Club members and guests, I hope you have had a chance to refresh yourselves and consume a bit of the cookies and lemonade of the Spirit Sisters Auxiliary. When you are all again in your seats, we will take another look at the meaning of *The Book of Amos*, maybe from a new point of view that we have not considered before."

The massive group heaved as one into a slow but determined maneuver back toward their original places.

The rats (who had not lost track of their invitation for cookies during the break) continued to graze at the food tables. Little Max motioned to Shaver to sit down beside him on the floor.

Moses began. "When we stopped for our break, we had just finished the story of the creation of Scraps."

"That was about you, Shaver!" squeaked Max. "That was really cool! The Book says that you guys looked like mice from behind!"

Moses scowled down at Max with a look that required instant quiet from the young mouse.

"There are three things beyond creation that we mice know today. First, we know that we mice live on Spirit's game ball. Second, we know that Scraps are our friends." Max nudged Shaver, who grinned self-consciously.

"Third, we also know that the Goodness, which Spirit intended for People, ended up in Scraps instead, right? We also know how that happened. This is, of course, the reason that The Big Game continues, with Fighter in a strong position. This is not good for the Goodness side. Am I right?" The Spirit Club nodded.

"This is what our book tells us," Moses stated slowly. "Because of this, it is my feeling that mice must naturally have a lifelong concern for the well-being of Scraps. A mouse was there at their beginning, and we mice should continue to be there for them. Am I right?"

"Right on." The rodents nodded in agreement.

"Until now, Scraps have not needed us to be anything but friends. This has always been a good thing." To make his point here, Moses reached down and picked up Shaver, the only Scrap in the room.

Moses held Shaver up in front of the congregation. "Take a look at this Scrap, a fine example of a Scrap, a wonderful being made completely of Special Clay. Where would *we* be as mice if we no longer had Scraps to share their Goodness with us?"

Shaver began to feel a bit odd being held up in front of the congregation for all to see. He squirmed, and Moses put him gently on the floor, but Moses was not through. "Imagine, fellow Spirit Club members, what our lives would be like if we had never met Scraps. Scraps have taught us much of what we know today about right and wrong."

"We would be exactly like People, I bet," whispered Max to Shaver a little too loud.

Moses wheeled around to face Max. "Exactly!" he agreed loudly.

"Exactly?" gasped the Spirit Club.

"Exactly!" repeated Moses in a strong voice that reached all the way to the back of The Hall. "People and the rest of us creatures were created with hearts made mostly of sand, just like it says in <u>The Book.</u>

"Scraps were the only ones created *completely* out of the Special Clay. Michael Angelo did that. That Clay contains the Goodness that was originally intended for the hearts of People! *That Clay* was the key to Spirit's Goodness, don't you see? That Clay held the knowledge of right and wrong!"

Shaver shook his head. "That's not what my mom says," he whispered loudly to Max. "My mom says that the knowledge of right and wrong is called Conscience. That's what my mom says, and my mom knows everything."

Moses heard Shaver. The Scrap had a point. "Your mom is smart, Shaver. Goodness *is* all about *the knowledge of right and wrong and acting on it*. From now on, we won't talk about Special Clay anymore. We'll talk about the knowledge of right and wrong. That knowledge was *in* the Clay. Scraps were created out of that very same Clay. From now on, *'Conscience'* will be our new word for the knowledge of right and wrong. That's what Scraps were made of. Thank you, Shaver, and thank your mom."

The congregation sat motionless, trying to absorb the new word for the Scraps' knowledge of right and wrong and what it could mean to them. They had always taken Scrap Goodness for granted.

"I know this new word is a new idea, but we know what it means. To me, the knowledge of right and wrong is what Scraps have and, actually, who they are. Does this make sense to you?" Moses continued.

"The poor, stupid River People didn't get enough of that good stuff in their hearts, did they, Grandpa?" commented Max. "They mostly got sand hearts instead of the Conscience stuff. That's what made them turn out mean and creepy. Do you think they could ever learn to be un-creepy, Grandpa?"

Moses was about to try to answer when, from the back of the crowd, a strong, angry female mouse approached the platform. It was Max's mother. She had been looking for him, and she was *not* happy.

"Maximilian Mouse, where have you been? I told you not to run off while I was getting ready! I have been looking for you for over an hour!"

Max could see that he was in big trouble. His mother was mad. She wasn't content that he was here, safe with Grandpa. Why not? What was the matter with mothers anyway?

Max's mother grabbed Max by the scruff of the neck and yanked him into the air. Just as Max was about to be grounded for life, Moses smiled and said softly, "Hello, Maxine."

Maxine Mouse was Moses's daughter. She stopped in mid-yank and looked at her father. She looked at Max hanging limply from her paw and awaiting his punishment. She looked around the room. For the first time, she became aware of the hundreds of mouse faces looking directly at her.

'Coach's family is making a scene. How embarrassing.' Slowly she lowered Max to the ground.

"It's good to see you, Maxine," Moses said with respect. "I am sure Max should be punished for not letting you know where he was, but your son has just asked an important question. I need to answer that question. It is a big part of my message for today. Please stay for a moment and contribute to the discussion. You have very good ideas. Maybe you can punish Max later?"

I think Grandpa just got me off the hook, thought Max. He was going to be happy but decided he better look remorseful. This wasn't a time to risk being cocky.

Slowly Maxine Mouse sat down, but she still had a firm grip on the fur at the back of Max's neck. Moses smiled and turned his attention back to the Spirit Club.

"Did we all hear what my grandson asked?" Moses continued with a serious tone. "He asked if the People didn't get enough of the Conscience material because their hearts had too much sand in them. Max was on point! People do *not* understand *anything* about right or wrong, quite possibly because their hearts *are* made mostly of sand. And why? It may be because *our* ancestor actually used up that material when he made *Scraps*! *Yes, our ancestor used up most of the Special Clay.*

"Would Spirit have come back the next day to use that Special Clay to *repair* the hearts of the humans? Would Goodness in human hearts have let Spirit win the Game way back then? No one knows." Moses surveyed the Rally members closely.

"The fact is simply that People did not get the Goodness in their hearts, and Scraps were made with it. This is a fact. This may be the reason that People are the way they are, as my grandson says. But, for better or worse, *our ancestor used up the Clay.*

"That leads me to today's question: even if the good stuff was used to make Scraps instead of human hearts, does that mean that Scraps don't deserve to stay alive today?"

The mice stood and squeaked loudly, "Of course not!"

"We love the Scraps!"

"Scraps are wonderful!"

"Scraps are our friends!"

Moses acknowledged the enthusiasm but moved on. "Right. Scraps *are* our friends, but now I feel that they are at least partly our responsibility. The problem is not the Scraps. The problem is what People are doing to Scraps, and we can't ignore it any longer.

"The way People got to be the way they are is something that happened way back in the day. We can't change it. What was, was. But there are too many People now. They are about to crowd out the Scrap population."

Moses paced his little platform. "That's why I've brought you here today. The Riverbank is overflowing with People, up and down the bank. Their numbers are growing fast. Our friends, the good Scraps, are being overrun and crowded out of their houses. Scrap Goodness is in extreme danger, and without Scraps, Goodness may be lost forever.

"Michael Angelo created Scraps, but he also promised to help them when they needed it. Now they need it. It is part of our heritage and duty to help!"

The Rodent Rally grew silent and thoughtful.

"You may not be aware, but in recent months, many Scrap homes have been crushed under the feet of People. Even worse, many Scraps themselves have been killed, ground into the ground. And by what? By growing herds of humans!

"Scraps have tried defensive action. They have moved farther and farther down the Riverbank, but even those houses have been flattened! Scraps have run as fast as they can, and they have even developed a warning system, but still, they continue to be killed. Families are being torn apart. They need to live by the River as People do, but they have run out of space.

"People are not good right now in any way. We all know that. Who knows if they ever will be? I would love to just forget about them until Spirit figures out the next Game Plan for their Goodness, but in this case, human rottenness is not the cause of today's problem. It's their numbers and size—too many big People.

Actually, People have no idea that there even *is* a problem. They don't know Scraps exist, but that is not the point. *Dying Scraps are the point!*

"A mouse made Scraps. *Our* ancestor was the one that did that, and now Scraps are going to die. They are losing their homes and losing their lives. If something is not done, Scraps are doomed, and if we don't help, it will be *our* fault. River People have lousy hearts, and they also have huge feet. They get more numerous and more deadly every day! Today the danger they represent has grown so great that it threatens the actual *extinction* of all Scraps."

The congregation gasped in unison. Max and Shaver covered their eyes with Maxine's apron.

"This much is fact. Michael Angelo Mouse took the Special Clay and made Scraps. He also promised to preserve the Scraps forever until they were needed on the game ball. As his descendants, we know this. It is in The Book. Whether or not the danger the Scraps are in now is our fault, we may never know, but *we* can't ignore the pledge made by our ancestor. Scraps are not only *our friends but our duty*! If something is not done soon, the world will lose their Goodness forever. The Big Game is not the most important thing, but without Scrap Goodness, Goodness will not stand a chance in the universe. If Scraps die, their Goodness will die with them."

Moses was on his feet, pleading and waving his paws in to the air. There was a great rumbling of concern among the mice as they thought about the horrible meaning of Moses's conclusion.

What should mice do? They now knew the meaning of The Book and their history. For the first time, they now knew that they were *obligated* by that history to do something. Obviously, as Michael Angelo's descendants, they *should* do something to help set things right! Michael Angelo had promised that they would.

Moses stood back and watched the importance of the situation sink in. Max and Shaver climbed onto Maxine's lap and huddled there.

Moses drew himself up to his full four inches and finished the most important speech of his life.

"After our recent study of <u>The Book,</u> we remember why River People are the way they are. But what was done was done. River People will always exist and increase. Now we, as lovers of Scraps, must make sure that Scraps continue to exist as well. It is time that mice stand up on our haunches and do something to help them," declared Moses. "What are we, mice or men?"

"Mice! We are mice!" cheered the Spirit Club. The mice came to their feet. Something must be done, and they were just the ones to do it!

But reality began to creep through the Hall and filter through the mice. What could *they* do to save Scraps from humans? They were small, too.

Moses, their Coach and mentor, was ready for this reaction. "I know that this is a big problem, but we also know how valuable our friends are to the Goodness of the Game. We all belong to the Spirit Club. Why are we in the Club if we can't rise up now and be the Players we need to be? We knew we would be needed some day. Here we are. Are we really a Spirit Club or not?"

With a rising chorus of cheers and shouts, the Rodent Rally accepted the challenge.

Moses Mouse, Maxine, and their fellow rodents began at once a great discussion about what they should do. Shaver and Max, now quite forgotten by their elders, looked at each other fearfully. They were not sure that they understood all of what Grandpa Moses had said, but they were pretty sure that it was serious business.

After many hours, the darkened Hall under the throne room was still full of rodents. The Spirit Club had divided into smaller groups around tiny straw torches and exchanged many bold ideas. Sad to say, however, no solutions had yet been found.

Coach Moses heaved a tired sigh. The play needed for *this* game was not going to come easy. Whiskers drooped. Eyes were glazing. It was late.

"Listen up, loyal members of the Spirit Club and Rodent Rally. We seem to have reached a need for a break in the action tonight. I know that you are all true to the Spirit Club and trying hard to help the Scraps. I know that you want to save them. And know that I am only your Coach. I am proud of our work tonight. We are all disappointed that we haven't found a winning strategy yet. But check this out. Tomorrow is a new day.

"Also, my staff tells me that time has run out on this, the 1st Quarter of The Big Game. Maybe what we need to do is go back to our respective field houses and give our challenge some real hard, strategy-type thought. Maybe when we are not so wrung out, we can get back on the field and *just nail* a plan that will knock Fighter's team out of our way and save our Scraps."

"Totally cool. That's what I'm going to do," whispered Shaver to Max. "I'm gonna go home and kick back, and then I'm going to ask my mom and dad what *they* think *we* should do to save us Scraps. I bet they will have some good ideas for the 2nd Quarter. They're pretty smart for parents." Moses heard the little Scrap and suddenly understood what *he* needed to say. He was a realist. He strode across his little stage with a meaningful look around the room. "You Spirit Clubbers have been given a real challenge. You laid out your best tonight, but here is a truth that blew right by me. Our friends the Scraps have always been superior problem solvers themselves. They even have their own branch of the Spirit Club.

"I will confer with the Scrap leadership in the morning. I see now that it is not necessary that *mice* decide what the Scraps should do. It is more important that *Scraps* decide what *Scraps* will do, and like true friends and loyal members of the Spirit Club, mice will be their backup as needed. Scraps and mice… We will be more than a team. Together we will be an *Army for Goodness!*"

The Rodent Rally burst into cheers. What a great idea. Why hadn't they thought of it before? Scraps and mice together. Moses Mouse was truly a mouse among mice, a real leader. The meeting was adjourned, and the mice filed out of the Hall. All scurried off toward home, concerned but quite satisfied with the results of their Rally.

Moses would meet with the leaders of the Scrap Kingdom tomorrow, but he knew one thing was true: He and the mice still had no idea how to solve the frightening dilemma that the Scraps now faced.

LEGEND II

The 2ⁿᵈ Quarter

The 2nd Quarter of the Game was beginning, but changes to the original lineups seemed eminent. There were rumors among the Fireflies about new players that might be getting ready to enter the Game, and neither one of the coaches even knew anything about them. These new players were Scraps.

More About the Scraps

—retrieved from Scrap Archives

Scrap Kingdom, as you know, was a tiny community hidden along the grassy bank of the River, where it had existed for centuries. Fighter and Spirit were not the only ones that didn't know about Scraps. Neither did the River People.

But Scraps definitely knew about River People. They had to. They needed to guard against them at all times if they wanted to stay alive. Scraps were taught from birth to watch for humans, avoid their big, clumsy movements and make themselves as invisible as possible. River People were dangerous.

Much like the River People, Scraps also had a King and Queen. But the King and Queen of the Scraps were a gentle, unselfish couple. They were loved by their subjects, and they definitely loved each other.

The current Scrap Royals were known as King Heart and Queen Concern (Heart and Connie, for short). Like most Scraps, they spent many of their days working in the fields with their subjects and trying to make life better for those around them. That may sound goody-goody, but that was how they were.

These Royals did not live in a castle the way the King and Queen of the River People did. Instead, they lived in a fallen log that had been hollowed out by worm contractors with the interior smoothed until it gleamed. Worms are talented.

Openings were burrowed through to the outside of the log so that air and light could enter, while the floor was carpeted with dried mosses to be very soft under tiny feet. Nut shell chairs, beds softened by duck down and toadstool tables completed the furnishings.

Their only symbol of royalty was an elegant carved heart with a crown etched on its surface. This formed the front door of the log. In honor of King Heart, Hearts had been adopted by Scrap Kingdom as their symbol and many Scraps wore a small heart around their necks or hung one over their doorways to show solidarity.

King Heart and Queen Connie were childless for many years and because of this, had ruled their kingdom as family, discovering many successful ways to serve and care for their Kingdom. They were kind and fair with each other and with their subjects. Their dealings were honest. They made important community decisions with the assistance of the Whole Scrap Council, a group of Scraps who had signed up for the job and the honor. There were no Castle Guards, however, because no one needed protection, except from the River People.

The nearby humans were a huge problem. King Heart considered his most important duty was to provide 'People Protection' for his subjects. To guard the Kingdom against the River People, King Heart selected and posted a security force of sharp-eyed Scraps, the Lancers. Their job was to spot the approach of River People and warn other Scraps by sailing lances (pointed grass shanks) through the air in a relay pattern. Noting the direction from which the warning lances flew, the Scraps would run in the opposite direction and away from danger. It worked beautifully, or it had in the past.

The Lancers were currently the *only* early security system for Scrap Kingdom. The Lancers were skillful, fearless, and ever vigilant. But King Heart had to admit that they were no longer sufficient protection. Too many People were living along the Riverbank and these People were now a constant threat to the Scraps.

There had been a series of disasters. In the past few months, seven Scraps had been killed, crushed to death by River People. Seven!

Scrap Kingdom and their Royals were devastated. These tragedies broke their hearts. Now the huge humans, who had always been a cause for Scrap concern, were threatening Scraps' very existence. The human population was growing fast. The Scrap population had found no other place to locate that would not endanger them.

King Heart worried daily about the future of his subjects. He was their King. It was *his* duty to protect them and he was feeling less and less able to do so. And he now had a new addition to his unsolvable worries. Yes, he had a new worry, but this worry was an unbelievable joy at the same time. Queen Connie, after many childless years, had given birth to a beautiful baby boy. King Heart was a new father. +

The Royals couldn't believe their good fortune. Connie and Heart were no longer young, so this baby was unexpected. They had been blessed and, indeed, Heart was joyful beyond words, but now, he had an even greater reason to fear. Until now, he had not known he could be any more fearful.

Of course, just like the human Royals, this child was the one thing that Connie and Heart had always wished for. But the King and Queen's protection worries now grew to an unbearable level. Their love and fear for their subjects was multiplied above all measure by the existence of this tiny boy. It's funny how that happens, but it does.

It was almost too much. They needed to protect their wonderful son. They needed to save the entire Scrap population at the same time. To do that, huge changes in their living situation needed to be made. But what changes and how? They could no longer live here on the Riverbank, next to the growing hordes of River People. Without a drastic move, all Scraps were doomed and so was their precious new baby. The Royals were so afraid of losing him that that they could scarcely take time to enjoy him.

"What would happen if one of the River People was not spotted by the Lancers in time, Heart?" whispered Queen Connie, gazing at her sleeping little bundle. "They are doing their best, but already the number of River People have increased to the point that living in our homes here on the river's edge has become too big a risk for all of us.

"The humans have multiplied and are so busy with their constant fights and squabbles that we could *all* be destroyed in an instant and they wouldn't even know it," Connie sighed. "I wonder if Spirit knows how much trouble we're in. We could be gone just like that. This fear has always been my nightmare, but now, with the baby, my nightmare is so real that I am afraid to go to sleep."

On the very same evening that the Rodent Rally was meeting in Mouse Hall, the River People terrorized the Scraps again in a way that almost turned Queen Connie's nightmare into a reality. There was a sighting of River People on the bank not more than a few yards away from the Royal Log and the humans were approaching fast.

The warning lances soared down the Riverbank. All Scrap homes were emptied as Scrap Kingdom, including the Royal Family, rushed to the roots of the Willow at the river's edge. Here the ground was damp and muddy, and the River People usually avoided the spot. That made the base of the Willow a relatively safe place for the Scrap community to hide in times of crisis.

Two happy young River People were chasing each other around on the riverbank, laughing and giggling as they caught up with each other. As they tried to avoid the watchful eyes of adults, they had wandered even farther upstream than usual. They were having fun, hugging and kissing and not thinking for a minute that their huge feet were within a twig of crushing a young Scrap couple out walking together in the same area.

In terror, the Scrap couple ran for their lives, dashing toward the Willow through the yards of their neighbors' homes. Behind them, the little Scrap houses they had just passed disappeared with the sickening crackle of broken cottages and crushed belongings. The young River People continued to laugh and tease and romp about as treasured Scrap homesteads crunched beneath their feet. At the base of the Willow, the Scrap population huddled in terror and misery.

Completely unknown to the Scraps, someone else sought refuge at the Willow on this eventful night. After the disturbing information that Spirit heard from the Rodent Rally, he had gone to the river's edge and settled high in the Willow's topmost branches. Unaware of what was happening below him, Spirit was lost in discouraging self-doubt and depression.

The Book of Amos, as faithfully read and discussed by Moses Mouse, had revealed a possible answer to the question Spirit had been asking himself since the beginning of the Game. Why were humans so slow to catch on to the idea of Goodness?

Now he had more questions. Was what he had heard true? Had *he* actually dropped the precious Special Clay before it could be placed in his humans' hearts? Were there really such beings as Scraps made of *his* Special Clay?

Spirit had never seen any Scraps. How could that story be true? He sagged into the branches of the Willow.

What if he had actually never created Goodness in his human creations as he thought he had? What if he had lost The Big Game even before the end of the 1st Quarter? Was he now in the 2nd Quarter just stupidly waiting for Goodness that was never going to happen?

And the mice at the Rally even had a Spirit Club. They were ready to be players. That was unreal. *And* if humans had no Goodness in them, what good could a tiny Mouse Spirit Club hope to do? The Game might already be lost.

Spirit needed to think. That's why he was here at the River's edge. This was where it had all started. This was where he had created so many wonderful things—plants, animals, People. All of this was good. He knew this, but with what he had just heard, he felt like a loser. Without any Goodness in the hearts of humans, Fighter would have no competition. The whole world would live in misery forever with no concept of right and wrong to guide it. Fighter would win The Big Game if he hadn't actually done so already.

Spirit was proud of what he had originally created, even though he had been dissatisfied with human slowness to learn things like kindness and honesty. Now he needed to admit that the *real* problem might be something he had not even thought of before...his own failure to create Goodness-equipped human players for the Game.

Spirit finally understood. Fighter had slipped a slick move by him during the monstrous storm that he had created for that very purpose. It was sneaky but smart. Spirit had been so sure of himself that he had let his guard down. What a lame player he had been...too much pride, and a stupid move on his part.

And what about these so-called Scraps? Was there such a thing? Were they players? If so, what part might they play in the Game at this point? Whose side would they be on? What *was* a Scrap anyway? A good guy or a bad guy? What did a Scrap even look like? Spirit shook the branches of the huge Willow in total frustration. He was such a loser.

As he sat there feeling sorry for himself, Spirit began to hear voices drifting up from somewhere below. Bugs possibly...People, probably. *Who cares? Forget about it.*

But, glancing down through the Willow's branches, he suddenly focused more closely. For the first time, he noticed that hundreds of tiny 'somethings' were gathering at the base of the tree and disappearing up into its branches like so many pieces of the Willow itself. They blended in with the bark so completely that they were almost invisible.

Upon closer inspection, Spirit was shocked to see that these little things looked like tiny People. He had never seen anything like it before. Where did they come from? They were not any species that *he* had made.

Directly below him, a little couple and their child were finding refuge in a nearby nook of the Willow. They appeared to be some sort of royalty, for they were treated with great deference by the creatures around them.

"They are beautiful," Spirit marveled to himself. "They are exactly like the humans I made, but so tiny that one would never know that they were here. But they *are* here, and *I* didn't make them."

There was no doubt. These had to be the creatures described perfectly in The Book at the Rodent Rally. After all this time, Spirit was seeing Scraps.

Now he realized with shame that, until today, he had known nothing about them. They were obviously here on the game ball that *he* had created. According to the mice, they had been here all along. How did they survive all this time without his knowing? How could he have been so blind? Trying not to scare them, he remained perfectly still and watched.

The Royal Couple appeared to have purposefully hurried up to their spot in the Willow's branches for a reason. From this high vantage point, they were peering down at the entire bank of the River, apparently trying to determine the status of their subjects below. Hundreds of the tiny people were now huddled together on or near the gnarled old tree. Why? What was going on?

After surveying the chaotic scramble below and being assured that their subjects were safe, the little King and Queen settled down on the Willow branch beside each other. As Spirit watched, the Queen tenderly checked her baby who was fastened securely to her body with spider webbing. Spirit eavesdropped on the couple with fascination.

"Well, tonight certainly confirms what we already knew, doesn't it, Connie?" growled the tiny King breathlessly to his Queen. "This is the second near miss this week." The portly little man wiped the perspiration from his brow.

"You're so right, Heart. The Riverbank can't be the place for us anymore. It just can't," the Queen whispered sadly, rocking her baby who was apparently sleeping through the ordeal.

"They speak!" marveled Spirit. "They sound just like my People. They have babies like my People. They have names. They are remarkable."

The little Queen gazed out over the riverbank. Fear wound its way up the Willow trunk from her subjects below. Queen Connie felt herself surrounded by that fear. What should they do? What *could* they do? *It isn't enough for me to simply know that the problem exists,* she thought anxiously. *Scrap houses are being destroyed as we watch, and we are doing nothing but sit in a tree. This is just wrong.*

Action was needed. *Action!* Their lives were threatened. They needed to do something different, but what? The problem turned itself over and over in her mind. Connie peered up through the Willow branches into the dark sky above. Spirit flattened against the tree, hidden but very near.

"What would Spirit say about our problem?" Connie wondered aloud. "This Riverbank has been home to the Scraps *and* the River People since the beginning. Spirit is the Spirit of Good. I know he didn't mean for Scraps to live in fear or be killed. He must have had some other plan for us, but what was it?"

"There it is," moaned Spirit to himself. "This little creature is *definitely* a Scrap, *and* she knows about *me*. But I am sure she would not be impressed if she knew that until now, I didn't even know that *she* existed."

Spirit stayed very still, but his mind raced. "And, indeed, what *would* I say about their problem?" he asked himself. "She is right. Of course, I wouldn't want them to live in fear or be killed, but why do they think they are in danger? What are they so afraid of?"

Spirit hadn't stayed to hear what Moses had said about this at the Rally, but now he was paying full attention. Why were these Scraps gathering at the Willow? He had no clue. They obviously thought that they had some sort of problem, but he had no idea what it was.

Spirit continued to watch these little creatures called Scraps. Yes sir, that is what Moses Mouse had called them. The more he watched, the more something else was revealed. These tiny people were actually being kind and helpful to one another. These Scraps seemed to possess the very Goodness that Spirit had always expected to show up in *his* People. He could not take his eyes off them.

Without knowing it, Spirit's fascination with the tiny Scraps began growing quickly into admiration. He was not sure how these beings came into existence, but instinctively, he knew that, if they had not been players in his Game for Goodness originally, they should be now.

But these Scraps were saying that they had a big problem. If they had a problem, Spirit needed to know what it was. Maybe he could help them.

Why did he care so much? Why was that so? He hadn't even known they existed until a few minutes ago.

Spirit realized in a flash that the reason he was so interested was simple. Scraps were exactly like his humans but tiny. He automatically cared about them.

And there was another strange but wonderful thing: He had pledged to let humans live their lives without his assistance, so he couldn't help *humans* at all. But he hadn't made such a pledge to these Scraps. If he couldn't help *his People* no matter how much they needed it, maybe he *could* help these *Scraps*. That would be great. It was in Spirit's nature to be helpful. He just needed to figure out what the Scraps' problem was. It would feel so good to be useful again.

Feeling energized by this generous impulse, Spirit forgot his gloom and hovered over the Scraps, hoping to discover a clue to the problem they were experiencing. They were afraid for some reason. He could hear and see that. But why? Who would want to hurt such marvelous little creatures? He continued to watch in fascination.

Hours passed, and at last, all Scraps were accounted for. The Lancers sent the all-clear signal through the grasses. The Scraps and their Royalty began returning to their homes or what was left of them. Many homes could no longer be inhabited after tonight.

Spirit had no idea about any of that, but he followed the Royal Couple, keeping well out of sight. *He* had decided that he would be there for them *and* their problem, (whatever it was) even though there was that annoying question about who created them.

Is it important who created them? Not really, Spirit decided next. What was important was the fact that they *were* created, and if their behavior was any indication, they might have actually been made of Special Clay as <u>The Book</u> of the mice had said.

Unbelievable. Maybe Special Clay was another reason that he felt so concerned about them so quickly. Special Clay had always been key.

Spirit watched as the Scrap King and Queen helped each other and their subjects struggle through the tall grasses in the night. There was that kindness that he had wished for but seldom seen in humans. Why could humans not behave like this? Spirit continued to hover invisibly, intent on more eavesdropping.

"We have to get smart quickly, Connie," he heard the King whisper as he lifted his wife and child over piles of debris.

"They need to get smart about 'the problem', whatever it is," Spirit guessed. He continued to listen for clues.

"I know," the Queen answered. "All Scraps are accounted for, alive and uninjured *tonight,* but look at these houses. They're shattered beyond repair. They're gone, and with more and more People moving closer and closer, where should *any* Scraps rebuild? There is no safe place for us here on the river bank any more. None."

Almost magically, Spirit noticed that Fireflies had arrived to light the way of the Scraps. *How strange that they should show up right when they are needed,* Spirit thought. *Very cool, though.*

In their light, Spirit could now see that the debris the Scraps were climbing over was actually the remains of dozens of crushed little cottages. *Dozens!*

Finally, Spirit understood. The 'problem' that Scraps were worried about was their very existence. They were being overrun by River People.

As the Fireflies continued to float above, King Heart grumbled. "I pound my brain, morning, noon, and night. All I *do* is study one idea and then another to improve our chances to survive with People, but I come up with nothing. I'm beginning to feel that we are doomed. We *have* to live near water. So do People. Where else is there?"

Queen Connie patted her husband with confidence. "I believe that Spirit would not have let us be made if we were destined to become doomed, Heart. We were made for a reason, I am sure, but I just can't put my finger on it. I have even studied *The Scrap Book* to find the answer, but I can't seem to find it yet. I really have a feeling that we are part of Spirit's Goodness Plan, but I don't know what that part is."

"She believes that *I* made the Scraps! She believes that *I* had a Game Plan for them." Spirit smiled.

"We were not made by Spirit, you remember," countered Heart, pushing aside some tall ferns and grasses. "*Michael Angelo* dreamed that *he* made us. Maybe *that* is the reason we'll go extinct. Maybe *we* were never in Spirit's Plan for Goodness at all. What if Michael Angelo made a mistake when he used up the Special Clay to make us?"

"*He* believes Scraps were made by the mouse." Spirit winced.

The little Queen halted abruptly. "I know. I know. I know all about Michael Angelo. But a *mistake?* No! Fireflies were there! Fireflies were watching. Fireflies are here right now! Fireflies know everything! I can't believe you said that we were a mistake!" she cried.

"Heart! Where is your faith? We are *not* a mistake! And we are *not* going to become extinct! We were made for a reason. Even Michael Angelo knew that. Special Clay was the most important part of Spirit's Plan for Goodness. He said so. *We were made out of Special Clay!* One way or another we will figure out what our future is supposed to be. We are *not* a mistake!"

King Heart hugged his wife and held her close. "I'm sorry, Connie. I am *so* sorry. I can't believe I said that either. I will never say it again. I am just so worried."

Connie took a deep breath and recovered. "We must have faith, Heart," she said gently into his shoulder. "You'll think of something. You always do. You thought of the Lancers. Now you'll think of something else that will keep us safe. Or maybe *we* will think of something *together*." She chuckled, kissing the little King softly on his cheek. "Sometimes *I* have good ideas too, you know."

Spirit was listening closely. In spite of his wish to doubt the historical readings of mouse at the Rally, he now believed that what he had heard was true. And these Scraps had read <u>The Book</u> as well. *They* believed that they were created by a dreaming mouse. There was no reason to doubt it...and these were the ancestors of those Scraps that had been created. They were proof.

Spirit thought back. The storm, the fumbling for Clay in the watery sand at the edge of the river—it all fit together. Spirit knew that he had needed this truth. Fighter must have been gloating about this for centuries. It had taken him too long to find this out, but it was so necessary. *He* had made a mistake, and his People had suffered because of it. These little Scraps were now suffering as well.

The original Plan for Goodness may not be in place as he had thought, but now Spirit had discovered that Special Clay still existed. It was not where he thought it was, but it was *here*, in these Scraps. Maybe this Clay could still be used for Good in some way. All might not be lost.

In gratitude for this new discovery, Spirit rose above the tiny couple and surrounded them with a warm protective breeze. *They* were made of the material he knew to be the source of Goodness, and somehow, he knew that these tiny creatures could be part of his Game Plan—a *new* Game Plan.

"Watch out, Fighter! I'm back in the Game!"

Connie could not hear Spirit, but she suddenly felt a surge of positive feeling. "We will find a solution soon, my dear," she announced softly, weaving through the towering reeds and cattails toward their log home. "I feel it, even though tonight was such a close call. We could have lost young Lovey and Stewart just like that! Who knows what those big, clumsy People were doing, wandering around in the dark down by the riverbank at night anyway?"

"They were probably doing just what Lovey and Stewart were doing," offered King Heart absently. "When River People are in love, they behave much like us. They weren't really trying to hurt us."

Spirit chuckled aloft at King Heart's wisdom.

Queen Connie smiled. "You have an understanding and forgiving nature, Heart, and you are wise in the ways of the River People. If they are not completely bad, there must be a way that we can live together peacefully *with* People rather than under their feet."

Spirit stopped and stared. Queen Connie had just said something profound. "We can live *with* the River People rather than under their feet." She was thinking what he was thinking.

'The Problem' for the good, gentle Scraps was the fact that their species was being crushed to extinction under the feet of the River People. 'The Problem' for the River People was their almost complete lack of Goodness. What if the two species could solve each other's problems together? This was a brilliant thought! How wise this Scrap woman was! She was truly made of Special Clay.

Spirit whirled into the sky and disappeared to consider all he had learned in one day, from a mouse at a Rodent Rally and a Scrap Queen. The Fireflies that he had noticed before seemed to dance among the grasses. The Royal couple continued on toward home, unaware that they had any company at all.

They were very near their log home when King Heart halted and addressed his Queen with fierce determination. "I *will* do what must be done to keep our people safe, Connie," he declared. "It is *my* duty, and I *will not* fail you or them."

Queen Connie nodded lovingly. "I know how hard you are looking for the answer, Heart. Why don't we call a Council of Whole Scraps? This is why we were all created out of the Special Clay. We have so many good minds and good hearts in our Kingdom that I know we can figure this out."

With a look of confidence, the tiny Queen raised her son to her shoulder, folded him in snugly, and scooted ahead. As they reached their doorway, she stopped, glancing back at her husband with a mischievous look. "I need to tell you a secret, Heart."

"I hope it's a good one," smiled Heart wearily as he pulled open the heavy heart door to their home. He was exhausted, but Connie seemed to have a new burst of energy as she scampered through the door.

"I hope so too. I wasn't sure at first. That's why I didn't say something to you before this. Don't laugh, but ever since our son was born, I have had a strange feeling. We know that The Big Game is still going on, right? My new feeling is this: *we* might have a bigger part to play in The Big Game than we know of right now, you and me and the baby...maybe all Scraps. Do you think I am silly to think such a thing?"

King Heart was not a deep thinker. He could not understand what his Queen was saying, but he did *not* think she was silly. She had insight.

"I am really not sure why," Connie continued, "but tonight, right now, my feeling about the Game is very strong. It's telling me that the time for Scraps to get into the Game is approaching. I know Spirit can't be happy with current Goodness on the game ball. If he still wants to win the Game, maybe *we* can help him make the world a better place, and *maybe* we Scraps can help ourselves in the process. Maybe it's all meant to be."

King Heart was trying hard to understand, but he had had a long day. Carefully he took his son from his suddenly energized wife and placed him in his crib. He knew that he and his son were ready to be down for the night.

But Connie was not ready for sleep just yet. "*We* must develop some new ideas for a Game Plan," she continued. "I just have a feeling that it's at least partly up to *us, you and me*. But we will need all the help we can get." She now began to pace.

"You must go to the Castle tomorrow and bring Coach Moses back for a consult on the Game. He is also an authority on <u>The Book,</u> *and* he is our friend. We will need his expertise and support. The way is not clear to me yet, but I am sure that Moses and his Spirit Club will be part of the solution. And they will *want* to do so. His Spirit Club is strong. They can help *our* Spirit Club if we get a plan together. We must not delay any longer.

I don't know how I know these things, but I do. I feel it, and we're in the Second Quarter of the Game, for heaven's sake! There is no time to waste."

Somehow, through the fog of his sleepiness, King Heart understood. Connie's feelings were not just feelings. They were more important than that. Tired or not, he knew that what she was saying could not be dismissed. Heart promised he would leave for the Castle and Mouse Hall at sunup the next morning.

Connie, still wide awake with her growing intuition, watched over her sleeping family. The Fireflies that had flitted in the meadow earlier returned and gathered above the tiny log castle. It was a sign.

The Fireflies and the Queen

How surprising it must have seemed to these two tiny creatures, Moses Mouse and King Heart, when they met each other midway between their two 'castles' the next morning. They had been friends for years, frequently arranging meetings to discuss issues of the day and chat about their respective responsibilities, but neither one had arranged this meeting.

There they stood in the middle of the road. They shook hands and exchanged small comments on the weather. They both knew that this was not a chance meeting. Without any discussion, King Heart invited his friend to return with him to his home, and Moses agreed. Together they began their journey back down the road toward the Royal Log.

The morning was bright and warm. On either side of their path, Scraps and mice were working side by side in the fields as they had for years. There were many places along this road where the two species shared the fields and the harvest from those fields. Bent over their work together, they were not easy to tell apart from a distance.

The Scraps and mice chatted together as they worked. This morning, they exchanged gossip about the close call that the Scraps had experienced *and* the Rodent Rally at the Hall, both having taken place the night before. The workers in the field glanced up to see their respective leaders walking by together and suspected what they would be discussing. The field workers nodded to one another knowingly.

As they strolled along, Moses began the conversation. "We had a mighty Rodent Rally and gathering of the Spirit Club in the Hall yesterday. There were hundreds present."

"A Rodent Rally *and* Spirit Club at the same time! What a sight that must have been." exclaimed King Heart appreciatively. He had been to the Hall for meetings several times and could visualize the scene. "You certainly do have a good turnout when you call the troops together. What was the occasion, Mose?"

"Well, part of it was our usual…you know, the reading of The Book, discussion, that sort of thing." Moses sounded like he was chatting, but as he walked, he scratched his whiskery chin. Moses Mouse was thinking deep thoughts. "You might be surprised to know, my good friend, that much of last night's discussion was about you and your Kingdom," Moses continued.

"You don't say." King Heart glanced sideways at his friend and continued walking.

"Oh yes, I do say," Moses responded. "And it was quite a spirited discussion too. There we were, hundreds of loud Spirit Club members, hollering and running around discussing *you Scraps*. Pretty strange for the likes of us mice, don't you think?"

"Now you have my interest aroused. Your Spirit Club gets pretty rowdy. What in the world did a hall full of mice find interesting about us Scraps?"

"Well, frankly, we were talking about the danger that you and your wonderful fellow Scraps are in," Moses stated matter-of-factly.

King Heart halted, wide-eyed. "*You mice* were talking about the danger that *we Scraps* are in? Why were you doing such a thing?" The King was beginning to feel disrespected. "Did you think that we Scraps needed your protection? If you were concerned, why didn't you talk to me about it? Did you feel that we couldn't protect ourselves?"

Now it was time for Moses to feel uncomfortable. "That is exactly where I went wrong," he said simply. "If I was worried about you, I should have talked to you about it first. I meant no disrespect. I am sorry, my friend."

King Heart stopped blustering and hung his head. "I'm sorry, too. I was talking like an ungrateful jerk to you, Mose. I guess, if I admit it, I need to say that I was flaring up due to guilt. I am the King of the Scraps, and you are right. We Scraps *are* in more and more danger, and I, their lame King, have done *nothing to* change that. We even had another close call last night. We lost some houses but no Scraps, thank goodness.

"The fact is that I don't *know* what to do. I am totally out of ideas. That is exactly the reason that I set out this morning to find you."

Moses smiled, causing his whiskers to tilt up. King Heart had always liked Moses's smile.

"Well," said Moses. "It looks like we are two 'great minds traveling on the same track' as they say. While we were all trying to get creative last night, I suddenly figured out that your kingdom was truly *your* business and that you certainly did not need our silly ideas. But I *do want you to know* that we mice will be more than ready and able to help you whenever you would like us to do so. I was coming to offer that help to you help in person."

King Heart looked gratefully at Moses. "You really are a good friend, Coach," he said. "Thanks for your concern and your faith in me, but come, why don't you tell me about the ideas that you and the Rodent Rally uncovered? I can use all the good ideas I can find."

Arm in arm, the two tiny leaders proceeded down the dusty road, the tall grasses waving above them on either side. Moses told the King of all the ideas that the mice had proposed the night before, and soon they were laughing together. Some of them were pretty crazy. For a moment, the two leaders felt youthful again.

But as the pair neared the door of the log, they became serious. They were both painfully aware that they didn't have a useful idea between them as to how the life-and-death issue of the Scraps versus the River People could be solved. There was no game plan at all.

The sunshine was warm on the heart-shaped door of the Royal Log. Among the sweet-smelling reeds and cattails nearby, there was a steady hum of bees and dragonflies as they traveled back and forth with supplies needed by nearby Scrap families. Insects were a very valuable delivery service in the daily life of the Scraps, and there was much appreciation between insects and Scraps. Together, they lived a life of mutual assistance. It was a very nice arrangement.

Queen Connie was seated on her throne with her baby as the King and Moses entered the home. It was a sweet sight. The only trappings of royalty that King Heart and Queen Connie possessed were the two thrones that had been created for them by their subjects. They were both made of twigs and soft mosses, but the Queen's chair had had reed rockers added to it for obvious reasons. There sat Queen Connie, on her throne, gently rocking her baby bundle back and forth, back and forth.

Moses Mouse was charmed. He had always considered the little Queen to be very special, but here, holding her child, Moses considered her almost as much *his* Queen as Queen of the Scraps. There and then, in his heart, Moses pledged his help and protection to her and her child for as long as he and his Spirit Club could provide it.

"Good day, Your Majesty." Moses bowed low with great respect. Queen Connie smiled. "For goodness sake, Mose," she whispered, her finger to her lips. "Haven't we been friends for long enough to be past such formalities? Come over here this instant and see how our baby is growing. Please excuse me if I don't get up. He just now nodded off, and I don't want to risk waking him. By the way, how is your grandson?"

Moses removed his cloak, gray with the dust of the road, and hung it by the door. Slowly he approached the delicate Queen and her child. The baby was so small. Moses had not seen a baby Scrap in a long time. Scrap babies were even smaller than baby mice. Hard to imagine...

"Max is . . . well, Max is Max." Moses chuckled, recalling his antics from the night before.

As Moses watched, the Queen looked with concern at her husband. "You both look tired, Heart. Why don't you and Mose sit and rest. In just a minute, I will pour you some honey water. You must be exhausted after your long walk."

The King did not go to his throne but sat down on a simple bench at the table near Moses. He poured some water for himself and Moses. The King took a long drink and then spoke seriously for the first time since he had entered the house.

"I met Mose on the road, my dear. He was coming to see *us* as I was traveling to find *him*. That's the good news. The bad news is that neither one of us have an idea what to do to save ourselves, our fellow Scraps, or our baby from the River People. I am beginning to think that I will never find a plan that will allow us to live safely near humans."

Again, Queen Connie smiled, but this time, her smile was a different kind of smile. She looked calm and relaxed, almost smug. She said simply, "Actually, I have been thinking about that since last night, my dear. I believe a plan might already exist."

Moses and King Heart both put down their water glasses with rather loud thumps and some sloshing. They stared in shock at the little Queen as she rocked back and forth with her mysterious smile.

"You have a plan?" Heart finally gasped. "*You* have a plan? What kind of plan? Do you think it will work? How did you get this plan? *When* did you get this plan?" King Heart couldn't get the words out fast enough. Moses just stared in fascination.

"My idea about a possible plan came to me last night, Heart dear, after you went to bed. I was sitting by the window with the baby, watching Fireflies. They were dancing right over our house and singing. It was amazing."

"Mouse Angels!" Moses squeaked in awe.

"Scrap Angels too, Mose dear," Connie whispered back with a grin. She had risen from her throne and was tucking the little prince into his milkweed pod bed. She smoothed the eider down blanket over her baby and came to stand by Moses and Heart before she continued.

"While I was watching the Fireflies, they suddenly flew off in the direction of the Castle. Right away, I had a very selfish thought. I wanted to say to them, 'Don't waste your beauty on those mean, nasty River People in that ugly Castle. They don't appreciate Fireflies like I do.'"

"What's wrong with that?" questioned Moses. "I have lived under the floor of the Castle all my life. That King and Queen have everything in the world, and they don't appreciate any of it. Why should they suddenly deserve *or* appreciate Fireflies?"

The Queen scooted over and plopped down between her husband and Moses Mouse. She was excited. "I am so glad you are here, Mose. You know practically everything there is to know about the King and Queen of the River People, don't you? More than I know, that's for sure. You are an absolute fountain of information and just what I need right now. Wonderful! Please, tell me all about them, everything you can think of."

King Heart was impatient. "No, Mose. Don't let Connie get off track. I don't want to hear about any human king and queen of anything. I only want to hear about the plan you said you had, Connie. For heavens' sake, spill it. Don't make us wait."

Connie just smiled her strange smile again and said, "Have patience, Heart. My idea from last night depends a lot on what Mose has to say. I *just now* figured out that this was why I asked you to bring him here. Mose knows things. He knows about the King and Queen of the humans. *And he knows about the Game.* I need to find out some of these things before I really believe that I heard the Fireflies' Plan the way I thought I did."

"Fireflies' Plan? You're kidding! What kind of crazy idea is that? How late were you up last night?" King Heart barked.

Queen Connie frowned at her husband. "You're being pretty rude and unkind, dear," she said calmly.

King Heart sat back in his chair and looked closely at his wife. She had a point.

"Sorry," he said. "You're right, as usual," he added with a grin.

The Queen smiled too and patted her husband's knee. "Patience, Heart. Now, Mose, dear friend, tell us *everything* you can think of about the King and Queen of the River People."

Moses checked King Heart once more, just to be sure that he should speak up. Husbands and wives had their ways. Then he rose from the table and clasped his paws behind him with his eyes to the ceiling, trying to conjure up just the right things to say.

"Well, let me see," said Moses, "the King and Queen of the River People are very big, and they dress in fancy clothes, but the King is totally selfish and has a horrible temper. The Queen is stuck on her own good looks. That's all she thinks about. Both of them are completely thoughtless. They are rude to everyone and pretty rotten to each other, and they yell a lot. They want an heir to the throne, and so far, they don't have one, and they both blame each other for that. They're pretty awful, for sure. I guess that's about it. Is there anything else you want to know?"

"Oh dear," sighed Queen Connie. "That doesn't sound good at all. Isn't there anything good about them?"

"Let me think for a minute. Something good about them . . . something good about them . . . *hmm* . . . if you can't say anything good . . surely there must be *something* good." Moses began to pace the room, still staring at the ceiling as though he might find a good memory floating there. "Wait for it . . . Wait for it . . . I'm working on it . . . Oh, I know! The Queen is very beautiful (for a large person), and she dresses in wonderful robes so she looks great. The King is thoughtless, like I said, but I *can* say that he usually lets people that he has thrown in the dungeon *out* before they die of old age. *And* I honestly believe that King Sol has never *actually* had anyone's head hacked off, although he threatens to do that almost every day."

Moses turned and smiled at Queen Connie. "How was that?"

The Scrap Queen rose to her feet and began to pace as well, shaking her head from side to side. She was no longer smiling. "How can this be?" she whispered mournfully, almost to herself. "I was so sure that I understood what the Fireflies were singing. How could I have been so wrong?"

"Wow! The Fireflies sang to you?" gasped Moses. "I have never *ever* heard of the Fireflies singing to anyone in my lifetime. The only record of them *ever* singing is in The Book!"

The Queen stopped and blinked three times as though something had just pulled her out of a trance. "The Fireflies *do* sing in The Books, don't they?" she asked.

"Absolutely! The Books say that they were singing when you Scraps were born," said Moses. "Some folks think that Fireflies might have even helped with your creation, itself. We mice call them Mouse Angels, as you know."

"Indeed . . . Mouse Angels *and* Scrap Angels . . . yes. Fireflies *were* there, weren't they?" Queen Connie stared at Moses and then at her husband as though she expected to find the answer to some very large question written on their faces.

"Sit down, my dear. You look pale." King Heart helped his wife to her throne and brought her some honey water. When she had sipped a bit, he asked softly, "Why don't you tell us *both* what happened last night and let Mose and I see if we can help you figure it out."

The Queen now gazed at the milkweed pod in which her baby slept and then stared at her hands folded limply in her lap. With a trembling voice, she began her story.

"When the Fireflies were above the log, I thought I heard them singing. I couldn't make out all the words, but they seemed to be singing something about the 'key to Goodness'. Then, as I told you before, they flew to the Castle. I was sad to see them leave because they seemed so happy and, well, full of promise. I was about to come away from the window when I noticed that they were coming back again, and . . . and—"

"And, and? Please continue, my dear! What happened next?"

"The Fireflies flew right into our window! The room was all aglow with them, and the air was filled with music. It was wonderful. They flew right to the baby. They hovered above him, really close to him, almost touching him with their wings. But he didn't wake up. He didn't even move. And because they were Angels, I wasn't afraid at all." Queen Connie smiled at the memory.

"You were visited by Mouse Angels personally?" Moses squeaked. "I can't believe it. Wait till I tell the Spirit Club. They will be sure it was a sign."

"Oh no!" the Queen cried in a startled voice. "You can't *ever* say anything to anyone, Mose. The Scrap Angels . . . Mouse Angels . . . I couldn't tell which . . . must be our secret. Promise me. Promise that you won't tell *anyone* what I am telling you today."

Moses promised.

"Did the Fireflies sing anything special to you when they were here in the house?" asked the King, his eyes wide with curiosity.

"Oh yes, they did. And I thought I understood what they meant. I even accepted it. Now when I hear Mose say those awful things about the King and Queen, I'm petrified. What the Fireflies suggested doesn't sound right anymore. It sounds horrible. How could I have *ever* thought that it was a good idea? Oh, my poor baby." The little Queen began to sob.

Moses went outside so that King Heart could comfort Queen Connie in private. He sat down on a lump of moss and tried to figure things out. As always, he scratched his chin whiskers and thought deep thoughts.

Something big was in the air. Moses could feel it. He knew he couldn't let the Queen's experience with the Angels end like this today. He stood up, brushed the moss fragments from his haunches, and marched back into the log.

The Queen still sat on her throne, dabbing her eyes with dandelion silk while the King sat nearby, fiddling with his glass of honey water. They said nothing.

"Maybe you could tell us what the Fireflies sang, Queen Connie," Moses said respectfully. "Fireflies *are* Angels, for either Mice or Scraps. It doesn't matter which, but what they say is always important. I would never presume to say anything against the Fireflies. Did *I* say something stupid to make you upset?"

Queen Connie looked up at Moses, her face pink and damp. "Oh no, Mose. It wasn't anything that *you* said. That's not it. It was what you *know*. I think I knew it too. I just wasn't really wanting to admit what I have always thought to be true. The Royals of the Castle are *not* good people. But with the Fireflies singing their beautiful ideas here, I didn't want to think anything negative."

"Why don't you tell us what they actually said," soothed King Heart. "Tell us the whole thing. We both love you. We won't judge."

"What they sang didn't seem bad at the time." Connie sniffed. "Now it seems awful. The Fireflies were singing and floating around the baby. Their song said that he was very special and had been born to us so that . . . so that . . . we could *share him* with the River People."

"Share our son?" exploded King Heart, jumping up and waving his arms. "How in the world could you *ever* think *that* was a good idea? *Sharing* our son with those ridiculous People? Were you crazy?"

"So much for not judging," sighed Connie.

King Heart sat again. "Sorry."

"Now *I* wonder what I was thinking, too," Connie agreed. "I *must* have been crazy. Forgive me, my dear. Believing that I heard Fireflies singing must have deranged me."

"Please wat, Your Majesty," offered Moses softly. "You say Fireflies visited you, and they told you something that sounded wonderful. I am sure that you actually *did* see Fireflies. I *know* you didn't imagine them. Did they sing about anything else to you besides the scary sharing stuff?"

"Indeed, they did," reflected Connie slowly. "That was why it all seemed so wonderful at the time. They sang about Scraps being made of the Special Clay that was missing from River People and that it was now time for us to take our place *with* People, to live *with* them instead of under their feet. I have said that exact thing before myself. I liked that part." Connie looked at the mossy floor of the log. "The Fireflies said that living *with* People was our destiny."

"Our destiny? That sounds impressive," mumbled Heart.

"Uh-huh."

Moses began immediately to scratch his chin. Was this it? Was this the idea that had been just beyond the reach of his thinking for months? Not yet. There must still be another piece. Thinking very deep thoughts, Moses asked, "What part did they want the young Prince to play in this destiny?"

"They wanted our baby to learn the ways of People. Then, when he was grown, they said that our son could show other Scraps how to help People discover their own Goodness. *This would make life safer for Scraps and better for the whole world.* It sounded very positive. It sounded like the Plan for Goodness that Spirit wanted from the beginning of The Big Game."

King Heart was still frowning and doubtful, but he stammered out, "The Fireflies said that? The Fireflies said that *our* son would make life better for the whole world?"

"That's what they were singing," sighed Connie. "It was beautiful, and it sounded like such a noble cause that even the sharing of our dear son didn't sound wrong. But how could I have thought that I understood something so foolish? I could never share my son with a heartless King and Queen."

The Queen walked over to her son's cradle to gaze at him. Love poured from her face. The little creature in the milk pod seemed to glow in her love light.

The Rescue

Throughout the day Moses, King Heart, and Queen Connie discussed everything: River People, babies, Fireflies, and Scraps. They also discussed the future and how frightening the future appeared to be for all Scraps. As the morning became afternoon, the riverbank turned unusually warm, and the air in the log home became stuffy. It was time to take a cooling wade in the River.

As King Heart, Queen Connie, and their baby neared the cooling edges of the river with Moses, they realized that they had lots of company. The River was dotted with hundreds of tiny heads. Every Scrap in the area must be taking a swim, as well. Moses was already up to his haunches in the cool water when disaster struck.

From out of nowhere came the sounds of laughter and whooping. The ground began to shake. The Scrap Lancers began targeting the Willow in warning. The huge, flopping bodies of the River People began to hurdle through the air, landing with immense tidal wave splashes in the swimming holes all along the shoreline! There was no doubt about it. The River People were going swimming too.

As the Scraps ducked and scrambled for safety, they became sickeningly aware of the sound of crunching and crushing and cracking. In their rush to jump into the river, the River People were destroying more of the Scrap homes that were dotted along its edge.

Dripping and terrified, hundreds of little pink Scraps struggled to the shore and onto the protective area around the roots of the Willow as they had the night before. Soon they gratefully spotted their King and Queen, safe and sound, hurrying toward them out of the shallow water with the little prince in their arms.

But Moses. Where was Moses? The word passed from Scrap to Scrap with concern. Everyone knew Coach. They loved him. They had seen him enter the water with the King and Queen. Where could he be now?

Then they heard an ear-splitting screech. On the bank near the Willow stood a young boy and girl, two of the River People. Dangling from the fingers of the boy was Moses, hanging by his tail!

The young girl screamed again. "A mouse! A mouse! Get that awful thing away from me!"

"Aw, it's only a stupid mouse. What are you afraid of?" teased the young man, waving Moses dizzyingly in front of the girl's face. She covered her eyes with her hands and continued to scream.

As the taunting continued, King Heart scampered up the trunk of the Willow and out onto a branch over the head the jeering boy. Heart knew that at any minute the youth would tire of his teasing and fling Moses far into the river to drown.

The little Scrap King scurried out to the end of the limb over the huge boy's head. Bravely, he jumped down into the hair of the young man, intent on rescue. It was only as he wove his way through the tangled, wet hair on the boy's head that Heart realized that he didn't know what he was going to do.

At the base of the Willow terrified Scraps watched the drama. What was their King's plan? Would he be able to rescue Moses and live to tell about it? Should they climb out on the limb and try to help him? Just as a brave group of little Scrap men was about to scamper up the Willow, King Heart had made his move, diving into the boy's hair. Now, what could they do?

Queen Connie hugged her infant close to her and prayed that her husband would survive his bravery.

Heart suddenly had an idea. Carefully he slid down a lock of hair to a place near the boy's left ear.

"Put the mouse down," ordered King Heart in his most authoritative voice.

The boy stopped short and looked suspiciously around him. "Who said that?" he asked.

"Who said what?" responded the girl, peeking out from between her fingers.

"I'm telling you, put down the mouse!" King Heart again commanded forcefully in the boy's ear. This time he added, "How would you like it if a big giant picked *you* up and swung you around by *your* tail?"

"I don't have a tail!" the boy answered angrily, swatting the air around him as though trying to do away with the voice in his ear.

"I should hope not," laughed the girl.

"Then how would you like it if a giant swung you around by some *other* body part?" Heart offered. The boy winced.

"Now put the mouse up on the tree, carefully. And one more thing... you shouldn't tease the girl you love."

Slowly, without really knowing why, the boy reached up and put Moses on the Willow branch above his head. Unseen, Heart jumped up to Moses, and they both hurried toward the Willow trunk and safety.

The boy shook his head, a very puzzled look on his face. Then he reached out and for his girlfriend's hand. "I'm sorry, Molly. I don't know why I tease the girl I love."

Molly peeked again from between her fingers. "You what?"

The young man grinned. "I love you," he repeated, now suddenly shy.

The girl named Molly hugged her young man and both splashed, hand in hand, down the riverbank toward their friends.

From her spot in a bend of the Willow's branches, Queen Connie snuggled her baby and knew she had just seen something new and wonderful.

Moses shook himself dry and thought about two things. King Heart, a Scrap, had just saved his life. But more important than what King Heart had done was *how* he had done it. Without knowing it, he and Queen Connie were thinking the same thing.

Remorse and Inspiration

The rescue had, indeed been amazing, but, equally amazing was the fact that Spirit had also been there to see it. He had been in the water of the river all morning, struggling among the rocks and sand. He had been looking for Special Clay.

Frantically he had combed the sandy shores since daybreak, hoping against hope to find at least a bit of the wondrous Clay he had dropped so long ago. This is where he had found it before. Maybe...

As he had expected, he had had no luck, but he *was* standing in the sandy water near the far side of the Willow when he had watched the unbelievable in amazement. The tiny Scrap King had actually rescued the same mouse he had listened to only the day before.

It had been truly inspiring. In contrast to his disappointing search for Special Clay, a beautiful moment had occurred and he had been there to see it. The brave little Scrap King had risked his life to save another, been welcomed by all his subjects and then appreciated by the grateful mouse, himself. It was a scene of joy and love and gratitude. Spirit had not seen that much Goodness expressed among his humans... ever.

Bravery, ingenuity, kindness and thankfulness—what other wonderful traits do these Scraps possess that my humans do not? Spirit thought with wonder. *They must, indeed, be made of Special Clay. Look at them. Their behavior displays all the ingredients of the Clay that I dropped.*

Spirit drifted with his regret to the top of the Willow above the Scraps. *All that Special Clay is in these Scraps below now,* he admitted to himself sadly. *Obviously I failed to make good use of it when I had a chance and a smart mouse used it, instead. How embarrassing.*

What the Fireflies showed me back then was a one-time opportunity and I blew it. They will never show me another. I don't deserve it. And with no more Special Clay available in the river, the chances of getting these qualities into today's humans is impossible.

Spirit sulked. *Now I know that I will never win The Big Game. That is certain,* he thought angrily.

Below him, the children of Spirit's humans were now chasing one another with angry threats and humiliating jibes.

"Come here, fatso! You float like a wad of blubber!"

"Shut up or I'll drown you. I'll make you swim like a rock."

"Better than floating like a fat spit bubble like you."

"Go ahead and drown while I watch. No one will miss you."

Spirit watched the two boys fight and struggle and yell in the shallow water, continuing to call each other names and scream for their mothers. No mothers came. The mothers were arguing over who was going to sit where and also calling names. It was a hopelessly common scene, but, in the Willow's branches, the Scraps continued to happily congratulate each other on the wonder of the rescue and the fact that they were all safe, even if they were once again hiding in a tree. The contrast between Scraps and People was depressing.

Spirit sighed. He had come today full of the hope of re-discovering some of the magical Special Clay that might mean a comeback in his side of The Big Game. He knew now that this was never going to happen. This bitter realization threatened to overtake him.

Gradually, however, looking down on his miserable humans and the happy Scraps beneath him, Spirit began to make an unexpected discovery. The importance of The Big Game seemed to be fading. The Big Game was all he had worried about for centuries, but now, Spirit could not help but simply pine for the memory of the peaceful humans that he *thought* he had created here so long ago. Today's unhappy humans no longer made him worry about losing the Game. They only made him sad, very sad for the loss of what these humans could have and *should have* been. And it was all his fault.

Spirit focused. He concentrated. Then, he decided. He must stop sulking and do something!

Suddenly he knew that today he must now stay here in the branches of the Willow. He must watch these Scraps. He must learn from them. The Game was no longer important. Winning the Game was not enough. He must help his humans. He must begin a new mission.

He had caused his People to be unhappy and thoughtless so *he* must find a way to repair his mistake. Today had shown him that he couldn't find any more Special Clay in the river, but Scraps were *made* of that Special Clay!

Spirit was now in a position to see Special Clay at work. If he observed them a lot and worked hard, maybe these Scraps could give him the inspiration and knowledge that he needed to fix the damage he had done.

And Spirit suddenly *did* have a very creative idea. *What if River People could learn to imitate Scrap behavior?* Humans were not stupid. At least, they had good brains even if their hearts were faulty. Spirit was sure that humans could *learn* to be nicer. Maybe their insufficient hearts could be fixed with their intelligence. Maybe his humans just needed some training. Again, Spirit thought Scraps might be the answer.

What if there could be a training camp? First, Scraps could teach River People the ideas about the Goodness that he had seen today. Then River People could practice some of these ideas, and Scraps could coach them. They could do this every day until humans actually learned all the good practices that Scraps already knew. Coaches—that's what Scraps could be!

What a brilliant plan! Spirit could already see that Scraps were kindhearted. He was sure they would be willing to help if asked. Scraps and People might actually learn to like each other.

Spirit began to imagine a training session for Scraps and People. After all, they were so much alike...but wait... Reality set in.

What about the skills Fighter had already taught People: their awful temper that always led to violence, their dishonesty, their cheating and lying, *and* then there was their selfishness and meanness. Would People be willing to sit still for even a minute and be coached?

Spirit decided that this coaching idea needed more careful study. Listening to the mouse read The Book of Amos yesterday had revealed to Spirit what his early operating style had been. He had created things quickly. He had enjoyed being creative. He had loved the competition with Fighter. But thinking ahead had not been part of his creative processes at the time. He needed to get better at that.

And Spirit had learned that he could not just blame Fighter anymore. *He* was the one that had made The Drop. *He* was the cocky one who had left the Game before it was won. This time, if Goodness and happiness for his people were ever to have a chance, Spirit knew he must think everything through and create a new Plan that would *really work* this time.

Winning The Big Game had been a selfish goal for him, but it was not as important a goal anymore. Good, happy People were his goal now. Spirit smiled as he thought about his new understanding and the part that Scraps might play, Scraps were wonderful. He thought back on his discovery of them last night. That had been such a lucky coincidence. Then he remembered something else.

Scraps had their own problems. They were being trampled into extinction. Spirit had almost forgotten. They were in danger of being killed by the very People that Spirit now wanted them to help him. What if they were wiped out just when he had discovered them?

There was no doubt about it. Visualizing the wreckage he had seen last night, there the future looked dim for the tiny Scraps. Spirit focused again. Protecting Scraps from extinction must also be part of his new goal. The seriousness of this situation was becoming even more evident.

Scrap protection would not happen overnight. Spirit needed to concentrate... and what was Fighter up to? He cringed. Fighter must really be loving the destruction of the Scraps' world that Spirit was just now understanding.

But wait a minute. Think about it. Spirit had not known about Scraps until last night. Maybe Fighter didn't know about Scraps either.

This was unbelievable yet totally believable. The more he thought about it, the more Spirit was sure that Fighter knew nothing about Scraps. If he did, Scrap Goodness would have been trampled out centuries ago.

Spirit paced the cosmos. He was re-energized. He was even more determined than ever that Fighter would not destroy his precious earth. It was too bad that it had taken him so long to understand things the way he did now, but he had a new focus. Spirit *would* get Goodness into position to hold its own against Chaos. Scraps had shown Spirit that this was possible.

Spirit romped through the cosmos...at least he did until he remembered a very important old piece of his new reality. He returned to the Willow with a thud. He had completely forgotten the huge limitation that *he* had put on himself back in the day...*his own pledge to not interfere with human development.*

He had been so smug, so sure of himself.

He was sure that he had given humans all the tools they needed for Goodness.

What an idiot he had been!

If he was true to his pledge, what could *he* actually do to help his People now?

Nothing.

Why had he made such an ignorant pledge?

He was cocky, just plain cocky.

This was another in his long list of flaws. But this was a big one. It was a sacred pledge to the cosmos. As a spirit in good standing, he could not interfere with Mankind now, no matter what. As a spirit with honor, he *must* stand by his pledge. Why had he done such a stupid thing?

Spirit slumped again against the Willow. Not only had he made a Game-changing mistake during his creation of human hearts but he had tied his own hands so that he couldn't fix it. Now, he couldn't do anything to help his beloved humans *or* Scraps.

But wait again!

He hadn't known anything about the Scraps when he was creating humans, had he? His pledge had nothing to do with Scraps, did it? Fireflies had been with him since the beginning, and they had made no such pledge to anyone, either. Perhaps Fireflies and Scraps could help humans *and* Scraps in ways that would not go against his pledge. This *could be* a win-win.

The more Spirit thought about it, the more cooking up a new Plan for Goodness with Scraps and Fireflies sounded like a eureka moment. He must run this by the Fireflies. Fireflies were cool. Fireflies were smart. They had been here from the beginning. They would certainly be willing to help him figure something out.

A new Game Plan must start soon, though. He had already waited too long. He owed it to both the River People and the Scraps to get a revised Plan ready.

Spirit sailed away from the riverbank. Scouting time was over. Dedication time was here. This was a time to get busy and create. He would discuss his new ideas and understanding with the Fireflies. He was out of here.

Spirit had no idea, but the Fireflies were way ahead of him.

The Great Fire

The Game may have become more meaningful and personal for Spirit, but it was still very much The Big Game for Fighter. Until now, Fighter had encouraged all evil freely with little competition, and he had become very good at it. He had even developed Laziness, Cheating and Distrust to go with Basic Mayhem and Violence while poor Spirit just waited for his Understanding of Right and Wrong to show up.

What a laugh! Obviously, Fighter knew that that trait never would. He was loving this Game the way it was working out, and that was a fact. Sooner or later there would be a major skirmish and Fighter was certain that this would give him final control over everything in the universe. In the meantime, Fighter enjoyed the day-to-day misery he could cause on a regular basis, and it was still only the 2nd Quarter.

Today, the River People continued to splash away the afternoon in the river, whooping and hollering and pushing one another around, unaware of the Scraps huddled in the nearby Willow. Occasionally, a fistfight or wrestling match would break out, but there was less bloodshed than usual.

Fighter observed the humans from a nearby hillside and was bored with the whole scene. There was no really good violence going on. There was no blood. Everything was ridiculously low-key. As the Chaos Coach, he needed to stir things up. He decided to get busy.

He stole somebody's pants and tied them in knots. No reaction.

He pushed somebody else into a plate of his neighbor's food. Nothing much.

There was lots of cussing and a few beatings but nothing worth watching.

Anger and unhappiness were Fighter's usual brand of enjoyment, and this group of humans was not making the cut. What could he do to get a misery party up to a higher level?

As the sun settled toward the edge of the sky, Fighter thought of an old standby...bad weather. Quickly he stirred up a sudden gust of chilling wind, and the warm day on the Riverbank became cold and harsh. *This could be great*, he thought. Chill and discomfort usually got people going. They would get mad that their good time was being ruined. They would steal one another's clothes and deny it. They would drink too much. All these things had the potential to start fights—bloody noses, more chasing around, more catching and rolling in the dirt, fractured jaws, etc., etc.

Instead of fighting and arguing with one another, however, the River People decided to build a bonfire. This was a dull, peaceful counter move that Fighter had not thought of. Drat! These weird humans were using their brains too much. Stupid people were so much easier to get riled up. Again, Fighter cursed the fact that he hadn't kept the Special Clay *out of human heads* along with the hearts back in the day.

The Scraps and Moses Mouse watched the River People from the branches of the Willow while some Scraps continued to huddle unnoticed among its roots. All were waiting to feel safe enough to return to their homes or what was left of them after last night. Shivering in their damp hiding spots, they were becoming more miserable in the sudden cold wind that Fighter had stirred up, but they could not venture out. It just wasn't worth the risk.

As the Scraps stayed hidden and shivering, the River People scavenged for dry wood to build their bonfire bigger and hotter. They found a large hollow log and dragged it to the fire. Smoke began to curl out of both ends. It was the Royal Log. Snapping and popping could be heard from within as household items exploded with the heat. Soon the flames of the bonfire began to leap and dance much higher than they had before.

Queen Connie, King Heart, and many of the Scrap Kingdom could only crouch tearfully in the mud and on limbs and watch as their beloved castle—thrones, cradle, and all—was consumed by flames. Fighter would have been pleased with their misery if he had known.

About the edges of the fire, the River People circled happily, enjoying the heat on their faces. As the Scraps comforted Queen Connie and King Heart, the River People laughed and teased each other. Someone in the back of the group pulled out a bigger jug of brew than the one they had drunk during the afternoon and passed it around. More jugs were found and drained. With each jug, the River People became louder and seemed to want the fire bigger and bigger still.

The potential for things getting out of hand was increasing. Fighter was finally beginning to enjoy himself. "I like a lot of booze at a party. Activities might get even wilder now if I put my mind to it. How's this for a great idea? I'll just join the party myself and add my own 'party power' to the whole thing. I'll be a player-coach! They'll never know it's me. A big batch of strong wind will make this group of losers more interesting, cold in the nose and hot under the collar, ready to fight and destroy stuff. Then this party will be really cookin'."

Fighter snickered with evil. "Here I go. I'll give 'em the good stuff. Let's hear it for unpredictable gusts of wind."

He blew a swirling, angry blast toward the growing blaze. A patch of the Riverbank grasses at the edge of the shore immediately erupted into flames and began climbing up the dry hillside with amazing speed.

The bonfire was quickly out of control. For Fighter, this was a wonderful thing. Leaping and dancing in his own fiery windstorm, Fighter now celebrated his ability to whip simple carelessness into high drama and destruction. He appreciated his own talent. "Burn, baby! Burn!"

At first, the River People just continued to laugh, brought out more jugs of brew, and chased one another with flaming branches, but suddenly, they realized that the fire had become bigger than they thought and it was heading in the direction of the Castle!

"Forget about the stupid Castle!"

"Let the fire burn!"

"If you just let it rip, it'll burn down the Castle gate!"

"Do it! Nobody likes the King, anyway!"

Fighter whipped the flames faster as they raced up the hill. "This fire is great. I am a genius!"

Higher and higher, the flames roared forward. No one cared if the Castle burned. They cared even less about the King and his piles of riches.

But a sudden thought caught up with the drunken crowd. The King would be furious. If anything happened to *even one piece* of Castle property, heads would roll…their heads!

"Oh my god! It's almost at the Castle Gate!"
"The Gate is made of wood!"
"The King is going to put us all in the dungeons!"
"Or he'll kill us!"
"Or both!"
"I'm gonna tell 'im that you started it!"
"I'll burn yer house down if ya do . . . with yer wife in it!"
"Yer too drunk ta find my house! Now shut up and put out this fire before the Castle Guards come after all of us with hatchets!"

Stumbling around in a drunken scramble, the River People began stripping off their clothes and wetting them in the River. Time after time, they soaked their garments with water and ran to the grassy edges of the fire, swatting at the flames with their wet rags.

Fighter was furious. The obnoxious brains of the River People were ruining his fun again. "These fools are going to put the fire out. There's no fun in that. How dare they wreck my beautiful fire?" He jumped into the flames with a vengeance.

"I'm not done yet!" he cried and shifted the fire with another huge blast of wind. Sparks and burning debris flew into the air and down the riverbank. "Let's see what they can do with this," he snarled. The fire roared off again, sideways…toward Scrap Kingdom.

Fighter leapt into the fire with a dry tornado of whirling winds. They went this way. They went that way. Marvelous! This could even improve his long-range plans for the riverbank. Fire! Ruin! These were the ingredients of Chaos that would double his goal of misery for People beyond the anger and greed he had already put in motion. *Let it take their houses. Let it spread to their families. This amount of fire could destroy a whole town.*

Fighter was no longer worried about the possibilities of intelligence thwarting his plans for Chaos. He was past that and in control of The Big Game and the world's future. There would be no interference from Spirit tonight or any night. No one had seen Spirit since who knows when. What a sore loser he was.

Rubbing his hands together with satisfaction, Fighter blew another fiery explosion into the monstrous grass fire that was roaring its way down the bank. Helplessly, the Scraps watched as the fire consumed one after another of the Scrap homes and fields, swirling through the grasses until it finally hissed to a stop at the water's edge.

At last, the huge fire burned itself out. The hillside was black up to the Castle's gate but had not actually touched it. Feeling that nothing serious had been lost and really too drunk to care anyway, the River People stumbled off to their homes, leaving behind the scorched remains of the riverbank.

Fighter was disappointed. It had all ended too soon. Tomorrow, the King would be ticked off about his hillside. That would be fun to watch. But Fighter became bored now, angry that he had failed to burn down some of the actual homes of the River People. That would have been so much more satisfying. He should have sent the wind in the direction of the village. Drat! Next time. That would have been a perfect ending to the evening.

The destruction of the Scrap Kingdom would have thrilled him if he had seen it, but he had not. Too bad. He would try for more destruction again soon. He thundered off in a noisy burst of heat lightning.

The Scraps were in shock. Just like that, *their entire village* had been destroyed. From the Willow's branches, they surveyed the smoldering scene below. They could see that they had lost everything. The ruined grasslands were still too hot and dangerous for them to step foot on the charred ground. Miserably, the Scraps huddled together, ready to spend a wet, cold night stranded in the Willow. Slowly, they climbed up higher and settled into its branches. They really had no choice.

Without thinking for more than a moment, however, Moses, who was huddled with them, offered a temporary refuge at the Castle to the Scrap Royals. The Scraps loved their King and Queen and now their new Prince. The little pair denied Moses's offer at first, but the Scrap Kingdom needed their Royal Family to be safe. The Whole Scrap Council insisted. King Heart gratefully relented.

Too much had happened to the little family today. They couldn't refuse. Like lost children, King Heart and Queen Connie followed Moses slowly through a secret, underground mouse passage to the Castle. There they and their tiny son would spend the night, miserable refugees from a Kingdom that was no more.

The Morning After

Before dawn the next morning, Spirit, unaware of the tragedy that had happened the night before, returned to the riverbank for another day of observing Scraps. He and the Fireflies had been in conference all night. They believed they had the beginnings of a plan that might use Scraps and *could* make earth into the place Spirit had always wanted it to be.

As he arrived, however, Spirit realized with shock that the idyllic life of the Scraps no longer existed. Scrap Kingdom was gone.

In horror, Spirit hovered high over the black. deserted ruins of the little kingdom. He could see what the Scraps had lost—their homes, their way of making a living, everything. Worst of all, had they all lost their lives?

Spirit was shaken by the awesome toll the fire had brought upon the area. He was sure that the fire had been caused by the River People, but something this terrible must also be the work of Fighter. Did Fighter know what he had done, how bad this really was? Had he killed all the Scraps on purpose?

What tragic misery the Scraps must have experienced last night. Were they all dead? Spirit was in despair. He should have been here. Perhaps he could have done something. Sorrowfully, he sank into the branches of the Willow again. Only then did he notice with relief that there were tiny creatures gathered below him.

They were alive. Hundreds of Scraps were still alive, scurrying to and fro, shivering, tending to wounds, drying tears, and holding one another tight. Spirit was thrilled that so many had lived.

But agony for the remaining Scraps soon followed. Spirit knew that he wanted to help these poor creatures, but with sudden clarity, he realized that he had no idea what to do for them. He wanted to find Fighter and beat him up.

Really? Violence? For the first time ever, Spirit of Good could think of nothing Good that he could do to help.

He was overwhelmed by the crisis below him. The Scraps were homeless. They were wet and quaking with cold. Without a major change, they might not survive. Most of all, he groaned helplessly, right now they were cold.

Yes, warmth... They need warmth. I can do that.

Quickly, Spirit reached down over the distant edge between the River and sky and pulled the fat sun up out of its resting place. The air began to warm. The Scraps began to stretch their stiff, cold arms and legs and move about more freely. And what were the first things they were doing? They were caring for one another.

Spirit spun away from the ruined riverbank. The sun had helped in one small way, but panic and guilt set in with Spirit. He had waited too long. The Scraps' way of life gone forever. There was now no hope for Good in the universe. He must inform the Fireflies of this disaster.

Moses Mouse was out and about in the Castle early, shopping for supplies among the foodstuffs left in the Castle kitchen. He now scurried back to his cozy apartment under the kitchen floorboards, his arms laden with supplies.

As the morning sun slanted through the Castle floor above Moses's rooms, he began to hear the faint whimper of the Scrap prince behind the curtain where he and his parents had spent the night.

"Good! Just in time," sighed Moses to himself. He had carefully picked out the fresh tidbits that he knew Scraps could digest. By experience, he knew that they simply could not tolerate the dried corn and beans that were *his* favorite. They had such particular needs.

Tidbits of cheese, butter, and bread, all were carefully balanced in his paws, threatening to tumble down about him. Carefully he eased his prizes onto a saucer, a special find that had been in his possession for years. He hurried over to his guests' room.

"Your Highnesses," he whispered, standing respectfully on his side of the curtain. "I've brought food. I am sure that you and the baby must be hungry since you didn't eat last night. Please come out and see what I have brought. If there's anything more you need, I'll get it. I know where *everything* is in this Castle."

Very quickly, the drapery covering their room parted, and Queen Connie stepped out with her baby, looking fresh. She smiled gratefully at Moses and began preparing the tiny offerings that would keep her baby healthy.

"Thank you so much, dear Mose."

King Heart now emerged from his bedchamber. He did not look nearly as fresh as Connie.

"What a night," growled Heart. "Lives lost... burned-out homes... what's next? I need to get down to my people and assess the damage. May I borrow some of this cheese and bread before I go?"

"Certainly!" exclaimed Moses. "It would be my honor. And while you eat, may I thank you again for your courageous rescue of me from the sure death that I expected yesterday. How brave and noble you were in the face of danger. You were unbelievable."

Queen Connie joined in. "Oh my goodness, yes, my dear. You were wonderful. Do you remember what you did and how you did it? Mose would have been thrown into the river to drown if it had not been for you. What *did* you say to that boy?"

King Heart blushed nearly purple under the praise. "It wasn't much," he grumbled into his cheese sandwich. "I simply said what any sensible person would say. That is, 'Don't hurt the mouse because the mouse didn't hurt you *and* don't scare your girlfriend with it. She might not love you any more if you do.' Something like that. It was nothing much really."

"But you risked life and limb!" exclaimed Moses. "And as the mouse that got rescued, I find your suggestions to the boy to have been brilliant and above average in creativity."

"I agree, my sweet," seconded Connie. "In fact, I dreamed all night long of the possibilities that I saw shown by your brave deed. I even think that I might be getting closer to understanding the song of the Fireflies."

Moses and Heart snapped around to face Connie. She was quietly feeding the baby tiny crumbs of milk-soaked bread.

"What are you saying, my love? Whatever could the lucky rescue of Mose yesterday have to do with Fireflies today?" asked Heart.

Moses said nothing. He was beginning to get that strange feeling again, the one that told him something important was about to happen.

"Think about it, husband," spoke Connie gently. "Yesterday you spoke in the ear of a giant, and he did your bidding. You *said* and he *did*, right? You asked him to stop doing something bad and to do something good and you told him why. The human changed what he was doing because of a little voice in his ear. Don't you find that amazing?"

"Not so amazing," answered Heart. "You say things in my ear all the time, and I do them." The King smiled slightly, not understanding the full importance of what his wife was saying. Moses sat very still and listened.

King Heart was through with early morning chitchat. He was consumed with worry. Praise for what he had done yesterday did not interest him. His kingdom was a burned and tragic mess, and it was *his* duty to help his subjects salvage what they could of their ruined lives. That was what kings were for... to lead their people when times required leading.

With a kiss for his wife and baby and a paw shake for Moses, King Heart turned his attention to the grim responsibilities awaiting him. Off he went to the blackened remains of Scrap Kingdom. He must comfort his subjects and search for life among the still smoking pieces of rubble that had been Scrap homes. The King was a man of action.

Moses waved goodbye to King Heart with a heavy sigh, knowing how difficult the task before the little King would be. Even the Royal Log had been torched and was gone forever. Who knew how many other Scraps had lost their homes and even their lives to the thoughtless "fun" of the River People? Moses promised Heart that he would bring a squad of mice down to help soon.

When King Heart was out of sight, Moses turned his attention to Queen Connie and her baby. He must make sure these precious souls were safe before he returned to help Heart at the riverbank.

On a small white patch of down spread on the floor, the Scrap baby was now placed, naked as the day he was born, beautiful, perfect, and happy. The Queen stood above him, looking down at him with great love and tenderness. Slowly she dropped to her knees, her hands running softly over his pink skin, pausing to allow his little fingers to curl around one of her own. The sunbeams slanted in through the floorboards above and captured the picture, putting both mother and son in a soft glow. Moses Mouse knew he would remember this sight as long as he lived. It was a picture of motherly love that needed no words.

While Moses stood watching the gentle scene, he suddenly became acutely aware of noises from above. People were dragging heavy tables and chairs about in the throne room. He decided to take a quick run up into the main part of the Castle to see exactly what was happening. Knowing what was going on at all times was the best way for a mouse to stay safe.

Quietly he slipped through the drapes that separated his private quarters from the rest of the maze of rodent scurry-ways under the main rooms of the Castle. This area was very busy. Below the floorboards, a community of rodents and various types of industrious insects traveled to and fro on their daily jobs and activities.

In general, by reason of size and numbers, the mouse population tended to occupy most leadership positions in this community. Rats did not, not because of a lack of leadership ability but more because of their insistence that they did not "have time for such unimportant things as politics."

Rats had very little patience with unnecessary socialization and had never become involved in the day-to-day problem-solving of the community. They were, however, very ready to pick up anything of value that was left lying around.

Who knew what they do with what they find? Moses thought smugly.

Rats as a group could feel the mouse distrust around them and resented what they felt was their second-class position in the world of rodents. Their resentment of this status caused them to primarily live with their own kind, away from other rodents.

The underfloor of the Castle was, therefore, divided into sections, much the way many towns are, with mice in one area and rats in another. No one said that this segregation was the way it should be. Mice liked to believe that rats preferred to live with each other. No one tried to explain why the rats tended to live closer to the sewer in the Castle while the mice were closer to the Castle kitchen.

The insects were basically immune to the rodent-segregation controversy. They lived and traveled freely, conducting business between and among all areas and with all rodents, not taking sides.

Moses had a feeling that all was not as it *should be* in terms of equality between rats and mice. He knew he *should* do something about it. It was probably an issue of pure prejudice. Rats *should* be equal to mice. Scraps knew this was so as did Moses. There was no doubt about it. But so far, no one had made any moves to change things.

This idea was running through Moses's head as he left his quarters to investigate the noise from above. For that reason, you can imagine his shock, surprise, and even fright when, right in front of his own doorway, he found a very large rat.

Ramon Rat lay sprawled to his full twenty inches, nose to tail, impressively blocking the scurry-way in front of Moses's home. His size was intimidating.

Ramon had been born in a rough area at the edge of the river. He and his twin brother, Reardon, carried in their bloodline the genes of the river rats, a much larger and more physical specimen than many other rats who had been born and raised within the Castle, itself. He was huge.

For a moment, Moses forgot his reason for leaving his hole and assumed a defensive stance. Why was a river rat here in this part of the Castle? Did he mean to harm Moses? Did he mean to harm Queen Connie? What should he do?

Be polite. Don't show fear. Be ready. Anything else? Speak up.

"Hello, Ramon. Were you waiting here to see me?" Moses tried to make it sound casual, as though he was ordering a cookie from the Spirit Sister's Auxiliary. Cool… Very matter-of-fact.

Unexpectedly, however, Ramon rose to full offense position, rounded his back, and stared directly down at Moses.

Moses knew that to show fear was to invite disaster, but his first desire was to turn and run back into his hole. Because of the tiny size of the opening, this huge rat could not follow (a designed safety feature of most mouseholes).

Before he could make his move, however, Moses noticed that Ramon did not appear to be his usual, intimidating self. Instead, he seemed to be somewhat dazed, as though awakened from a deep and troubling dream. Had he been sleeping in front of Moses's door? Ramon's dark furry brow was deeply creased, and for the first time, Moses saw a side of Ramon he had never seen before. Ramon looked sad and confused and frightened.

Moses could not help but feel some sympathy for this enormous rat with troubled eyes. The creature was trembling. "Ramon, you don't look well. Where is your brother?" The two were seldom apart.

Ramon blinked several times as though trying to erase his bad dreams and bring himself back to the question. Then he took a deep, shuddering breath and pushed his misery out of his mouth in the form of words.

"Last night, my brother and everybody in my family was killed," he declared bluntly.

Moses was dumbstruck. He couldn't say a thing. Before his eyes, the giant rat crumpled and seemed to flatten onto the scurry-way like a bag of melting butter, his huge paws over his face. There was no doubt. Ramon was in misery.

Moses no longer saw a rat. He saw a fellow rodent in distress. Gently he put his nose close to that of the bigger creature and offered all he could in comfort.

"Oh, Ramon. I am so sorry! How did it happen? What can I do to help?"

Ramon, unaccustomed to such gentle words from a mouse, drew himself up and tried to act dignified, but the attempt failed. He sat crookedly on half a haunch and looked at his paws, snuffling uncontrollably.

"I dunno. It all happened last night," Ramon related dismally. "There was some sort of swimmin' thing happenin' with the River People. There were hundreds of 'em runnin' into the river, splashin' and yellin' and chasin' each other around like usual. That was all right. We've lived 'round People all our lives. No problem. We know how to dodge 'em. We're good at it."

"Yes, I know." Moses nodded sympathetically.

"It was the fire! It was the freakin' fire that done it! The stupid River People started a fire! They could've gone home and stoked up a fire in their own fire pits, but no. They had ta make a fire on the riverbank, right on top of the dig where my whole family was livin'. They ran from the fire and smoke, but the River People caught 'em. They stomped on 'em. They burned 'em. They threw 'em into the fire and watched 'em cook. There's no one left. I am the only one still alive out of my whole family. I would've been dead too, but I was gettin' down to the bank late. Even my brother's gone. He wasn't much, but he *was* my brother." The rat was sobbing.

Moses shuddered as he remembered his own close call and the roaring fire that followed. Almost forgetting his distrust of rats, he edged closer to Ramon and cautiously tried to put his arm around Ramon's heaving shoulders. Moses was too small. Just the same, he patted the big creature gently. "I am so sorry for your loss," he said. "Is there anything I can do?"

Moses was not prepared for Ramon's answer. Ramon gathered himself up to his full height, displaying all the pride and determination that he could put together. He made a statement that sent shivers down Moses's spine.

"I want Rodent Revenge against the River People!" Ramon growled from deep within. "We're both rodents, you and me. Are you with me or against me?" He focused hard on Moses.

Moses swallowed. Revenge was not something that mice practiced. Moses had spoken before with Scraps on this subject. They had concluded that revenge tasted sweet but could make you sick. This was what Moses had always believed. But here was Ramon, and Ramon wanted revenge for his dead family. For the life of him, Moses could not come up with a good reason to say no.

As Moses tried to sort out his feelings about revenge, he heard a small rustling behind him. He turned to see Queen Connie, standing in the doorway of his home. Seeing her sweet face, Moses felt guilty about his thoughts of revenge. She would not think that way, he was sure.

Suddenly, Moses feared for the little Queen. Ramon towered over both of them. He could snap her like a twig with his huge teeth, and he was not in a good mood. Moses began to wave his paws and gesture for her to return to his hole.

Consciences—and the Legends of The Big Game

Connie did not seem to be at all worried, however. She glided past Moses and reached up toward Ramon's scraggly cheeks as though she had known him all her life. Surprisingly, Ramon lowered his huge head. With great compassion, the Queen held his face in her tiny hands, brushing at the hot tears that were matting his fur.

"How sad you must be to have lost your family," she murmured. "How heartless the River People are. We must do something to keep sadness like this from happening. No one else should die because People are so thoughtless and cruel. Last night, the River People burned *my* home and, I fear, killed many of the dear Scraps in my Kingdom as well. We can no longer stand by and do nothing. Perhaps we should all work together."

"No, no, Queen Connie! You must not become involved." Moses squeaked protectively. "Ramon, she is the *Queen* of Scrap Kingdom. She doesn't understand how dangerous things might be. She is very small. She breaks easily." He began running back and forth, trying to distract Ramon's attention.

Queen Connie shot Moses a very queenly look, giving him solid notice that no one needed to protect *her*. As protective as Moses felt, there was nothing he could do. Ramon and Queen Connie were nose to nose.

"I know who you are, and you are right, Queen Connie." Ramon responded firmly. "This here *should never* happen again. We *should* all work together. And I thank ya fer yer offer." Ramon began to pace, his long, snakelike tail whipping back and forth across the floor. Then he rose on his haunches and stared down at the Queen and Moses.

"But I demand Rat Revenge! *Rodent* Revenge! *You* are not a Rodent. Are you and your people ready to wage war on the River People? It's a just cause. There's strength in numbers. Even if we are all small, there's a bunch of us. We gotta show the River People that they can't step on us no more!"

"Yes, I am ready," stated the Queen. She held her head high.

Moses couldn't believe his ears. Ramon was ready to wage a revenge war upon the River People, and it looked like Queen Connie was going to help him. Moses felt his understanding of things spinning out of control. He needed to slow things down. *He* was not ready to wage war, and he couldn't believe Queen Connie would even consider it. But just as suddenly as the war clouds gathered, Queen Connie whisked them away.

"You are so brave and strong, Mr. Rat," Connie stated with sympathetic respect. "I feel reassured already that we can develop a plan among all of us, a plan that will resolve your anger and allow us all to live in safety. I am so glad that we have decided to work together. I will explain everything we have said to each other to my husband, and I am sure that he will be happy to join in a plan with you. Thank you so much for including us in your preparations. We will speak with you soon."

Ramon shook his head a bit as though he wasn't quite sure what he had just heard, but he said, "Thank you, Your Majesty." Then he bowed low and walked slowly away. He had never had much to do with Scraps, but if they were all like this little Queen, they were all right.

"What just happened?" sputtered Moses almost to himself as Ramon disappeared around a corner.

"We have begun to make a friend," stated Connie and slipped back into Moses's mousehole to check on her baby.

Shaking his head, Moses turned in the direction of the scurry-way upstairs and the noisy throne room above. He must evaluate the situation. With the Queen here in the Castle, security measures were essential.

The Royal Yesmen

In the throne room of King Sol and Queen Luna, heavy benches had been set around massive wooden tables and were filling rapidly. Tall and short, fat and thin, young and old, nearly one hundred male members of the Royal Yesmen were shuffling into place. They had no choice. They had been summoned at dawn by an angry King, and they knew better than to not show up.

The River People, still sleeping off their party from the night before, had been rudely awakened by ear-shattering blasts from a shell horn, one of the enormous shells that existed in great abundance along the Riverbank. With much grumbling (but no hesitation), the men rolled off their sleeping mats and began trudging up the hill toward the Castle, most of them still dressed in the rumpled rags they had worn the night before.

King Sol the Selfish was not a late sleeper. It was his habit to rise before daylight and survey *his* Kingdom from *his* Castle windows, appreciating the fact that it was all *his*. The sun was just rising. Everything he expected to see from here to the river would be reflected in golden sunlight, marvelous as it should be.

Imagine his horror then when he discovered that a great wide patch of *his* hillside was scorched black.

His hillside! Who could have done such a thing? How could anyone *dare* to do such a thing? King Sol never stopped to wonder if anyone had been hurt in the fire that had caused this. All he knew was that a huge stretch of ugly burned hillside was still smoldering and completely ruining *his* view.

This could not be tolerated. Someone was to blame. Someone must pay. He gave the order for the shell horn to be blown immediately. The Royal Yesmen must deal with this without delay. Heads would roll.

The Royal Yesmen were King Sol's Advisors, or at least, that was what they told themselves. The eldest males from each household in the village formed the group. Each took his position as a Yesman very seriously. Not only was it a position of honor but being part of this group was the only way to protect oneself from King Sol's anger in times of crisis.

The households of River People often contained several generations huddled together under one roof or gathered near one another in small huts. Since there was safety in numbers, children simply continued to live with their parents after they were grown and had their own families. When the oldest male of the family group died, the next oldest male took his place among the Yesmen and was accepted as a Yesman from then on.

There were no term limits to the position of Royal Yesman other than those imposed by death or stripping, but there were two ways to be stripped off a position in the group. The first way was to tell the King something he didn't want to hear, such as 'no' if he requested something. Thus the name, '*Yes* men'.

The second way to be stripped was to be found guilty of a crime. A 'crime' consisted of doing something the King didn't like. The rules were very simple.

Consequences for being stripped from the Yesmen were swift and harsh. First, the offending Yesman was thrown into a dungeon to await his real punishment. Most of the time, he was never seen again. Next, the family whose Yesman had been thrown in the dungeon became a *non-*family. In other words, the family no longer had a representative among the Yesmen. The family simply did not exist anymore.

Because these non-families were shunned by all their neighbors, they usually drifted off in a clump to the outskirts of River Kingdom and then disappeared altogether. It was always very sad.

Stripping and banishment of families had happened regularly throughout the years, however. This may account for the spread of the population farther up the River's bank and even the development of new villages.

The results of Yesmen meetings were dependable. For every major unhappy incident that involved the King, someone had to be blamed, whether that person was guilty or not. The person blamed could deny that he had done anything wrong, but the remaining Yesmen would agree with one another that they themselves were innocent and the blamed person was, indeed, guilty. It worked that way all the time.

"Yes! That man is certainly guilty! I knew it all along."

"Yes! He has the look of a guilty man for sure."

"Yes! You are right. I never liked him anyway."

Fairness was never looked for, attempted, or considered to be necessary. All verdicts were final and enforced by the Castle Guard. Stripping would occur soon thereafter.

No one was sure what lay farther down the Riverbank where the banished families went, but all were sure that they didn't want to go there.

It was thought that there were probably murderers or thieves or even highwaymen up there.

Of course, there were many violent and dishonest People *in* River Kingdom, but no one was worried about the evil People that they *knew*. They were much more concerned about those People up the road, the ones they *did not know*.

As a matter of fact, that's why the Storytellers were so popular. They came and went up and down the bank on a regular basis and told everyone how terrible those *other People* were. The evil of 'those people', whoever they were, was common knowledge.

So on this early morning, with the scent of smoke still mixing with the mist, the Royal Yesmen wound their way obediently up the hill to the Castle, prepared to do their duty—find a guilty party, hand him over to their King, and avoid being blamed for anything, themselves.

From a far distant edge of the cosmos, Fighter for Chaos heard the King's shell horn and also hurried to the Castle. This gathering of the Yesmen was not to be missed. These meetings never happened without the Chaos he loved, and today, after the mess that he had helped to cause last night, men would be forced to lie like crazy to save their own skins. Accusations. Denials. Liars.

Arguments and family feuds would follow. Maybe a fistfight or two. It would be spectacular.

Someone would surely be sent to the dungeons and banished. An inspiring display of nastiness and accusations would create awesome distrust that would last for months. Bribery and threats could be counted on. This is what Fighter lived for. His People had been developing these skills for years. He had trained them. Every one of the Yesmen was a player on the side of Team Chaos. These were *his* people.

Strangely enough, Spirit also slipped into this Castle gathering today unnoticed. He had just come from the Fireflies where they, too had discussed the fire and the damage it had caused, particularly to the Scraps.

But, in the face of all the unbelievable destruction last night and the unfair punishment that would follow, the Fireflies had also insisted that this Yesman meeting might somehow be involved in a Plan for Goodness. The new plan might help both humans and Scraps.

The Fireflies had seemed to believe that the battle lines between Goodness and Chaos were now more dangerous than they had ever been.

Human Goodness needed to be found and developed, but even more important, Scrap *lives* needed to be preserved Scraps had no more time

So far, Spirit couldn't quite understand the Fireflies' whole concept, but they had hinted that he might find some helpful aids to his understanding here. Fireflies were very smart. Spirit was trying to get a handle on their idea, and he wasn't sure he got it yet, but he was here. Spirit found an inconspicuous corner.

King Sol had not yet entered the throne room as the first of the Yesmen arrived, but Moses Mouse was already in position in its rafters. Attending these meetings was always informative as well as necessary for protection. It was one of the best times to study the behavior of River People, at least the male members of the line. For Coach Moses, Yesman meetings had also been a Big Game Scouting Mission. Moses scrambled to a vantage point high above everything where he could see and hear all that went on.

And Moses would be taking notes. For years, he had kept a journal on the activities of the River People, much in the way that Michael Angelo had done before. He thought his observations might expose weaknesses in Team Chaos and be as informative to the future of the Game as Michael Angelo's notes had been. Today could be very meaningful, considering the horrors of the night before.

Moses had seen these meetings many times before, but they always fascinated him. These People never made deals because they would help someone else. They only made deals to save their own skin. River People were so odd and dangerous

As the Yesmen of the River People straggled in, their conversations were no surprise to any observers.

"Here we go again. I suppose that someone is gonna have ta pay fer that fire last night," commented one creaky elder, shaking his shaggy gray head.

"Well, it's not going to be me or mine, I can tell you that. Sure, we all threw things into the fire, but when it spread, it was not *my* fault. I aren't gonna take no blame," answered his crotchety partner, pulling his rags up around him. "A wind came up. Did ya see that? A wind came up." Fighter snorted happily from the shadows.

The two early arrivals dragged benches close to a rear table so that they would be farthest away from the King. These two were very old and had been Yesmen for a long time. They knew how to survive these sessions.

Others continued to arrive and began clustering in small groups right away. The bargaining began. Who was going to take the blame this time? Arms were twisted. Old debts were called to account. Alliances were formed. Everyone furtively scanned each newcomer for a likely looking scapegoat. Wind or no wind, someone was going to take the heat for that fire.

"I stood up and made sure that someone else got blamed last time when yer sons stole food from the King's storehouse," one of the elders whispered to the two men near him. "If a lie needs tellin', I expect ya both ta stand up fer me this time or else. And ya both *know I* got the goods on ya if ya don't." The speaker leaned back with one eye squinted shut and the other eye in a threatening stare.

The men he was addressing nodded knowingly. They didn't feel that they owed this man anything. They never felt they owed *anyone* anything, but they just knew what would happen if they went against him. Right and wrong did not enter into the thinking of the Yesmen. They were only intent on keeping themselves alive, no matter what.

Spirit watched closely as deal after deal took place. Threats and promises slithered back and forth. Each elder eyed his peers with a look of distrust and self-protecting determination. Things were not looking Good in any way.

They don't even like each other. There are no real friendships here. This is so sad, thought Spirit.

The Yesmen rose from their chairs. At last, King Sol had arrived, followed by Queen Luna, looking extremely beautiful in a splendid rose gown with gold braid. The roomful of men all inhaled with one breath, a wonderful response to the glowing appearance of the Queen and just the response she wanted. She smiled radiantly at all the Yesmen, enjoying their gaping jaws and bulging eyes. It was great fun to be the only beautiful, well-dressed woman in the Kingdom. She might as well enjoy it.

King Sol took his place on his throne. Queen Luna followed to a smaller throne at his right. Moses scampered to a rafter directly across from the Royal Couple so that he would not miss a word.

"The meeting of the Royal Yesmen is now in session," announced a large Castle Guard to the left of the King. The Yesmen respectfully took their seats again on the benches around the tables. All faced the King and tried to look innocent. Although they hadn't thought of it yet, the elimination of one of them had just started.

As was expected, the King was fuming. "I have demanded you dimwits to be here at daybreak because of the fierce fire fiasco that has been promulgated on my property. No one has the right to grievously gross out my glorious grasslands. This outrage is an outstandingly outrageous occurrence! *Who* was responsible for this reckless ruin and rubble? *Who,* in particular, must be punished…and *perhaps perish? Whose* hapless head should be hacked?"

King Sol pounded his fist on the arm of his throne and scowled at one Yesman after the other. Beards quivered. Eyebrows twitched. Beads of sweat began to pop out on many a brow. Each man looked at the others around him and then said, in a jumble of grunts and groans, "It weren't me or mine, Sire."

This was not true for most of them, but of course, lying didn't bother them. That wasn't the point. They had been there, and they had watched the fire swirl out of control. None of them had done a thing to stop it until it reached the Castle Gate. Was anyone going to admit that? Of course not. This was one of those questions that no Yesman was going to say yes to. They needed a scapegoat, but who?

Just then the answer to their question walked in the door—a *new* Yesman. This one had been recently appointed to his post. Opening the throne room door a crack, he tried to slide into the hall without being noticed. Being new, he didn't realize what usually happened to those who were not there early enough to band together and form strategies.

He was new. On top of that, he was Homer, the Teacher. He was a perfect scapegoat. His first Yesmen meeting would be his last.

"There's the one that done it, I 'spect," croaked the old craggy spider man that had positioned himself at the far end of the room. It was a strategic declaration.

"We all thought he was gonna put out the fire, but he was too busy takin' care of his kid. Look… The fool even brought his kid with him to this here meetin'," offered another.

"Shoulda' left'r ta home," commented several more, smugly.

Spirit recognized this Teacher. He was the one that the parents had dragged before the King a while back for not teaching. Immediately, Spirit took a keen interest. This was a man who had still loved his wife and child. This was a River Person who had shown some heart.

All the veteran Yesmen pointed to the Teacher who now fell on his knees in a very deep and terrified bow before his King. And peeking out from the satchel on his back was that same baby girl.

"Is that the King, Daddy?" she chirped innocently.

"I beg your pardon for being late, Your Majesty. This is my daughter, Awake. My father died and her mother died just yesterday. This is why I wasn't at the fire. And today I couldn't find anyone to watch her."

The little girl peeked at King Sol and Queen Luna. Spirit was seeing something very rare. He had heard of it happening, but he had never seen it. He was watching one of the River People who was showing that he still cared for his child for more than a year. Amazing! On top of that, he was telling the complete truth. Even more amazing... Spirit made note of this to tell the Fireflies.

But this beautiful moment couldn't last. The father of the baby was being accused of today's crime. The other Yesmen were shaking their fists and snarling toward their neighbor, even though all of them knew that he was not guilty of anything. No one remembered seeing him at the bonfire the night before because he hadn't been there, but that didn't matter. The young father had no allies. He had no strategy. He was doomed.

King Sol arose from his throne and addressed his advisors. "I see that you all agree that this rogue is responsible for the blistering and burning, searing and scorching, ravishing and ruining of my gorgeous grasslands? You all say that he was the cause of the complete catastrophe in my Kingdom last night?" Sol roared his question with frightening fury.

"Yes! Yes! Yes!" they all shouted in chorus and on cue. "He must pay the price! He must be punished! Yes, yes, yes!"

It looked as though the Yesmen had easily determined who was going to be blamed this time. The King appeared satisfied and was nodding sagely in complete agreement with their brilliant conclusion. Homer. The Teacher, and his baby just stood in one spot as though rooted to the floor. The baby girl gripped her father's neck, eyes widening with fear.

The King was just about to order the deserved punishment when a sort of miracle took place, one that changed not only the outcome of that day but eventually the course of all time to come.

Queen Luna had watched the proceedings with her usual boredom, until the moment when the newest Yesman arrived with his young daughter. At that moment, the childless mother in her awoke. She had seen this baby before. She recognized the baby. She became focused. Suddenly, she did not care what happened to the father who was being wrongly accused, but she *did* care about his little girl. She really cared about *her*.

"Wait!" Queen Luna shouted in a most unusual fashion.

"Wait!" she said again, more slowly, as though not quite sure what she was going to say next. She rose from her throne and walked slowly forward, her eyes never leaving the face of the baby girl. All eyes turned toward the Queen. Even the King just stood and stared. No one had ever heard the Queen speak in a Yesmen meeting. Most men there had never heard the Queen speak at all.

Queen Luna glided toward the dumbstruck young Teacher and his daughter, her beautiful rose-colored gown swirling around her. Gently she removed the child from her father's arms. The little girl wiggled in protest, but seeing the sweet smile on the Queen's face, she stopped and smiled back.

"Me's Awake," she announced proudly in her baby voice. "You the Queen? You berry purty. You not hurt my daddy, OK?"

Queen Luna snuggled the toddler to her, smelling the sweet baby smell of her hair.

"Thank you," she responded. "You are very pretty too and very clean. Who takes care of you?"

"My daddy mostly. Sometimes Auntie, but mostly Daddy."

Awake liked the pretty Queen in the beautiful dress. She gave Queen Luna a big hug. "Please don't let Mr. King hurt my daddy," she whispered to Luna.

"I won't," Luna whispered back and turned to face her husband, who was still staring in amazement. She held the child to her breast a minute longer as though listening to her own heart.

"Sol, this little girl is so beautiful," she said at last. "And she needs her daddy. Must you punish him? If you punish *him*, he will be sent away and her family will be banished. You will be banishing *her!*" There was a tear in the eye of Queen Luna, probably the first tear she had ever shed for anyone other than herself. There was no sound in the room. No one moved.

Moses crouched on the rafter overhead, chewing nervously on his pencil. Spirit leaned forward nearby. Fighter stared at the whole thing in wonder. What would happen? What would the King do?

King Sol cocked his head to one side and scratched his beard, much the way Moses did when he was thinking deep thoughts. Time seemed to hold its breath. No one spoke.

Then the King spoke directly to Queen Luna with a tone that he had not ever used before.

"Harrumph, my dear. It appears that you choose to cherish this child. That is novel and new. Because of this, I believe I won't banish the baby or her fault-filled father. Harrumph." He cleared his throat, thought for another minute, and turned to his Yesmen.

"Upon further figuring, I further find that the flames of the fantastic fire caused little lasting loss to my lovely landscape. Therefore, no person in particular will be punished for it. I *do* insist, however, that you Yesmen who modify the mess immediately. When the dirty deed is done, I will have cider and sweets served to those of you who clean up the catastrophe. We are concluded."

Queen Luna smiled a beautiful smile and returned the baby, Awake, to her father tenderly. "Take good care of her," she said to him. "I'm sure she will make a lovely young woman when she grows."

erupted into cheers of "Yes, yes, yes!" No one was being punished or banished! It was a wonderful day! The King his and his cider were even more wonderful!

They were still cheering, throwing their hats in the air, and chattering happily as they paraded back down the hill and began the cleanup work on the burned areas of the hillside. King Sol and Queen Luna left the throne room arm in arm for the first time in months.

After the Yesmen

What?.................... The throne room was now empty...or almost empty.

"What in the heck just happened?" Fighter snarled in shock. "*This meeting of the Yesmen was a complete washout. I have never seen such wimpy behavior from my team. No blood...no fist-fights...nothing.* Sure, the Queen is a knockout, but that degree of female influence and thwarting of great unhappiness is off the charts.

"What about the charred hillside? What about the need for *hard, undeserved, misery-producing* punishment for the *wrong person?* What does '*This little girl needs her daddy'* nonsense have to do with anything? Where is Spirit? I call 'penalty for interference'."

Fighter stormed away from the throne room in disgust. For the first time, his best players had dropped the ball...and in front of a huge crowd. This was humiliating for a coach not used to botched performances from star players. With a clap of frustrated thunder, he retreated to consider his options.

Spirit, on the other hand, wasn't leaving. Something wonderful had just happened for his side of the Game and he was lucky enough to have witnessed it. *His* River People had shown compassion and kindness toward each other. Not everyone had done so, of course, but the Queen's gentleness and the King's forgiveness were all-time firsts.

Spirit blended in with the rafter where he had been perched and basked in the glow of what had just happened. No one had been punished. The King and Queen had left together. The Yesmen were happy. Was this a sign that his People's hearts might finally be using some of their small stash of Goodness?

What has caused this? he wondered. *Could that cause be duplicated?* Spirit's mind began to race. He needed to relate this immediately to the Fireflies, but he couldn't bear to leave the throne room. This was the site of his *first real success in The Big Game*, even though he had told himself that the Game was no longer important, Moses was still excitedly scribbling the whole thing down in his journal when he heard someone beside him. He glanced over just in time to see Queen Connie, her baby strapped to her back, settling down on the rafter beside him.

Moses stared at his notepad and chewed on his pencil. The Queen was here? Had she seen what just happened? What should he do? What should *he* say? He chewed his pencil some more.

Spirit couldn't believe his eyes—the Scrap Queen and her baby were *here in the Castle?* What in the world were they doing here on a rafter with the mouse called Moses? Spirit had no idea. This was the most successful day for Spirit's team in years but the little Queen had just been burned out of her kingdom. Now she was here in the Castle with that mouse that kept popping up. How did that happen? Why? This was all very confusing.

And the Scrap Queen was not even looking at the mouse. She was smiling a very mysterious smile and gazing down on the room below. Spirit could not help but stare at the pair in wonder as they began chatting.

"Queen Connie!" Moses now squeaked. "What are you doing up here? And your baby is here, too?" Why? I thought you two would be resting." He tried to look calm and collected.

As Spirit watched, the Scrap Queen smiled at Moses. She and this mouse *were* obviously friends. Amazing. Spirit leaned closer to listen.

"I am afraid for you up here." Moses continued. "Should you and the baby be way up in the rafters? It is very high, you know. Do you need something? Can I help you?" If she fell, he would never forgive himself.

For a moment, Connie surveyed the empty throne room, ignoring Moses's questions and concerns. Her mind seemed to be elsewhere. Now she looked at him and came directly to the point.

"Did you see that, Mose? Did you see what happened just now?"

"Indeed I did," stammered Moses. "I was up here during the whole meeting. I never saw anything like it. Did *you* see what happened? Queen Luna actually *helped* one of the River People and his little girl. The Queen was kind. The King was forgiving. I couldn't believe what I was seeing." Queen Connie glanced at Moses with an impish grin stretching from cheek to cheek. She was dangling her bare feet over the edge of the rafter and swinging them back and forth. She looked like a little girl.

"What would you say, Mose, if I told you that *I* had something to do with what just happened with the King and Queen?"

Moses waited. He could tell that she had more to say.

"What would you say if I told you that *I* might have even *caused* things to work out the way they did?" Now she stared at Moses, awaiting an answer. Her smile shone and her eyes twinkled. She waited. Spirit waited, too.

Moses thought for a minute. He scratched his chin whiskers. "How?" he asked.

Connie stood and began pacing the rafter, her arms clasped behind her under her baby's bottom. Now she looked like a tiny field general recalling a recently fought battle. The little Prince gurgled happily on her back, but his mother's face was serious.

"We went down among them, Mose. The baby and I were actually there on the Yesmen's tables, on their shoulders, even in their hair. We were everywhere, but they never saw us. I only went down there to watch and listen, but before I knew it, I started talking to People."

"You didn't?" Moses squeaked.

"I did." Connie confirmed. Her wide grin returned with a flash. "Did they say something back to you?" Moses sputtered. "Who did you speak to? You were in danger! King Heart would never have allowed it. You might have been killed!"

"But he didn't and I wasn't," Connie interrupted. "The baby and I were in no danger at all. No one saw us. No one even knew we were there. And here is the best part. I actually talked to only two of them. They heard me, but they didn't know they were hearing me. I spoke to them, and they listened to me, but they didn't know they were listening. Then they thought about what I said and decided to do something nice."

"Just like King Heart did yesterday...?" questioned Moses incredulously.

"Exactly! Just the way Heart changed that young boy's thoughts about you! They thought it was their own idea. Can you believe it? It worked the same way. I thought it would work and it did."

Connie began fairly dancing on the rafters. "Who do you think I talked to?"

Moses understood immediately what Queen Connie had said and who she had said it to. Spirit did not. He leaned in even closer for the answer.

"Queen Luna and King Sol?" Moses asked with a grin.

Spirit sat back, incredulous. So that was what happened. Unbelievable.

The little Queen nodded and sat down again beside Moses. Once more, she looked him in the eye.

"You are very smart, Moses Mouse," she said, kissing him sweetly on the end of his nose. But she was suddenly serious again. "You have a good mind and a solid heart. You have much knowledge. You understand just what I did. I know you do, and I think that you also know why."

Queen Connie was silent for a moment. Both friends looked to their own inner thoughts. At last Connie confirmed their thoughts. "This was the trial run of a much bigger idea. I am going to need your help, Mose. Will you help me?"

Moses scratched his chin whiskers. "Does King Heart understand your 'big idea'?"

"Perhaps not yet in detail, Mose, but of course I will not do anything without his approval and help."

Moses was fighting with himself to keep his focus, but it was very hard. He would do anything for the little Queen, but he could barely wrap his mind around the impact of what they both might be thinking. He stared at her. So did Spirit.

"Remember, Mose?" Queen Connie continued. "Ever since I heard the Fireflies sing two nights ago, I felt that they were trying to tell me about something that had to do with the River People and this Castle. Heart and I knew too well that it was *our* duty as King and Queen to help our fellow Scraps, but we just didn't know where to start. Today I think I discovered not only where to start but who to start *with*. We Scraps are destined to help all River People in general and begin with their King and Queen."

"Scraps *help* the River People? Their King and Queen? Help them do what? With all due respect, Queen Connie, what you did today was fine. But it was only two People. You saw what happened yesterday with crowds of them. You must stay away from crowds like that!"

Moses rose and stood face to face with the Queen. The hair on his neck was sticking out in all directions. He started speaking again but stopped with a gurgle, waving his paws and dropping his pencil. What was she thinking? Moses was now truly beside himself.

Connie waited for a minute and then spoke very slowly. "Calm yourself, Mose. I was down there among them all and they didn't hurt me. They didn't even *see* me or the baby.

"Just think about it that. Don't mice and Scraps do things for each other all the time? Don't we help each other think and do good things like I just did? Don't all mice and Scraps work together and share ideas like that?

"There are still many living Scraps after that horrible fire, more than one for every living human alive today, I would guess. Couldn't we Scraps learn to work with humans the way Scraps and mice have always done?"

Spirit heard the tiny Queen and was stopped in his tracks. Was this the answer? Did this wonderful Scrap woman somehow know the answer to what he had been trying to figure out? The possibility of these two species helping each other filled Spirit with hope.

The Scrap Queen stood very still. She looked royal, shining with the same glow that Moses had noticed the day before in her small log home. Now she relaxed, turned, and grinned. "And you must admit, Mose, working *with* people would be much safer for us Scraps than *dying under their feet* as we have been. (There was that saying again.)

"Yesterday, my dear husband did a very similar thing when he rescued you. We have much to plan and many details to work out, but I will share what I did just now with Heart this evening. I believe he will understand our idea."

Spirit was not sure he understood the idea. He was elated by everything he had seen but confused by what seemed to be the beginnings of an actual plan. He was only sure of one thing. He knew he had to relate *everything* he had just seen and heard to the Fireflies immediately.

After The Great Fire

That day on the riverbank, both Scraps and People performed somewhat similar duties, cleaning up the remains of what came to be known to all as The Great Fire. The River People did as they were ordered by the King, clearing burned brush and trees from the hillside and joyfully guzzling the cider that the King had provided by the barrel. But the People's positive spirit predictably evaporated, dissolving into an ugly, drunken brawl. Fighter felt better now that his People were back to normal. He perched himself nearby to cheer for one bloody side of a fight and then the other. "Hit him again!" This was more like it.

Arguments broke out on every patch of scorched turf, ending with the arguers rolling in the soot and mud. They fought about who worked the hardest, who worked the fastest, and who got the most cider. They pulled hair, socked noses, and called one another names. When they had finished, they crawled home or sprawled out in a stupor, blaming one another for work that was not yet done.

From the beginning of the day, however, there wasn't time for arguing among the Scrap workers. While the River People were involved in drinking and fighting, the Scraps dodged them and worked with a horrible sense of urgency. They couldn't hesitate. There were fellow Scraps trapped in the ruins.

Narrowly escaping the feet of drunken River People time and again, the brave Whole Scrap Rescue Detail, under the personal leadership of King Heart, climbed from homestead to burnt out homestead, often finding tragedy but occasionally finding pockets of life where the little Scraps had burrowed in and let the firestorm blow over.

By noon, they had reunited many grateful families. These families then turned with concern and comfort to those who had not been as fortunate. There had been many lives saved but many were lost too.

Spirit decided that he must stop by the charred hillside on his way from the Castle to the Fireflies. He needed to see how the Scraps were doing after the horrors of the night before. He hovered over the ruins unseen. There was sadness everywhere. Scrap homes were gone, lives were gone, a way of life had been destroyed.

A moment ago, Spirit had been thrilled by the positive prospect of Scraps' ability to help him encourage human Goodness. Now, seeing this misery around him, how could he expect the devastated Scrap community to come back from such losses to help solve *his* problem? It may be too much to ask.

Spirit watched the Scraps at work. He was impressed by their dedication. But he also watched the drunken River People. Again, he was embarrassed and disgusted by the contrast between the two species. He was ashamed.

Spirit remembered the glow of the promise he had just seen and heard in the throne room but making use of Queen Connie's wonderful ideas now seemed impossible. The lives of the Scraps had been too damaged. The need for reform of the River People was too great. He would bring the new ideas he had heard at the Castle to the Fireflies, but he was full of doubts.

King Heart, on the other hand, had no time for doubts. Time after time, he dove into clumps of still smoldering grass, thinking he heard a voice. The Scrap men and women labored heroically to save their families and the families of others, knowing it was something they had to do. No one had to ask them to help. They just did it.

As the day progressed, the exhausted ranks of the Scraps were nearly doubled by squads of mice who were rounded up by Moses and accompanied him to the scene. Gratefully, Scraps and mice worked side by side tugging, and hauling, pushing, and pulling, but over time, they came to a heartbreaking realization. In addition to the loss of life, all the homes and farms of Scrap Kingdom were gone forever, and there was no place or materials in the scarred remains where they could rebuild any of it. The way Scraps had lived since the beginning of time was gone forever.

Amazingly, Queen Luna and Queen Connie were both focused on the tragic, violent cleanup process as well...and together. Watching from a Castle window above, each woman believed she was alone. The two Queens shared a deep sadness but for different reasons.

Connie could not really see the work of her tiny Scraps from this far away, but she knew what was happening and she was too sad to do anything but look wistfully in their direction. She knew her people were helping and comforting one another, but she was also aware that she would never see many of her beloved subjects again. Tears rolled down her cheeks, and she let them flow, sadly snuggling her infant into his corn-silk wrap and holding him close.

Queen Connie was so deep in thought that she was not aware that Queen Luna had moved to the very window where she and her baby were hidden.

Quickly Connie scooted into the folds of the window hangings and peered up at the giant woman next to her. She had never been in a place where she could study a River Person up close like this...and it was surprising. Watching this Queen was much like watching a larger version of herself.

Connie was even more surprised, therefore, to see that Queen Luna was also crying. *Why would such a beautiful, large Queen be so sad?* Connie wondered. Nothing of hers had been burned. She had lost no one. Why did she cry? Did she really care that much about her fighting subjects?

Soon another human approached Queen Luna, a serving maid by the name of Thistle. She was staggering under a load of mirrors and combs and dresses. Carefully she lowered these items onto a gilded lounge nearby, puffing a little from her labors.

"How goes the cleanup, Your Majesty? Would you like to change your dress? How about a hair comb?" she chattered, staring past the Queen's shoulder to the hillside below. (Thistle had a boyfriend from town that was working on the fire-cleanup crew, and she was hoping to get a glimpse of him.)

Queen Luna did not respond and continued to stare out the window at nothing, the tears running in crooked trickles down her cheeks.

Now the servant girl noticed her Queen's tears. "Your Majesty! Why do you cry? Did you stub your toe? Did you lose a hair comb?" The girl backed off a bit, sure that an outburst of bad temper would soon follow. The Queen usually went from sad to mad in a flash.

But Queen Luna did not lash out. She simply continued to cry, mumbling softly, "Will it ever happen, Thistle? Do you think it will ever happen?"

"What's that, Your Majesty? Will *what* ever happen? What are you asking?" Thistle stood still in one spot, shifting from side to side with nervousness. The Queen had never addressed her by her name before. Thistle wasn't even aware that the Queen *knew* her name. She *was* sure that she was going to be in trouble for something, any minute.

"Will I ever have a child?' sobbed Queen Luna. "I have tried so hard. I want a child so much. Did you see that beautiful little girl today? Why am I so unlucky? I am doomed to be childless all my life. I know it."

Now Queen Luna began to cry harder, covering her face with her hands. Thistle noticed that the Queen's hair was tumbling down in every direction. She was not demanding assistance. She was not shouting. This was not like the Queen. Something must be very wrong.

The Scrap Queen watched this display of human misery in astonishment. She had never known that River People had strong feelings of any kind other than anger. This sincere sadness was unexpected. Moses had undoubtedly never seen this side of Queen Luna. And these tears were all because a childless woman yearned for a child of her own. Connie remembered her own feelings in the years before she had conceived. So similar. How amazing.

As Connie watched, Thistle whisked out a comb and approached her mistress carefully. She was hoping to do something that would make the Queen more content. She didn't really feel sorry for Queen Luna. To be honest, she didn't like her at all. But she *was* aware that a happy Queen was much easier to work with than an unhappy one. She had learned to employ many tricks to keep her Queen content.

"How about a nice upsweep for your beautiful hair," she murmured in cooing tones, inching forward with a smile. "That 'do' is always so good on you. It makes you look so young."

Now Queen Luna began to cry even harder. "Young? Young? Now I need a hairdo so that I will look young?" she wailed. "Even *you* can see that I am becoming so old that I have to *make* myself *look* young. And I *still* don't have a child! My husband despises me because I am childless. Every day I become older and older and more and more *un*loved. All is lost, Thistle. I will never have a child of my own."

Thistle was confused. She didn't know what to do. She had a crying Queen in her hands. She just watched helplessly as Queen Luna's beautiful hair came completely undone and toppled in loose golden ringlets. Thistle had no idea now what other tricks she could employ. More combs? More mirrors? What?

Queen Connie watched Luna and Thistle with sympathy. Her heart went out to this woman who was so much like herself and the young girl who was trying to please her but couldn't. Sympathetic tears welled up in Connie's eyes and spilled down her cheeks. How sad Queen Luna was. How terrible it must be to have no child, a selfish husband, and no one but a worried servant girl for comfort.

Connie looked down at her own infant, sleeping contentedly in her arms. He was so good and beautiful. She was so lucky to have him. But Queen Luna was talking again. Connie scooted closer with her baby and peeked around the edge of the curtain. She did not want to miss a word.

"If I had a son, Thistle, my life would be complete," Queen Luna whispered as Thistle began to work again on her hair. "I would not need my hair combed. I would spend all my days caring for my baby instead, keeping him safe and loving him. My husband would be so happy with a son that he would again be the man he was when we married—sweet and lovable, easy to charm and easy to please. He would love that baby so much that he would love me again and I would love him. We would be a family."

Thistle forgot her usual shyness in her fascination with what the Queen was saying. "But how could this be so, Your Majesty?" she asked. "How could one small baby do so much? How could a baby do all that?"

"Babies do that, Thistle. They make people nicer . . . and kinder . . . and more . . . loving," Queen Luna answered sincerely. "I don't know why exactly. They just do."

Queen Connie listened quietly. Could it be that she was hearing something she was supposed to hear? The mysterious feelings she had had this morning returned.

By the end of the day, King Heart was worn and torn and used up. His subjects were homeless in one place, and his wife and child were refugees in another. He was bone weary and needed in both places. But he was a King. He knew his duty, and he would do it. He must do his best to rally his bedraggled subjects.

"I will be returning to the Castle soon to check on your Queen and the Prince," Heart told his fellow Scraps. "I feel terrible about leaving you all here on the riverbank. This is the darkest day for Scrap Kingdom since our creation, but we will find a way to rise above it, I am sure. I will return tomorrow. Together we will find new places to live and build a new life. It may take time, but I know we can do this. Keep heart."

The exhausted Scraps nodded but seemed to be dissolving into the soot and mud of the riverbank. Where should they go? What would happen to them?

Heart felt their pain. As their King, he must say something to give them hope, at least for a moment.

"My fellow Scraps" the King began. The weather is warm. The Willow will welcome all of us into its arms tonight as it always has and perhaps shelter us for some nights to come while we work together to find housing and heal our community. The riverbank is our birthplace. The Willow has always been our friend. My wife, your Queen, says that there is a Plan for us in the cosmos and that we will know it soon. She believes that our lives have meaning. After all, we are Scraps!

"Be brave, fellow Scraps. Be strong. Remember, we are made of Special Clay and destined for special things. It says in The Book. that we *will* find a good solution for ourselves! We *will* become strong again! Maybe from this tragedy, we will find a whole new life, something full of purpose that we have never even thought of before!"

Heart needed and wanted to believe that this pep talk was true. His exhausted subjects watched their King and listened. They nodded hopefully and tried to trust that King Heart would help them find a way.

"They say that every setback is an opportunity if you can just see it in the right light. We will find that light and that opportunity!" King Heart concluded with as much enthusiasm as he could muster.

The Scraps rallied a bit with these hopeful words and began to work their way back to the Willow where they would probably be living for a while at least, as refugees from The Great Fire. At this point, they needed to console one another and rest from what had been a miserable and sorrowful day. They had buried their dead. They had mourned for the lost that would never be found. Now they would take the time to be grateful for those that were still alive. Housing solutions could come later.

"Who says that every setback is an opportunity?" whispered Moses to Heart as they trudged up the scorched hill.

Heart shot him a glance. "*They* do," he answered glumly.

Moses decided not to ask any more questions. By early evening, King Heart and Moses had arrived at the Castle. Once inside, all the enthusiasm and determination that they had shown to others during the day faded away. In its place was only exhausted sorrow and pain that they could no longer deny.

Scrap Kingdom was gone. Its families had been broken, their houses destroyed and their spirit crushed. King Heart's guilt was great, knowing he had left his subjects huddled in small groups in the branches of the Willow as he returned to relative luxury with Moses. It was a warm fall evening, so no one would freeze to death. And Scraps were resourceful, but no one would be comfortable. Through no fault of their own, they were homeless.

Moses and Heart ducked into the scurry-way of the Castle. The light was dim as the day was fading but the lamps in the Castle rooms above had not yet been lit. Slowly Heart pulled himself away from the dark wall against which he had been leaning to get his bearings. He helped Moses do the same.

Moses and Heart were beginning to slow down. They could feel it. Although the two appeared to be the same age, they did not age in the same way. Heart was twice as old as Moses, but Moses was already a grandfather, while Heart had just become a father. Mice aged quicker than Scraps. It was just a fact. Sometimes they both forgot this difference. At times like this, Moses really felt it.

King Heart looked at his friend with gratitude. "You were a great help today," he said sincerely. "And the refuge that you are providing to me and my family is appreciated for sure. I don't know how we will ever pay you back for everything."

Like the Scraps, Moses was uncomfortable with compliments. "You know you are always welcome to anything I have," he mumbled as he led Heart down the dim scurryway. "Anything at all."

They had arrived at the curtained mousehole that Moses called home. Listening intently, they could hear the sounds of a lullaby from within. For just a moment, Moses thought back fondly to his own children, who were all grown now with children of their own. He envied King Heart coming home to this sweet mother and child, even if they really had no home at the present. Moses scratched his chin whiskers as he did when he was thinking deep thoughts.

As though reading those thoughts, Heart said, "You were a good father in your time, Mose. How you must treasure your little grandson, Max. I would love to have a chance to see him before we leave your hospitality."

"Certainly," Moses answered. It always surprised Moses when Scraps seemed to be able to read his mind. "Max *is* a wonder! I would be honored to have him meet you, although you may have seen him already today. He was down with us in the ashes, helping to look for his friend, Shaver. Losing Shaver is such a shame. Shaver was so young and with such a bright future. Max will miss him terribly," continued Moses, shaking his huge ears sadly. He thought of the sweet young Scrap who had danced back and forth just out of his reach at The Rodent Rally. "I will miss him too."

King Heart followed Moses into his quarters. "No need to miss him at all," Heart snickered with a tired smile. "I saw him wander off toward the Willow just a few minutes before you and I left. He was arm in arm with a handsome young mouse."

"Max and Shaver?"

"I think so." The two old friends smiled at their shared good news.

They found Queen Connie waiting for them. "I am so glad you are back at last," said Queen Connie softly as they entered. Her eyes were fixed on her sleeping baby. She was staring at his face and stroking it as though trying to memorize every detail. "I have been waiting for you and I have something important to share with you."

King Heart knelt wearily by his wife's side. "This has been a horrible day for Scrap Kingdom, my dear. You have no idea how many souls we have lost."

"Yes, I think I do," Connie replied sadly. "I can feel the pain of it. That pain makes it even more important to discuss what we have to discuss now. We have no choice. We cannot wait any longer. The Fireflies have spoken."

King Heart put his arms around his wife and child, resting his head on them both. "What are you saying, my love?" he asked in an exhausted tone.

"Can't we wait to talk about this in the morning?"

Moses watched his two friends. They needed to be alone. He turned and quietly slipped back out into the scurry way. Looking above, Moses almost thought he saw Fireflies. *Fireflies here? In the Castle?* He shook his head. He must be wrong. He moved down the hall. These were trying times.

Moses was not wrong. Up in the rafters, he *had* seen Fireflies, but Fireflies were not the only visitors to the Castle. A hopeful Spirit had also arrived. This was an important moment. He had to be here.

The Fireflies had decided that there was no more time to waste. The urgency brought about by The Great Fire had pushed them to a decision. Yesterday, humans were out of control, and tonight, Scraps were homeless, jobless and futureless. Completely ready or not, this was not a time to hold back.

Fighter was obviously getting stronger every day. If a Goodness Plan was not at least started, there might not be an earth or humans worth saving soon. In addition, there might be no Scraps to try to help. Both humans and Scraps were in grave danger. The Great Fire had proved it.

The Fireflies knew they couldn't wait, and they thought they had a plan. After this afternoon's consult and sharing of the morning's activities, Spirit now agreed.

Spirit watched as Moses left the King and Queen alone for a while. They needed this time. Moses helped himself to leftovers in the kitchen. The somber togetherness of the Royals seemed to Spirit to go on forever, but, finally, Spirit watched Moses venture back to his cozy living space. King Heart, still dusty and obviously in a very emotional state, had just tracked Mose down and asked him to return.

Moses was worried by his friend's look. So was Spirit. King Heart was past tired. He was miserable.

Queen Connie greeted Moses warmly as he entered, but she didn't rise. She was rocking her sleeping son and patting him gently. King Heart sat down beside them both, staring at them intently even as he spoke to Moses.

"Come sit with us, my friend," he said. "We need to talk."

With some hesitation, Moses squatted across from them. He was concerned with the way King Heart was acting. The King's face was creased with worry. His head occasionally lowered to kiss his sleeping child and his shoulders slumped.

"What is it?' Moses questioned gently. "What is it that we need to talk about tonight of all nights?"

"We need to share something with you, Mose," responded Queen Connie. "You are our closest friend. We value you. All Scraps value you and your wisdom, your knowledge of <u>The Book,</u> *and* your knowledge of the River People. Tonight we ask you to listen, using all your friendship for us and all that knowledge. We need you to hear and evaluate a very special Plan that Heart and I feel will help us all. We need your wisdom tonight. Will you help us?"

Moses sat back. He looked at the faces of his two tiny friends and shrunk under their praise. "You overvalue me, Your Majesties."

"No, we do not," replied Heart. "Your friendship and qualities are key to what we are about to tell you and ask of you. If we had any doubt about you or what we are about to say, we wouldn't say this. You are about to receive a request that may alter the history of the earth and the People who occupy it. Do you think you are ready?"

Without hesitation, Moses answered, "If you think I am worthy, then I am ready."

The Book of Moses

This chapter is adapted from notes provided by Moses Mouse.

To Moses the honor was given that night,
as Fireflies sang sweet and the moonlight shone bright,
to hear of a gift far more precious than gold.
This was unexpected, if the whole truth is told.
An old mouse was given an honor that night
to help right a wrong that would change wrong to right.
A gift would be given with heartache and care
and sacrifice almost too painful to bear
and Moses was honored to even be there.

Queen Connie now spoke through her doubts and her fears,
saying, "Now is the time." She choked back her tears,
but she stood strong and proud while the King's sad eyes glistened.
Now, the Queen told a tale. Moses sat still and listened.

Queen Connie:

"Fireflies have explained to me what I know now is true...
They have had a plan for us, that we Scraps never knew,
since the first days of The Big Game when Fighter then created
a storm to destroy every lovely thing that Spirit had created.

"The Fireflies, you see, knew our Spirit so well
that they knew what he wanted. They were there. They could tell
"Spirit chose Special Clay to be used for the heart
that he knew would work well to set humans apart
and give them the knowledge of right and of wrong.
It would be in their hearts, just where it should belong.
With this Special Clay, human hearts could then be
the source of Man's love as he meant them to be.

"But Fighter caused a terrible storm that caused Spirit to drop the Clay.
He didn't know he used sand instead before he went on his way,
So the hearts weren't made as they should have been.
They never got enough Clay
and that is why People lack Goodness in the way they act today.

"After Spirit left that day, Fighter's storm still blew,
Michael Angelo Mouse, alone, saw what he should do.
Michael Angelo then worked hard and rescued the supply
of Special Clay that had been dropped and was melting there nearby."

"Though Goodness for humans was truly at stake,
Spirit was gone. He had made a mistake,
but nobody knew to request a remake
of these faulty hearts that were already made.

Goodness in Man would be more than delayed,
and the loss of that Clay would be more than a loss.
The Goodness of Man has become its great cost.

"Fireflies watched the mouse as he started to sleep.
Then they read his dream, so hopeful and deep,
and decided to use his dream and his care
to help him make creatures so they might prepare
to someday help Man. They might need to help do
the work human hearts were alone meant to do
to make Spirit's Plan for Man's Goodness come true.

We Scraps, since the start, have been part of that Plan,
which was meant to complete needed Goodness in Man.

"Poor Spirit didn't know until now what happened on that day,
or why no one practiced Goodness, with such meanness on display.
He had expected the Special Clay to be in every heart
of his nearly-perfect humans right from the very start.

When Spirit learned about Scraps, he quickly came to see
that they led the life of Goodness he had always wished could be
in all his hapless humans. He wondered if he could
ask Scraps to help his humans. He was hoping that Scraps would
help to save his humans from all their evil strife.
Then, as you know, The Great Fire destroyed Scraps' way of life.

"How could Spirit ask Scraps to help him now. It was too much to ask.
What his People needed would be too great a task.
But the Fireflies had a secret that no one ever knew.
They had always had a Plan to make Spirit's Goodness true.

"Today, the Fireflies told me and finally explained
the Plan all Scraps are part of. In spite of recent pain,
their songs made it very clear to me what *we Scraps* must do.
And, though it makes my heart ache, I believe that they spoke true.

"Since the time of creation, Mankind has shown
that Man's heart was not meant to live on its own.
The Special Clay, from which all Scraps were made,
was *saved in us Scraps*. It was not just mislaid.
Scraps were created to someday play a part,
as the Consciences needed in each human heart.
Moses looked at Connie and said, "I don't understand
why the Fireflies waited centuries to do what they had planned."
"I wondered that, too", Queen Connie replied. "As Consciences from the start,
we could have helped out right away in everybody's heart."

"Fireflies showed me then what I needed to see.
We Scraps weren't as Good as we needed to be.
We needed to practice. Scrap skills were still rough.
Fresh Clay from the river was not quite enough.

"Scraps needed to live and, so that we wouldn't lose it,
find out what the Clay knew and learn how to use it.
There was practice in living that we Scraps would need
before our real mission with Man could succeed.

I wish the Fireflies would have told me all this earlier," thought Spirit to himself. Then he chuckled. *"I guess it was better kept a secret. Learning is good and patience is not my strongest suit."*

"I had no idea Scraps were practicing Goodness with their Practices," sputtered Moses.

"Neither did we," King Heart replied with a wry smile.

"We needed to learn about life by living it, Heart. That was a good thing," explained Connie.

"If you say so."

"I do. The Fireflies explained it all to me today before you got home."

"And to me too," Spirit agreed. "I had no idea. Fireflies know how to keep secrets, that's for sure."

King Heart hung his head. He knew what Connie was going to say soon. Moses sat very still as Connie continued:

"So we Scraps learned of love by just letting it grow.
We learned of forgiveness and letting it show.
We learned to show kindness when times were sad.
We learned to find Goodness in good times and bad.
We learned to be patient, support, sympathize.
We learned about truth, and we learned about lies.
We learned to choose peacefulness over a fight,
to search for the difference between wrong and right.
But we're now in danger... We learned that last night....

"This new 'Conscience Mission' for which Scraps were created
may never occur. Scrap world is ill-fated.
Scrap lives are in danger, so the Fireflies now think
that our species, at this rate, may soon go extinct."

Moses gasped. Spirit shook his head but then nodded. They both knew that the Fireflies were right, as usual.

"And also, the future of Mankind is bleak.
Their hearts grow more faulty, their Goodness more weak.
Without a new way to improve on Man's thinking,
the fate of all Mankind may also be sinking.

"Fighter is planning for wars without end.
Wars kill, greed corrupts, lies and torture extend
to the ends of the earth, warping all in their way.
He will win The Big Game and go on to *Doomsday!*

"Fighter will wipe out all Goodness on earth
unless we step up to teach Man what he's worth.
So today Fireflies told me. There's no time to wait.
Scraps' role has been chosen and this is our fate."

Connie almost stopped breathing. Her head was bowed low,
but she lifted her eyes to Mose and Heart as she spoke sure and slow.

"*Someone* must go first in this hour of need.
He must learn about Man and get ready to lead.
One Scrap must go first. *He* must learn what to do
for the Game Plan of Goodness to start to come true.
To become the first Conscience, <u>one</u> must live as the son
of the Royals of this Castle. When this night is done,
we must give for all others...*Our son is The One.*"

Moses rocked on his tail! What had he just heard?
He backed up and stumbled. He must hear every word.
The Queen smiled with sorrow and held out her hand.
"You have heard it all now, Mose. Do you understand?"

"What do you mean by "Conscience? Do you mean, 'your son?'
Your son is just a baby. How can he be *The One?*
How can your son help Mankind as you say must be done?"

Connie shook her head and sighed.
"You ask very good questions, Mose. That can't be denied.
I don't know all these things yet, and right now, I can't say,
but I trust in the Fireflies of <u>The Book</u>. They sing what they need today
is a babe that is young enough to learn
the ways that People think and then, in turn,
he can help them change with his Special Clay
to discover a kinder and gentler way...
to live here on the earth in a kinder way.

"We *know* our son is made of that Special Clay,
He must *learn* how to think and *learn* what to say
to turn Man around and create a new way
to live with more Goodness on the earth
and at last show all Man what a Good life is worth.

"The way that our son will learn how to give
is by watching and *learning* how Mankind now lives,
by listening and noticing ways to improve,

by thinking of others with care and with love.
When our son has learned all that he needs to learn,
he'll become the First Conscience... a role he must earn.

"When he knows what to do, he can help all the others
and teach what he knows to Scrap sisters and brothers.
Scraps can then live *with* humans, not under their feet,
As they help Man survive with their hearts more complete."

Moses was stunned. Could this plan be true?
And what in this plan did they want *him* to do?

King Heart started groaning. "This is too much!" he cried.
Queen Connie went to him and clung to his side.

Heart moaned, "I can't do this—give our baby, our own,
the fruit of our love to these creatures who've shown
that they have *no heart!* They are selfish and wild!
How *can* we give *humans* our beautiful child?"

No one had the answer. No charm could be found.
Nobody spoke. No one uttered a sound.

Spirit drew back. This was too much to ask.
How could *he ask Scraps* to embrace such task?

Then the room began glowing. Songs filled the air.
It was most clear to all that the Fireflies were there.

The Queen dried her eyes. She must try to be strong
if Mankind was ever to learn right from wrong.

"This is our mission, Heart, where we belong.
It was always intended. Spirit's Plan from the start
was that **all** Special Clay was in each human heart.
So the sand hearts of humans must someday be mended
to know right from wrong as Spirit intended.

"Our son must go first. Yes, it's his destiny
to live with the humans. We must pray that he
learns his role as a Conscience until folks can see
the kind Good souls they were all meant to be."

King Heart just listened, his head in his hand.
He was trying his hardest. He must understand.
But it was too hard for this Scrap to conceive
of this frightening plan, much less believe
that he should now donate his only dear son
to the cause that the Fireflies now sang should be done.

"If Spirit of Good feels that this Plan is true,
why doesn't *he speak* and tell us what to do?
If Spirit needs *my son* to help humankind,
he should say so out loud and not lead from behind.
He can't take *my* son, *my* whole life and betray it.
If Spirit wants this, *he* should step up and say it!"

"He's right," Spirit groaned. "I now understand
the whole glorious goal that the Fireflies have planned.
My People all need this. There isn't a doubt
that this is a plan that they can't do without.
Heart speaks the hard truth. I know I should say it.
But *I made a pledge*. It is wrong to betray it!"

Spirit felt shame about what Heart had said.
He felt dark and full of confusion and dread.
Would he break his pledge if he now intervened?
His course was not clear, not as it had once seemed.

He wished to speak up now. What was right to do?
But the Fireflies knew history. They knew the pledge, too.
The Fireflies remembered the pledge he had made.
They knew that such pledges should not be betrayed.

So they sang this to Moses to help him recall
this part of <u>The Book</u> that had started it all.
Then they followed this thought with their glorious sound.
The mouse heard them singing. His answer was found.

Quietly Moses said,
"Remember the words of The Book, Heart, my friend.
Spirit made quite a pledge just before The Book's end.
He promised that he would not come to Man's aid.
His work had been done, and his cards had been played,
but the Fireflies were there. They knew there would be
a crisis when Man was not all he should be.
This was their solution. At least, that's what I see.
Because of his pledge in that moment, Spirit can't interfere.
We hear only Fireflies, but Spirit is also here."

Now Moses continued in his quiet way.
He knew he had just found the right words to say.
"I know there will never come a day
when you *want* to give your son away.
But I know you both, and I know you care
for the fate of Mankind. That is why you might... *share*.

"*Share* your child with the humans. Though he lives as *their* son,
you two can stay near and guide all that is done.
You can stay by his side but stay out of sight,
making sure your son's safe and is growing up right.
If *he* feels your Goodness, he will feel secure.

You can help teach *your* ways. Then you both will be sure
that tonight's gift was worth all this pain you endure."

The tears slowly dried on the face of the King.
This suggestion of Mose was a wonderful thing.
Heart suddenly knew that, in spite of his loss,
sharing might make this a bridge he could cross.

"Thank you, dear Mose. Your thought shows great merit.

With my son in my sight, I believe I can bare it.
If I can stay near him, I believe I'll get through it.
For the sake of Mankind and all Scraps, I must do it.
There is no better mission that I'll ever find
for the future of Scraps as well as Mankind."

King Heart and Queen Connie embraced their sweet son,
kissing and loving him. Then it was done.

The Gift

King Heart placed his small son in the arms of Mose.
Mose was the friend that the King and Queen chose
to deliver their son with tenderness, keeping
him safe to the bed where Queen Luna was sleeping.

In the darkness, Moses carried the little Prince there.
He nestled the babe on her pillow with care.
Then Moses stood guard. He watched the babe doze
until, in the morning, a new day arose.

Queen Luna awakened and sat up in her bed,
knowing another sad day lay ahead.

Moses watched her arise to her usual day,
knowing nothing of joy would be coming her way.
Every day now, the young Queen had to hide
the tears of her sadness, deep down inside.

Each night she'd petitioned the moon up above
to send her a child, a sweet baby to love.
And still she had nothing. It pained her to know
the childless old lady her future would show.

The Queen began crying in outright despair
at the sad, lonely life she expected to share
with a King who would no longer love her or care
because she could never produce him an heir.

Life was so miserable. Life was unfair.
Moses stood in the shadows and surveyed the scene
then awakened the baby. Moses prayed for the Queen
and then quickly returned to his corner unseen.

Imagine the wonder, the thrill, and surprise
when a baby appeared right before the Queen's eyes!
A baby? Yes, baby! He was smiling and sweet
but with such tiny fingers and such tiny feet.

"This cannot be real! This can't be what it seems.
I must still be sleeping. This is one of my dreams."
Now the Queen looked about. The new sun shone bright
as if to dispel all the gloom of the night.
Of course, what she wanted the most was a son.
But was *this* the way that such magic was done?
She had never before seen a newborn at all.
Were they always this tiny, always this small?

Consciences—and the Legends of The Big Game

(When surprise gifts arrive at their destination,
the receiver may seek to find *some* explanation:
How did I get this? Who would deliver
a gift such as this? Just who was the giver?)

But . . .

Luna asked nothing. In her heart, she just knew
that she had *her* baby. *Her* dreams had come true!

Queen Luna was sure, in her new-mother's way,
she'd love this small babe until her dying day.
Just how she knew this, she didn't quite know,
but the Fireflies were singing. The room was aglow.

"I love you, dear baby," she whispered with bliss.
She raised him up gently and gave him a kiss.
And as Fireflies sang her a song overhead,
she gazed at the child in her hand and she said,
"I have no idea just how you came to be,
but I *am* your mother, and soon you will see
that I'll be the best mother that a mother can be.
This I now promise you, right from the start,
I will love you forever. I give you my heart."

Hearing this pledge, Moses Mouse slipped away,
relieved at the motherly love on display.
Only *he* knew the meaning of this special day.

Queen Luna's excitement, now filled her with pride.
"I, at long last, have a sweet son!" she cried.
"*No... We* have a son!" she quickly corrected.
She prepared for the welcome she surely expected,
the joy of her husband when she gave him the news
that he had a son. There was no time to lose.

She raced off with her baby. She must tell the King.
Their lack of a child and an heir was *the* thing
that their marital problems were always about.
King Sol would be thrilled now. There could be no doubt.

But . . .

The King on this morning was in a foul mood.
He roared and he threatened. His language was crude.
The scars on his landscape still looked far from good.
The Yesmen had not cleaned the grounds as they should.

The servants were quivering. They knew nothing would
make their King happy. Clearly all understood
that today was a day, if they knew what was best,
they would stay very quiet, not make a request,
not offer suggestions, not get in his way.
This day from the start was just not a good day.

But Luna dashed into the throne room with glee.
She couldn't wait for her husband to see
the wonderful child that they had conceived—
their 'miracle birth' as Queen Luna believed.

And so, when the joyful Queen burst through the door,
most of the servants just dove for the floor,
knowing for sure how King Sol would react.
He would roar in a rage. They knew that for a fact.
He would throw things and holler and blame everyone
for what they had done or, what's worse, left undone.
Today they could see they were in for much more
the minute Queen Luna danced in through the door.

She was holding a cloth like a fine piece of gold,
smiling and joyful, her face proud and bold.
With an air of sweet triumph, she sailed to the throne
and spoke with a joyfulness she'd never known.

"My husband and King, my soul mate, most dear.
Step down from your throne now and join with me here.
You must come to my side. Hear my joyful command.
Our dreams have come true in a way quite unplanned.
Come see the blessing I hold in my hand!"

"Why?" the King bellowed. "Why do you reckon
that I want *you* in here? Did you hear me beckon?
No! You didn't! I'm mired in affairs of the state.
My landscape was torched... Its repair was not great...
They drank up my cider but did not clean the mess
or repair any damage from their carelessness.
I've recalled the Yesmen. They'll be here right away
and now you waltz in, interrupting my day
with some trifle, some nothing. Turn around. Go away."

Luna stopped for a moment then lowered her head
and marched toward the throne where she quite firmly said,
"*You* are my husband. *I* am your Queen.
I bring you a gift that must *right now* be seen.
You have said you want children. Don't you want an heir?
Well, if you really want one, it's time that you share
with me this great news that I hold in my hand.
Just take one look and you *will* understand."

Luna spoke the word '*heir*'. Luna knew very clear
that this was <u>*the word*</u> King Sol wanted to hear.

Sol leaped from his throne with a single command.
"Show me, my Queen, what you have in your hand!
Do not keep me waiting even one minute more.
What news do you bring as you burst through my door?
Is it a message? Do you bring me a sign
that the son I have always desired will be mine?"

The Queen slowly lifted her hand and revealed
the source of her joy, now no longer concealed.

There in her hand, the most tiny child rolled
over and wiggled, a sight to behold.

The King simply stared. "Is this toy meant for fun?"

The Queen simply answered, "No. This is your son."

Did his wife think it funny to pass off this toy
as a child even though it *did* look like a boy?
"What do you bring me? What is this thing
that you hold in your hand and present to your King?"

"Dear husband, just look," said the Queen with great care.
"Look very close at this treasure I share.
He is not a toy. No. This is the one
gift I can give you. This is your son."

"Harrumph," growled the King in a sinister tone.
"You present *this small thing* as an heir to my throne?"
The King's face now warped to a cruel, hateful wince.
"Surely you can't think *that this* is a prince!
Look... He's much smaller than the smallest bird.
This can't be *my* son. Please don't be absurd.
Go! Just remove this bad joke, this small toy.
What I need for a son is a real, full sized boy!"

The Queen was now pleading. "Sol, this is your son!"

"Not so!" snarled the King. "This thing's quite underdone!
"Did you not notice his un-prince-like size?"

But Sol looked at his wife, and he saw in her eyes
that she spoke with a love that she could not conceal.
Could this *thing* in her hand be a child that was real?

King Sol now squinted and brought his face near
to much better see this small object more clear.

And as if the babe knew, this infant Scrap child
looked up at the King, waved his hands, and just... smiled.
(One fact should be known: this smile was the start
of this tiny child's capture of his father's heart.)

King Sol began pacing, quite clearly undone.
"How can you be sure that this babe is our son?
He is too small. Tell me how he can be
the heir to my throne that I need him to be?
He'll be too small for combat. A small King can't lead.
Our foes will not fear him. He'll be no use indeed.
I see that you, Luna, do love him dearly.

"So, keep him as a pet if you want, but quite clearly,
I very much hope that you can now see
that this child is not nearly 'enough son' for me."
The Queen drew up firm. Her cheeks blazed bright red.

"You *will* now accept and love *our son!*" she said.
"He *is our son!* I say that it's so!
It's a truth, Sol, that only a mother can know.
It's true that he's small, but I'm sure he will grow.
He will be a fine Prince. He'll be loyal and true.
And besides...I am naming him 'Sol', after you."

She placed her small son in the palm of his hand,
in the hope that King Sol would at last understand.
Just then the babe looked into his father's eyes
with a strange knowing look that was both sweet and wise,
as though he was saying, "You'll do the right thing.
You know I'm your son. That's why you are the King."

Holding the child, Sol instinctively knew
that all that his Queen had declared was quite true.
And as he fondly gazed into his new son's face,
all King Sol's doubts vanished without a trace.

"You are right," the King whispered. "I should have known.
He is truly quite perfect. He must be our own.
And though I can see that he's overly small,
and I also predict he'll be underly tall,
he is our perfect son and, like me, is named Sol.
And one day, he, too, will rule over all.
This I am sure of. This is my belief."

Queen Luna secretly sighed in relief.

The New Prince

King Sol kissed his son and, at once marched away
to prepare an announcement of *Prince* Sol's birthday!
His worries of landscaping melted away.

"There must be a party! Of course, there must be!
I'll present my new heir for my subjects to see!"

(Now here was a problem Fireflies should have forecasted.
The joy of The Birth was just fine while it lasted.
But the gossip soon spread through the homes down the bank
with the gossip from all Castle servants to thank.

They whispered together and then spread the word
of what they'd been told but had *not* seen or heard.
They had *not* seen a baby, no girl or no boy.
They had *not* seen a thing but two parents with joy.
They *had* heard the Royals laugh, watched them cuddle and sing,
but they'd *not* seen a baby. No, they'd *not* seen a thing!)

"But the King *does* seem happy. He acts nice without trying."

"The Queen sooths a pillow when there's *no baby crying.*"

"The Royals work at caring *for nothing* all day.
But... plans for a party are well underway!"

In truth, all the servants had not seen a thing.
They had not seen this 'Prince' who might someday be King.

The Royal Day of Announcement soon dawned bright and clear.
River People assembled from both far and near
to hear the announcement they had heard they would hear
and to be at a party that would serve them free beer!

King Sol stood proud on his balcony
to show off his new Little Majesty.
The townsfolk gathered up close to see
their first good view of their new King-to-be.
The King held the little Prince up to the skies
as all new dads do, a proud look in his eyes.

"I bring you *my son!*" he announced to the crowd.
(The crowd squinted hard to see *why* he felt proud.)

"He is such a fine son that I know you can see
why he is named Sol, Number Two after me."

Scrap Royals watched it all from the grasses nearby.
King Heart blew his nose and tried not to cry.
"Now it begins," Connie said with a sigh,
"Our *son is still ours, so we won't say goodbye.*

But he'll live with the humans. He must learn their ways.
Be asleep in their nights and awake in their days
and we will be helping him stay good and true"
to the skills he was born with. He must be a Scrap too.
"I am not sure just how all this will be done,
but we will stay near as we share our dear son."

"Moses was wise," sighed tiny King Heart.
"*Sharing* our son was the key from the start.
His skills are Man's future. We won't go away.
We will help to complete the goal started today."

Spirit heard these parents' pledge, and he knew
that what they believed in would surely come true.
Spirit was thankful deep down in his soul
for the sacrifice shown by this child-sharing role—
a gift from two parents, so small but still there,
watching over their son with invisible care.

Consciences—and the Legends of The Big Game

Mose watched the Scrap couple now walking away.
I'll record this, he thought. And I know what to say.
I'll tell of this loss for a dear King and Queen
who gave up their son on a night quite unseen
to win <u>The Big Game</u> with the Fireflies' sweet song
so that humans might learn what is right and what's wrong.
Human Conscience will help the whole world get along.

* * * *

That was an elegant thought. For a while Spirit rested well with less aggravation and concern than he had had in centuries. His humans were going to have Consciences. That would be a miracle. These little Scraps that he had dropped from his original construction of human hearts were going to be returned to his humans as Consciences and do the job that he had intended them to do in the first place. Finally, he could look for Good in his humans and actually expect to find it.

This was a good place for 'Halftime' in The Big Game so Spirit took advantage of it. But a flaw in Spirit's Game Plan had not yet surfaced. Had he not noticed that this new 'miracle Conscience' was only a baby?

LEGEND III

The 3rd Quarter Begins

- as noted in Scrap journals

The 3rd Quarter started out with little observable change in the action. Human beings continued to learn and grow, but most of their accomplishments were brought about by their brain power. Hearts were still underactive.

River People had gone back to fighting and brawling soon after The Birth Announcement for Prince Sol. Fighter, laughed at the announcement, calling it a Royal Hoax of some kind. Completely unaware of the changes that had been put in motion at the Castle, he didn't miss a minute of his favorite activity, coaching his humans in new and subtle negative skills such as cheating...and lying and taking advantage of their neighbors. Violent behavior also increased, of course, and there were still no refs and no penalties in the Game. Because of that, Fighter was 'moving the ball', as he liked to say.

There was no end to the talent of Fighter's violent players. They were never satisfied, never ready to just do 'the right thing' even when it was obviously the best thing to do. Fighter's game plan was getting so strong that he now declared that his prize for winning The Big Game on earth might be a World War... but he was not in a rush. This was only the third quarter. He would enjoy letting his Chaos build slowly, right up to an explosive

4th Quarter. Then, kaboom! That would signal his control of everything. Marvelous!

Spirit snorted at Fighter's confidence and the fact that he knew nothing about the new Plan for Goodness ('the Plan'). *And he never will know until it's too late,* Spirit thought confidently. *He* knew that he was developing a 'secret weapon' that would make all the difference in determining the ultimate winner of the Game, even if it took a while.

In the meantime, however, Spirit did notice that many of the People's attitudes toward their King were improving a little. They now enjoyed new gossip, marveling at the unbelievable changes that had taken place recently in their monarch.

For some reason, the King seemed less hostile.

He wasn't throwing People in the dungeon.

He was seen smiling frequently.

They couldn't see a reason for all this, but they liked it. Spirit was encouraged by what he heard and saw. Hopefully it was a sign of more Good things to come.

The King's changes had started, the People said, the day he decided not to punish anyone for The Great Fire. He had actually served cider to everybody. That was totally unexpected. Cider, mind you! That was an all-time first. "We could get used to a monarch like this!"

Another topic of conversation was, of course, that whacky birth announcement for the baby that no one could see *and* the big party that followed to celebrate it. That party had been so amazing that everybody would talk about it for years, even if there *was* no new prince. The King had looked happy, the food had been good and nobody had been thrown in the dungeon. The fact that there was no visible prince was not much of a problem as far as anybody could see. No harm, no foul.

Eventually, everybody concluded that the King didn't really have a new son. There were a few suspicions that he had slipped a bit mentally, but he was in such a good mood lately that no one was going to ruin the current good times by doing anything about it.

And he wasn't talking funny anymore. That was a welcome change.

There was no reason to say anything about that.

And they also decided they were never going to make a point of the fact that no one had seen the baby, either. The fact that there was no heir to the throne didn't bother anyone. Why should it? What the Royals did wasn't their business...if they left their People alone,

The gossipers actually began to speak of "The Prince" as though he existed. Why not? The King liked it. He was being nicer to People. What harm could it do?

"The Prince will probably grow up to look like his father," they snickered.

"It would be better if he was good looking like his mother."

"That will never happen. All the men on the Royal Family Tree are as ugly as him."

"That's too bad. I was hoping for somebody that at least *looked* like he knew what he was doing...even when he didn't."

They all laughed and rolled their eyes as they spoke, knowing that this 'Prince talk' was going to be a running joke and was their best way of keeping their King happy, and out of *their* business.

Strangely, Fighter liked the rumors, too. "A King who is going through great changes of personality and is showing off a baby that doesn't exist is definitely losing his grip. This craziness will eventually bring on a complete breakdown in any kind of order. There might even be a revolt!

"The King's temporary, 'happy behaviors' are a good thing...a false sense of security for poor Spirit", Fighter snickered. He had it all figured out. The 3rd Quarter was starting out well.

Abandoned Scraps

Was this new Plan of Spirit's as problem-free as it originally appeared or did it have a flaw? Indeed, it had several flaws.

Slowly, Spirit's realization of the Plan's problems set in. With astonishment, he become painfully aware that his wonderful new Plan would take *much* more time than he had originally thought. Scraps matured at the same rate as humans. The Scrap baby at the Castle would take years to grow up and provide the leadership needed.

And Scrap Kingdom was homeless right now. Nothing in the new Plan had addressed that. Half time in the Game and a party at the Castle had allowed him to take his mind off this huge issue, but Spirit was now back in the Game. He finally noticed everything and what he saw was frightening.

Helping the Scrap Kingdom is an underlined immediate need! he suddenly realized. *Why didn't I understand this right away? I lost my focus. I need to get on this, now. But how?*

Panic set in.

Fortunately, Scraps weren't waiting to be rescued by Spirit. In the days following The Great Fire, the Scraps simply huddled in the branches of The Willow by the river. Soon, however, Scrap creativity took over and they began building themselves temporary 'homes' with leaves and twigs and spider webbing. They were relatively safe, being off the ground and out from under the feet of the River People and they were ready to 'make do'.

Spirit returned to The Willow and took note. With relief, he became increasingly impressed by the Scraps' ability to adapt and find positive solutions, but this was only temporary, he knew. Winter would soon be whistling through The Willow. Frozen Scraps could not practice their Goodness, no matter how Good they were.

Spirit knew that he was in 'over his head' again. He definitely needed to get some help. Carefully, he pulled together the issues of his concern. He would present them to the Fireflies for assistance right away. They were proving to be important problem solvers and he wanted to show them that he was up to the new issues he was discovering.

Issue One: Scraps are as slow to mature as humans and Prince Sol is a baby. It's going to take him a long while to become useful in his intended role.

Issue Two: The Scrap population must survive until the new Plan is actually ready. Right now, they are stranded in The Willow and the fall weather is getting colder. (He had not thought of this until now.)

Issue Three: The *Scrap Royals* are focused on the Plan for creating a *Scrap Leader* with their baby son so they probably have not had time to focus on the rest of Scrap Kingdom.

With his list of unsolvable issues in hand, Spirit hurried to a consult with the Fireflies.

Because Spirit was new at 'Scrap Watching', he had no idea, however, that Connie and King Heart were completely aware of all of these problems and focused on their subjects' untenable situation, themselves.

For only a day, they remained "camping" with Moses in his home under the kitchen of the Castle, making sure that their little son was safe in the hands of Queen Luna. They were consumed by guilt, however, at their own comfort. They knew that they needed to take care of their subjects right away.

The kindly Scrap population did not question their King and Queen about their living conditions. They had faith in their leaders. They were sure that their Royals would somehow find better accommodations as soon as they were able and the time was right.

King Heart decided that the 'right time' had to be now, but the first thing that Scrap Kingdom needed was an explanation of the Plan. It was ultimately for them, too, after all.

The next evening, King Heart called together a meeting of the complete Scrap Kingdom at The Willow. Although many had died in The Great Fire, the gathering was massive. It was a swarm of tiny people, intent on hearing from their beloved King and Queen and completely unaware that their infant prince was going to be living in the huge Castle of the River People.

Spirit got wind of the meeting and sailed over to watch. The Fireflies had suggested it. They knew the Scraps better than Spirit did.

King Heart began with an apology. "I am really sorry that I was not able to consult with the Whole Scrap Council before making the decision that I am going to tell you about now. It has always been my practice to consult and I don't intend to change, but I hope you will understand the quickness with which this happened and what was my...our intent."

Tearfully Heart outlined the future that he and Connie had chosen for their Prince and their entire population the night after The Great Fire. He told of the pain and fear that had racked them when they put the Plan in place. The decisions they had made that night again became painful to him. He could not go on.

The Whole Scrap Council rose up and comforted him. They had not seen their King cry before. Queen Connie came to his rescue. She needed to be strong. Spirit watched the Queen and King with sympathy and admiration.

"The Fireflies guided us," Queen Connie explained. "They were there at the beginning when humans and Scraps were made as you know. They knew the need for a new Plan to correct the danger Scraps were in after The Great Fire, let alone the problems that had existed before that. They came to help us put that Plan in motion. Without the Fireflies, we would never have had the strength to do what we did, but, after understanding their knowledge of The Big Game, we could not refuse their idea. What we have done was part of Spirit's original Plan for the Goodness of the earth. We Scraps have always known that something was needed to complete Spirit's Game Plan. We just didn't know what it was. The Fireflies knew."

All Scraps were alert now and paying complete attention.

"But when I speak of need, I hope you will understand that I speak now of two species of creatures with need... Scraps *and* River People."

The gathering of Scraps mumbled. What possible need did River People have, and who cared? What did River People have to do with Scraps other than to step on them and cause trouble?

Queen Connie read their indifference well. "River People are violent and dangerous and have no understanding of right and wrong in their hearts. We all know that. For everyone's sake, they really need to change that, don't you think?" the little Queen asked quickly. The Scraps shrugged and nodded. This was a fact that no Scrap would deny.

"We Scraps have always been at the mercy of River People due to our size. Now that our farm lands have been torched, we also need to find new ways to be safe *and* earn a living. Am I right?"

At this point in time, living in The Willow, no one could deny what their Queen was saying. They nodded again and this time, more vigorously.

"Well, this was the reason for the new Plan that the Fireflies suggested to us. Their idea was to save Scrap lives by finding a way for us to live safely *and usefully*, perhaps by living *with* humans rather than under their feet. But they knew this would not be easy.

"To learn to work with humans, one single Scrap was needed to go first, to live with a human family, learn the way humans think and hopefully show them how to think better. Then that smart Scrap could teach the rest of us how to use what we call Scrap Practices to help humans. The idea is for humans and Scraps to live and work together. 'Safe housing and employment!' How does that sound?"

The Scraps turned to each other and then back to their Royals with so many questions that they could not be answered for hours. The meeting went on into the night, but Scrap Kingdom *did* have faith in their King and Queen. *The Prince was going to learn how to help People without getting hurt and teach everybody else how to do it...right?*

That actually sounded almost reasonable. Their Prince was safe and his parents were watching him daily to assure that all was well. That also sounded like a good thing. They decided to trust.

Spirit watched the Scrap meeting in amazement. The explanation of the Royals and the response of their subjects confirmed for him what he had already decided was true. Scraps were wonderful creatures. In spite of everything, this new Plan would succeed...eventually.

The Search for Scrap Real Estate

But, this would take time, and, meanwhile, what? The most important issue was, of course, current housing ...housing that Scraps could live in while the little Prince (who was now a Prince in two kingdoms) learned how to do *their* future job.

Daily real estate searches with the Whole Scraps began immediately, conducted by King Heart. Day after day they combed the Riverbank area with positive attitudes and enthusiasm but with less than satisfactory results.

Caves near the Castle were evaluated but rejected as too damp or already occupied by bats who were not particularly tidy.

A huge, decaying tree trunk behind the Castle was another possibility. It had many hollowed sections which would have provided a type of apartment house for many, but the trunk was over a day's walk from the Riverbank for the tiny Scraps. Hauling daily water to the site would have been nearly impossible.

"I should have thought of this problem earlier," Spirit told himself over and over again. "Once again, I lost track of important details." Frustrated, he hovered uselessly above the Whole Scraps and their house hunts.

So, the hunt for adequate housing for the Scraps continued day after day. The search was intense and the Scraps were not at all picky, but nothing seemed to be sufficient for a large group of such tiny, fragile beings. King Heart and his Queen were getting desperate.

But a miracle was about to happen that nobody expected. Queen Connie had already sown the seeds of an amazing solution, even though she was not yet aware of it.

On the day after The Great Fire, Connie had met Ramon, the miserable, big river rat who had lost most of his family to the fire. They had begun a strange friendship that neither of them really understood, but there it was, rooted in the fact that both of them had lost family, friends and home. Ramon had not forgotten the little Queen's kindness.

King Heart was completely unaware of this friendship. For that reason, he did not know how to react when he came upon the sight of his wife being carried in the arms of a rat over twice her size. The hair on his neck stood up straight and he clenched his fists. He stood tall and tried to look as fierce as he could. He would rescue his wife and then beat up on that rat, although he was not sure that he could survive either of those things. But it was his duty.

Imagine his surprise when the rat gently handed Queen Connie to him as though he was passing a small child to its parent. The Queen's face was puffy and red from crying. She was limp and crumpled, almost as if she had no bones to hold herself up.

"I found 'er in the scurry way, cryin' her eyes out and I thought I'd better bring 'er back here to Mose's place before one of the rat packs took 'er fer ransom," Ramon drawled. "We got *some* rats 'round this Castle that don't take kindly to no strangers."

Moses had come to the doorway to pull back the curtain for King Heart and was quite surprised to see Ramon and Queen Connie there as well. Knowing the history between Connie and Ramon, he would have invited them all into his hole, but Ramon wouldn't fit and it seemed rude to just leave the rat there alone, after he had been so kind to the little Queen.

The two rodents stood on one haunch and then another. Then King Heart recovered enough to say, "Thank you for bringing my wife back to safety." He turned to Connie and asked gently, "Whatever is the matter, my dear?"

Connie leaned sadly against her husband and started to cry again. "Oh, Heart, I am so sad. I have just been visiting our people down by The Willow. *We* still have no place to live and neither do *they*. I feel as though we are failing in our duties since The Great Fire.

"I am sure that we did the right thing with the baby," she sniffed, "but what should we do for the rest of our people *now*? They can't just hang about with no place to live and nothing to do, waiting to become useful to humans."

"Why should anyone want to be useful to humans?" asked Ramon.

Connie dried her eyes and patted Ramon's paw. "That is a very long story that involves our son, Ramon. You and I will need to sit down together and talk it over. As good a rat as you are, I know you will understand. It's sort of a project, but it's going to take a long time to complete. Maybe someday you can help.

"But right now, my biggest concern is for the rest of Scrap Kingdom. Our people that survived The Great Fire are stuck in The Willow down by the River. Their homes were burned as you know and so was the grass they would need to farm and build new homes. They...*we*... have no other place to live."

"I understand," nodded Ramon.

"It will take years for Prince Sol to grow up and learn what he needs to learn to complete our project. Who knows how long it will take for other Scraps to learn what *they* will need to learn from him after that? Our people need help *now*. They can't wait in the cold and do nothing. And the weather is getting worse.

"As their King and Queen, we must find housing for them...and for ourselves. We can't stay here forever and depend on the kindness of Mose."

"Yes, you can," said Moses quickly. "You can stay here as long as you need to."

"Bless you," King Heart answered Moses warmly, "but Connie is right. We need to find a more permanent home for ourselves and our people while we work on learning to do this 'project thing'. Yesterday I met again with the Whole Scraps and we searched all over the countryside. For some reason, we just have not been able to come up with a place to live, at all."

Ramon shook his shaggy head. "Prince Sol"? "The project"? He didn't understand any of that. He just knew that his friend, the little Queen, was upset. He had been watching and listening. Suddenly, in his slow, quiet way, he had something to contribute.

"Why don't ya move in with me?" he asked simply. "I can offer a place fer you and yer people to stay and maybe jobs, too, if ya want 'em." He stared at the floor as if waiting for his offer to be rejected.

"That is most kind of you," King Heart responded gratefully. "It is a most generous offer...and sincere, I am sure. But didn't I hear that *your* family was burned out of *their* homes in The Great Fire? You must be as homeless as we are."

Ramon hung his head. He had suffered great losses and *was* almost as sad as Queen Connie. Like her, he had lost many friends and family, but unlike her, he still had the home that he had been living in, in recent years...the sewer!

"I lost a lot 'a folks to The Great Fire back on the Riverbank where I was born. A bunch 'a friends and my brother that'd moved in with me in our part of the Castle were visitin' the Riverbank when the fire hit. They're gone forever. They won't be comin' back, that's fer sure," Ramon mumbled sadly. "That's why there's lots 'a room in 'The Sew' (Soo), if ya want it."

Moses Mouse did not believe his ears. Scrap Royalty living in the sewer? He could hardly put those thoughts together in his head. The sewer was dreary and dank, Moses was sure, (although he had never actually been there). Obviously, the big rat couldn't be serious.

But Ramon was very serious. There was no laughter in his beady red eyes, but there was no meanness, either. This was a sincere offer, even if it was a ridiculous one.

King Heart treated the offer with respect. He could see in Ramon's face that he had good intentions. Heart had never spent much time with rats, but he had no bad feelings about them. This was a very kind thing for this rat to do, and it was the first offer of housing he had had. He could not afford to ignore it.

"So, the place you live in is called 'The Sew', is that right?" he inquired. "What's it like? How big would you say? How many families of Scrap size would it hold?"

"Oh, Your Highness! You have never seen anything quite like it, I am sure!" Moses squeaked. How was he going to warn Heart about the place where Ramon lived without hurting the rat's feelings?

"It's a good place. You'd like it, I think," continued Ramon. "I've always liked it. Me and my mates had a lot 'a good-times there. A'course there's not as much sun down there as yer used to 'cause it *is* part of the sewer run for the Castle, but we all made it pretty nice and there's lots of room."

Queen Connie had not said a thing, but she had stopped crying and was paying very close attention.

"You said something about jobs, as well," she said. "Did you mean that there might be jobs for some of our people? That would be wonderful. Our

Scraps have nothing to do because they were farmers and their fields were all burned. It would be truly a miracle to find both housing and work in the same place." A hopeful smile began to tug at the corners of her tear-stained face.

Moses couldn't say a thing. There was absolutely nothing to say that would not be insulting. He scratched his chin whiskers as he always did when he was deep in thought. Before he could come up with something good to say, the little King and Queen decided to follow Ramon to the sewer. Moses had no choice but to follow.

The Sew

Within a few minutes of starting their travels to The Sew, King Heart began to doubt the wisdom of his decision to visit Ramon's part of the world. It was definitely not like anything he had experienced before.

First of all, there was the route, a twisting, turning, downward path which seemed to follow a series of rock structures into increasing darkness. It was an aqueduct. Second, Heart could tell that he was going down, far, far down, way into the earth. He felt like a mole.

Ramon led the procession with what appeared to be pride, unbothered and unashamed. When it became too dark, he simply pulled a small tar ball on a stick from the satchel under his robes. He then clicked his large teeth against the rock, creating a spark and caught the spark with the tar ball. It became an instant torch, casting a wide, golden glow that made the dark passageway almost welcoming. What other surprises would the rat reveal?

As Ramon led further downward, he lit additional tar ball torches that were pre-placed along the way. "You can use these to find your way out," he explained. To Moses, this was a very comforting thought.

Finally, Ramon stopped and turned around.

"Here we are," he announced proudly.

In the glow of the torch light, there was very little that was pleasant to see...or to feel. The air was damp with a fine mist, causing their robes to stick to their bodies. Strange, dark droplets dribbled from the bottom of the aqueduct that they had been following.

Queen Connie's heart sank. She had had such high hopes. Now they were quickly fading. Her rat friend had meant well, but she could never live in dark, wet gloom like this. She certainly could not ask her subjects to do so.

"Thank you so much for your kindness," Connie said sorrowfully, "but..."

King Heart tried to help his wife explain. "Yes, thank you so much for your offer, but..."

Suddenly Ramon began to chuckle. It was a very strange sound, somewhat like a hinged door that needed oiling. But it was not altogether unpleasant.

"Oh, my gosh," he chortled. Y' all think I meant for *you* folks ta live down here in *this?* This-here is no place fer fine folks such as yer self ta live. This-here really *is the sewer*. This is where *I* work. I *am* a sewer rat as well as a river rat, after all."

Ramon stepped aside and put his hand on a shiny black knob behind him, turned it and pushed. Slowly a door that no one had noticed before swung open, revealing a beautiful waterfall below and a glorious shaft of sunshine beaming down toward them from the canyon above. The air that whistled in through the door was sweet. It was a grand sight. "This," said Ramon proudly, "is 'The Sew'."

Looking down through the doorway, Connie and Heart could see a gurgling stream flowing from far beneath the waterfall and on out toward the grass lands and the River beyond. Over the years, the waterfall had carved a deep canyon in the clay. Both sides were lined with ornate sculptures.

Upon closer inspection, however, the sculptures were not merely decorations. They were apartments.

"These are the digs 'fer most of the rats who work in and around the Castle. They're sort of carved into empty spaces on the of the canyon wall so they don't have any yards to speak of, but they are pretty cheerful and clean on the inside. *And,*" he concluded, "like I said before, due to all the brothers we lost in The Great Fire, there's a bunch of empty apartments right now and room to carve a lot more."

Moses couldn't believe his eyes. Here was a whole piece of the world that he knew nothing about. And, even more important, here was a group of cousins in the Rodent World that he had looked down on. And they lived in a wonderful place that was clean and neat and very beautiful.

Moses hated to admit it, but these houses looked better than some of the places where he and his closer mouse relatives lived. Moses' eyes were as wide as they could get. He had misjudged rats as a group. He was ashamed of himself.

King Heart and Queen Connie were thrilled, of course, and began to discuss a plan to bring other Scraps down (or up from the valley floor through an intricate series of stairways) to see this thrilling surprise. After taking a quick tour, with Moses following along in stunned silence, the little King and Queen concluded that The Sew would be the housing solution of their dreams. It was truly a miracle.

Within days, all Scraps, including their King and Queen, had gratefully accepted Ramon's offer, moved into openings in The Sew and begun busily constructing new housing. The employment problem was still unsolved, but housing was the most important thing and this housing was more than adequate. Moses took note in his journal. Spirit was stunned and also grateful.

More Solutions Needed

Now the Scrap Royals and their subjects were housed, but the concerns of the little King and Queen were not yet ended. Their son seemed safe and content. They checked on him every day. Their subjects were also safe, but they were far from content. Scraps weren't working. That was not good.

Keeping busy was part of Scrap makeup. They couldn't just sit around. They were restless and unchallenged. And this was not their only problem. They were hungry. They had been able to scavenge edible tidbits from what was left behind by The Great Fire, but their supplies were running low.

"I had no idea that this new Plan would be so complicated," Spirit sighed. "These Scraps are not ready for their big job yet but they have to eat and work...and for how long?

"Why didn't I think of this?" Again, he watched and waited, hoping that the problem-solving nature of Scraps was as strong as it needed to be for yet another challenge.

Again, King Heart searched high and low for answers. Scraps had primarily been farmers by nature. They were living in a completely different place now. There were no farm lands on the canyon walls of The Sew. What could they possibly do to provide for themselves? King Heart pined for the simple days when farming had been such an easy answer to both food and occupation.

The solution came as a surprise. The Scraps had nothing to do so they just watched what was going on around them. What they saw were rats, hundreds of rats, and all of them working very hard every night...*on all-night night shifts*. This was a new concept.

As the Scraps watched, the rats hustled down to the homes of the River People, from dusk to dawn. All night, the same rats would struggle back in the moonlight with their loads. They carried food of all kinds, pieces of material and piles of cloth and leather. All of these things were hauled from the throw-aways of the humans and carried off on the backs of a very industrious group of rodents.

Although spent, the rats would drag their bounty to warehouses dug into the walls of The Sew where it could be stored until needed. They made trip after trip. By daybreak, the exhausted creatures would collapse into their homes to rest for the next night's labors. The Scraps watched the hardworking rats with admiration.

Moses, visiting frequently, was also impressed and ashamed of assumptions he had made about 'lazy rats' which were obviously untrue. No wonder the rats he had known always seemed lazy. They were tired. They had been working all night. Fortunately, Moses concluded, he was not too old to learn.

The Scraps were also learning…and acting like Scraps. Making note of the rats' hard work, they suddenly came upon a useful idea.

After a quick meeting of the Whole Scraps, a group of Scraps presented some rats with a proposal: Since the rats were being generous and sharing their housing with the Scraps, why didn't the Scraps lend a hand with storing and cataloguing the stuff that the rats were gathering so that it could be found and used more easily? The grateful Scraps were eager to pay back what 'rat generosity' had done for them.

The suggestion of assistance with the storing of supplies in the warehouses was approved by the rats right away. The rats accepted the offer as 'Scrap gratitude' which it was intended to be.

The idea of Scraps taking inventory took a bit longer for some suspicious rats to digest, but eventually, the rats decided to try that, too. That idea also worked. It helped.

The rats gradually learned that they now knew not only what they had but *where* it was. That saved time. They became a bit more rested during the days and grateful for the Scrap assistance. Friendships began to spring up.

After inventory began, it didn't take long for the rats to realize that they had more than enough edible food stuffs for their own needs and that some of it was spoiling. Waste was not a good thing.

It occurred to them that it might be in the rats' best interest to *share* some of their excess food with their new helpers.

Sharing? Amazing! The concept of sharing (a Scrap Practice which rats had never considered before) was also accepted, just in time to keep the Scraps from starving. Another miracle.

Moses looked at this development and called it to the attention of King Heart and Queen Connie. Moses was stunned and Heart and Connie were thrilled…but they were not amazed. A Practice of Generosity on the part of their subjects had resulted not only in solving their food and work problems but had helped the rats to become generous as well. It was a sign.

This truly wonderful solution was not expected, but it was appreciated by Connie and Heart. It was the natural sharing of Scrap Practices. They brought up the concept to The Whole Scraps Council who dubbed it "Big Job Preparation". Scraps were using their Practices with a new population. Moses documented this in his journal, as well.

Spirit smiled with understanding and appreciation. Again, whether or not the Scrap King and Queen thought so, these little Scraps had proved to be amazing. They had already adapted the concept of Scrap-type of behavior to rats and *their* lives. Spirit could see it. Maybe they would be as successful with humans when the time came. This off-grid workout to keep from starving did nothing to improve the Goodness of People, but Spirit thought these experiences might pay off later in the Game.

Prince Sol, the early days

- adapted from Queen Connie's memoirs -by M. Mouse

Meanwhile, back at the Castle...

Queen Luna was loving her new baby boy.
No problem could dull her great feelings of joy.
But, what should he sleep on? What should he eat?
These were questions this new mother needed to meet.

On her own, in her room, she took pains to prepare
the items her new babe would need for his care.
Each day she searched through the Castle to see
the things she could use for her small King-to-be.

Queen Luna decided to care for her son
by herself, not the way Royals had commonly done.
There wouldn't be servants to care for this child.

When the servants first offered, the new mom just smiled
and rejected the offers. And her manner was mild...

Those who had cared for the Queen before
just lounged now and waited outside her door.
She had stopped throwing tantrums and crying all day.
She had stopped getting mad when they got in her way.

She didn't need hair combs or changing of dresses,
or someone to praise her or clean up her messes.
She said please and thank you, amazing but true,
then returned to her room. This behavior was new.

The servants just watched her each day and would wonder
if there was some kind of deep spell she was under.

Though she spoke of her baby in tones sweet and mild,
no one believed that the Queen had a child.
And though they reported that they heard her sing,
all thought that she did this, to humor the King.

She became gentler...you might even say kind,
but why did she need what she asked them to find?

"Can you find me some thistle down? Pieces of fur?
Long lengths of spider web? I would prefer
birds' nests that are vacant. Soft feathers are nice.
And one flake of oat. I'm sure that will suffice."

At her door they would leave things but never go in.
They couldn't imagine what went on within.
They still sat by her door with a dress and her brush
to help her get dressed with the usual rush, but all rushes stopped.
The Queen now called sweetly,
"Please bring me an apron and slippers, completely
soft with no heels, built for comfort instead.

This mother must work, clean the room, make the bed.
And please bring some sea shells and goose down and thread."

"She's making a bed? A real bed for whom?"

"We've never seen anyone else in her room."

"Our Queen never, *ever* did housework before."

"Whatever is happening behind her closed door?"

The servants, dumbfounded, just walked away.
What had caused all these changes? No one could say.

This love Luna offered her sweet, tiny son
was changing her. (That's how 'baby magic' is done.)
The 'new baby happiness' Spirit noted before
was occurring with Luna. Such joy was 'a score'.

This Queen was determined, one way or another
that she would become *the* most excellent mother.
She bathed Sol each day in a large golden cup,
(being ever so careful to not drink him up!)
She made tiny clothing from pieces of silk
and carefully fed him from one drop of milk.
She emptied her jewel box to make him a bed
with pieces of goose down for under his head.
Nothing he needed was too much to ask.
Luna seemed to enjoy every motherly task.

Queen Luna invented a most clever plan to
house Sol 'just so' as he grew to a man.
She had decided to make him a suite
of fine tiny rooms that were playful but neat.
It was housed in her room with his movement secured
until he was bigger, his safety insured.

Safety became her most critical need
for a son that was small and quite fragile, indeed.

Sol's suite resembled a doll house that she set on a table
so that, if he needed something, she would be quickly able
to find what it was and, of course, above it all,
keep him happy *and* safe while he was so small.

"The Prince will grow out of this soon," she confessed,
"but, until then, I am making him the very best
fine, tiny world as a new mother should,
to show him a life that is his size...but good".

And, as she worked, she looked up to know
that Fireflies were hovering, providing a glow
by which she could care for her new son below.
She could watch him at night when no candle was there,

and the Fireflies were pleased with this Royal love and care
that just seemed to grow in a manner quite rare.

The Fireflies and Connie, the other Queen-mother,
had chosen Queen Luna, above any other
to raise little Sol and help him to grow
to the man that would rise up and someday would know
the knowledge required to complete human hearts.
Queen Luna's love was a very good start.

King Sol came to the Prince's quarters each day
to watch his son cared for in this gentle way.
He was charmed by the care that his 'new wife' was giving
to their precious new son, now his reason for living.

The King hugged his Queen and said, "I always knew
you would give me my son as I asked you to do.
I knew you were trying. I wish now that I
could take back my actions when I made you cry.
I had no idea that my new son would show
me what real love feels like. I never did know
I had this inside me, these feelings of care
but I'll use them more, now I know that they're there."

"I hear you, my husband. I can't now compare
our love from before this sweet child that we share.
It seems that we've just figured out how to care.
I love you, Sol. All past pain I'll forget.
Our child is so dear that I, too, regret
all the mean thoughts that I always had.
I love our dear son *and* his wonderful 'Dad'!"

King Sol called him 'perfect'. No matter how small.
No child of that time was more loved than Prince Sol.

And the servants all noticed. The Royals weren't as wild.
Their requests were more patient, their tempers more mild

as they cared for their truly invisible child.
..that no one had seen yet. (No servants yet knew
that the 'New Prince Announcement' had been real and true.)

King Heart and Queen Connie, looked down on it all.
As they watched from the shadows, they could easily tell.
These new parents now cared for their son very well.

Queen Connie helped Luna to think problems though
with Scrap child-care solutions she already knew.
King Heart sat nearby whispering to the new father
how to enjoy a small son without bother.

And at bed time, in ways that were tender and right,
two sets of parents kissed Prince Sol goodnight.

The Safety Issue

As the Scrap parents watched, they were both pleased to see
their dear son was growing up quite happily
but both queens began to soon understand
that *safety* for Sol might not go as they planned

As soon as the Prince learned to crawl, walk and run,
Queen Luna began to lose track of her son.
His hide and seek tricks became his favorite game.
He never sat still. It was always the same.

Over the table top, onto the floor
...finding new hiding spots, searching for more,
hiding where ever he found a small space,
loving the frown on his Queen Mother's face.

It was great fun to see that his gigantic mother
was so easy to hide from since there was no other

person nearby. She'd stand still with her fears
that her big feet might crush him. It brought her to tears.

"What about a tiny bell?" Connie whispered in Luna's ear.
"Being able to hear him, would make where he is more clear."

"I should tie a bell on you," said Luna, reflecting Connie's thought.
"No bell," little Sol insisted. "Bell noise will get me caught!"

Queen Connie decided that evening to whisper to her son.
"Your mother is sad when you hide from her. I know that this is fun,
but she's afraid that she'll step on you. It will be more kind
if you wear a bell for her sake. You can still play 'seek and find'.
Just find less frightening places to hide. That will ease her mind."

The next morning, Sol tied his bell on and proudly went to show
his very big mother what he had done. "Mommy, I didn't know
that you were scared to step on me, but now you can always tell
if I'm running on the floor. Now you can hear my bell."

Luna held him to her heart.
How did her little son get so smart?

The Pain of Small

Luna's love for her son grew day and night.
She had made up her mind she would bring him up right
so she watched him and fed him and sung him to sleep
with a motherly love that was tender and deep.
"With my love," she promised, "we we'll soon realize
a big, healthy boy that is just the right size."

But, although the Prince aged from one year to two,
then four and five as she knew he would do,
he didn't grow bigger, disappointing, but true.

So Luna continued to keep him safe in her room all day and night.
For sure, this boy was completely safe...Of course...*he was out of sight!*

He continued to live in his doll house. At first, he was unaware
of the rest of the world that existed in the bigger world "out there."
But one day, he discovered there was something more
that existed beyond his mom's locked bedroom door.
He could now hear voices... and footsteps... and more.

Sol was now a captive. The problem was quite clear.
His mother wouldn't let him out, due to her terrible fear
of big folks because of their most fearful size
that might crush her small son before they realized
that he was right there, underneath their big feet.
So she kept Sol alone in his miniature suite.

Queen Luna decided that she couldn't share
her son with the real world. This wasn't fair
for a boy with big energy cooped in one spot.
This boy needed action, whether safely or not.

He was spending each hour behind a locked door,
safe but alone. Prince Sol needed more.

Sol's world was a doll house behind a closed wall.
He had comfort and safety, but that's about all.
Sol had made his folks happy, but *he* had no joy.
Sol needed to run and explore...be a boy!

The Change

Luna kept Sol in her sight, day and night.
She completely gave in to her panic and fright.
They both became captives, but she couldn't avoid
her fear for her son. She was now paranoid.

Luna stayed in her room with the Prince, every day
and yelled out to everyone, "Just go away!"
Her protection of Sol was bound up in such fear
that it soured her nature. This, too, became clear.
She began to return to the earlier ways
she had used in the past, in her 'pre-Prince Sol' days.

She treated her servants as she had before.
She was yelling again. Her patience was poor.
She lashed out in anger. She threatened and screamed
at the servants who came to the door and it seemed
that she wouldn't stop. She was no longer trying.
The servants just shuddered and ran away crying.

Luna was a captive too, now, their world was no longer fun.
This was not the dream she had when she dreamed of a son.
Something was very, very wrong. Her world now came undone.
Prince Sol frowned and watched her. It made him very sad
when his mother was shouting at everyone, always mean and mad.
He wanted to know how this change came about,
why she no longer smiled
...why she didn't go out
...why they stayed here together, locked up in her room,
...why sunshine and playfulness turned into this gloom.
So, he jumped to her shoulder and asked, nose-to-nose,
why she did what she did, why she chose what she chose.
He just asked her questions. Like any young kid,
he wanted to know why she did what she did.

"Do you really like green beans?
Why do you brush your hair?
Why do you sometimes talk to yourself when there's nobody there?
And why are we always in this room? When can we go outside?
Why not meet other People? There's so much I haven't tried.
If I flap my arms fast, do you think that I could fly?
Why do you yell at the servants? Why do you *like* to make them cry?"

Luna blinked and sat up straight. "I guess I don't know why.
I simply say what comes to mind. Yes. I would say that's true.
I just say what I want to say. That's what Royal Queens do."

Sol now scratched his head a bit and looked her in the eye.
"Is it fun to make people sad then? Do you like to make them cry?"

"Not really." mused Queen Luna. "I'm really not sure why
I've begun to shout at servants. I guess it could be true
that I don't really need to yell, now that I think it through.
Sometimes, when I'm frustrated, that's just what I do.
"And I am *really* frustrated. That much is quite true.

"Maybe, if I am nicer, my maids will stop their crying.
I think, now that you asked me, that might be worth trying."
Queen Luna looked down at her son with a smile.
"I can see you don't like it, so I'll change my style."
And she did.

She again began to make changes in unexpected ways.
She began saying "please and thank you" again and offering words of praise.
She became much less demanding. She stopped being mean,
the most amazing turn about the servants had ever seen.

And the servants all were grateful for the changes that she made.
They now began to like her, (really?) and were no more afraid.
Why all these changes had occurred, they knew not then nor since.
They didn't suspect Prince Sol at all. (They had still not seen the Prince!)

Freedom

Connie, Sol's Scrap mother, knew that she could see
that her son was safe and healthy but he needed to be free.
'Safe and healthy' was not all a boy like him should be.

Sol's Scrap parents became now most gravely concerned.
Sol was locked in a bedroom. Needed skills could not be learned
with no one around him but his mother and his father
and Prince Sol was changing from 'sweet child' to 'a bother'.

The Prince began to sulk a lot. His days were becoming wild,
much like an animal in a cage, a frustrated, lonely child.

Sol started swinging on curtains, hiding under beds,
ditching his parents for hours, pulling the hair on their heads.
Queen Luna shrieked and chased him. She would hunt for him and call,
"I know that you're in here, you little scamp! Now *you come out here, Sol!*"

Sol would hide for hours, then out he would suddenly crawl,
and say that he was sorry, a Scrap child, after all.

Queen Connie became more worried. She and King Heart knew
that their son needed some freedom *now*. What could *hidden* parents do?
Safety wasn't enough anymore. Their Scrap son needed more.
He needed to meet and learn from what was outside the bedroom door.

Connie had waited long enough. She had tried to hold her tongue,
but she knew what was essential for an active Scrap this young.

So Connie whispered to Luna. "Please understand today
that your son *must* leave this safe place and learn to find his way,
first starting with this Castle. This Castle is his home.
He must explore every inch of it. It's time for him to roam
about the Castle daily. The servants will help him see
this part of the world that he lives in, the world where he will be
a King. He's smart. You know that. It's time for you to see
that your tiny son can survive this now. You *must* let him run free."

Luna heard Connie in her mind and reluctantly agreed.
"My baby boy is five now. I guess he must be freed
to see what else is out there. As much as I hate to see
my son exposed to dangers, this is not fair of me.

"I must let him wander the Castle, but he must stay inside
and be so very careful. I pray he can learn to hide
away from clumsy servants. And they must watch their feet!"

The Royals brought the servants together for a 'servants-only' meet.
The King spoke firm to the servants, "I request that you be discreet.
You must tell no one else about this. This news can't hit the street.
Our son will soon be out and about, and then you'll get to see
a very, *very* little Prince, your handsome King-to-be.
He will walk among you and watch the things you do.
You don't need to do anything special. Just *be careful with all you do.*"

The Queen now spoke with a shaky voice. This bravery was new.
"He's very, *very* tiny. *Please...* be careful where you walk!
This is my motherly warning, not just my idol talk.
He is our precious little son, worth more to us than gold.
We release him now with fear and dread. He is only five years old."
The King now added another word, telling *all* what they *must* hear.
"I am now *ordering this request...* in words most strong and clear!
"You *must not* tell the People outside this Castle's walls
that you have seen their future King. Because he's still so small,
you must never, *even hint* that you have seen our son at all.

"Our foes will take advantage. *We* all know Sol will grow,
but we must wait 'til he's bigger so that others just won't know
that he is still so tiny. They'll think that he's too small
to ever become a decent King, like me, 'the Great King Sol'.

"So his size *must* be our secret. I *order* you not to call
out the word 'til I tell you. Our foes can't know he's small.
This is for Kingdom Protection...*Security for us all!*"

The Castle staff smiled and nodded but their strong belief persisted
that Prince Sol was just a fantasy that never had existed.

All the gardeners and guards and servants and cooks
just rolled their eyes with knowing looks.

They secretly laughed. They couldn't resist.
They worked for some Royals whose son didn't exist!

To challenge King Sol, though, they still wouldn't dare,
even though they all knew that no Prince Sol was there.
King Sol had seemed kinder in these last five years,
but he still had a temper that kept alive fears.
So, they just played along and pretended they knew
that their King had a son. What else could they do?

They and the town all continued to say
that the Royals were both crazy...though just in this way.

The Reveal

For this reason, for servants it was a surprise
when Prince Sol popped up right in front of their eyes!
And, day after day, as he became older,
they saw him more often. He became bolder.

The gardeners would find him on top of their rakes.
Then he'd swim in their pails. Their pails were his lakes.
He would find a maid dusting and jump on her hand,
hanging on to her fingers when he couldn't stand
and riding her thumb as she dusted with care.
When any one saw him, each would declare,
"I just don't believe it! Prince Sol! You're right there!"
"I still don't believe this! It's been years, after all!
But I actually see you! There is a Prince Sol!"

One maid saw Prince Sol for the very first time
when she pulled on the rope used to make a bell chime.
Sol slid down the rope and flew through the air,
then laughed as he scrambled to land in her hair.

The poor girl just screamed and then came to a stop,
feeling quite faint. She let the rope drop.
"You're real! I can see you," she announced with a squeak.
Sol saw she was startled so hurried to speak.
"Don't give us away. If I do as I'm bidden,
my mother won't see us and I can stay hidden.

She's always afraid that you big folk will hurt me.
Let's play hide and seek, and you can desert me,
but please keep my secret and please do not tell.
If I would still let her, I'd still wear a bell."

The maid found Sol charming in his friendly way.
"He a pretty nice kid and as real as they say."

In spite of their doubts, staff began to enjoy
the presence of this very active small boy.
And, as time went by, nearly all of the staff
got to know their small Prince and they learned how to laugh
at seeing him pop up in very strange places,
even though there were times that he caused some red faces...

Hiding lovers *alone* could not be assured
that the Prince was not watching, not saying a word.
And secrets, though whispered, were frequently heard.

And...
some servants had a bad habit of stealing,
taking trinkets and jewelry and never revealing
they had stolen things right out from under the nose
of the King or the Queen. They just took what they chose.
They had no Conscience so none of them knew
that stealing was really a bad thing to do.

"The Queen has so many. This one won't be missed.
There's no reason to leave this. Why should I resist?"

But, imagine how this 'stealing' might feel if you
were happily sneaking a trinket or two.
There you would be, acting clever and sly,
pocketing jewels that you happened to spy.

Then you spot Prince Sol who's just standing nearby,
watching you steal without batting an eye.

"Would you like to have that?" the small Prince might say.
"I think that my mother wore that yesterday.
We could easily ask if she'll give that to you.
Let's ask her and see if that's what she will do."

The maids knew for sure that the Queen wouldn't say
she was willing to give her fine jewelry away.
So, the maid who was caught with the jewels in her hand
would put them back fast. She could now understand
that she shouldn't do this again as she'd planned.

Spirit observed this. This was a sign
Sol could help folks learn honesty with this design.
This was Spirit's hope. Now he prayed that Prince Sol
was creating the skill he could teach to all,
the rest of the staff in a way that was new.

Yes! After a while, staff instinctively knew
that stealing just wasn't the "right" thing to do.
Suddenly stealing was not as much fun.
Had a 'Prince Sol Effect' in the Game just begun?

Figuring it Out

The Castle Kitchen was an interesting place
where Sol met a servant named Cook, face to face.
Sol could tell right away. He naturally knew
that a kitchen was where there were *great* things to do.

He found a cupboard where he could go
and roll in the flour like it was snow.
He used the kitchen for his back yard
and left tiny prints as he ran through the lard.
He jumped off pan handles to land in the green
of large leafy salads. He rode a stringed bean.

Cook started laughing and shooed him away.
"You are a scamp! You must watch where you play!
If you don't take care, you'll get eaten some day!"
Sol also laughed, scooting out of her way.

But, little by little, the kitchen changed to a most unhappy place.
There was no more laughing left on Cook's sweet, chubby face.
Sol now heard through the grape vine that Cook was in disgrace.

At the dinner Prince Sol heard the King's harsh lament.
"The meals that Cook sends me should never be sent!
There is not enough sugar. There's way too much salt.
This stuff lacks in flavor and is dry to a fault!"

Prince Sol now noticed what had rearranged.
His kind, gentle father had definitely changed.
The King was now grumpy with affairs of the state.
He never seemed happy or liked what he ate
so he frequently dumped what was served on his plate
and threw plate and everything into the air.
This became common and no longer rare.

He growled at the Cook, "You're no longer able
to place a respectable meal on this table!"

Sol finally decided to check with Cook.
He sat on a shelf out of sight for a look
at what she was doing when she made the next ration
of food that was causing his dad's aggravation.

CONSCIENCES—AND THE LEGENDS OF THE BIG GAME

Sol saw Cook looked angry and he wondered why.
He jumped to her counter. "Hi, Madame Cook! Hi!
I heard you were busy. I just thought I'd stop by
and watch what you do when you boil, bake and fry."

Then Cook and Sol chatted. She spoke of the days
when she made the King meals that were worthy of praise.
"But he's has such a temper, when he feels bad,
he throws my creations! That makes me mad!"

"I make him a masterpiece. He throws it and then
he tells me that I should go make it again.
When he's angry at others, why should I get the blame?
Throwing my meals is an insulting shame.
And why can't he say he wants sugar or salt?
If he doesn't say anything, that's not my fault."

Sol hadn't noticed this, he told her.
He was eating with parents now since he'd become older.
And his dad *always* threw things whenever he got mad.
Sol thought that this was common and done by all dads.

Sol at last knew what all this was about
and Cook was in danger of being thrown out.
That wouldn't be good and quite sad in the end.
Sol loved his dad, but Cook was his friend.
And Sol saw that food would never get better
if his dad didn't stop doing things to upset her.

Queen Luna knew the Kings temper was wild.
She also feared he might hurt their small child
with tempers and tantrums quite out of control
but what should she do now? What was her role?
Could her son be damaged? What might be the tole?
She wasn't as worried about the Cook's food,
but upset with her husband, so dangerously rude.

Though he loved their son, his behaviors were crude,
left over from times when his son wasn't seeing
his frightening behaviors that now sent the boy fleeing
for somewhere to hide where he wouldn't be hit.

There was 'Kingly Behavior" and this wasn't it!

Little Sol understood the Royal Cook's angry mood,
and he knew that his father would like better food.
He also thought, in his little boy's head,
that, if he didn't duck, he might someday be dead.
He now knew that dinner was something to dread.

He tried to find something that he could say
that might show his dad a bit calmer way
of fixing the problem he now understood...
plus keep *him* alive. All of this would be good.

So he dined with his parents as he'd usually done
on a small, tiny plate they had set for their son.
He munched on a crumb that was passed to his side.
This was all that Sol ate to keep satisfied.

Then his father got angry. Prince Sol jumped from the table
to a space he could hide. He was quite fast and able
but the tantrum continued. Sol watched the plates fly.
This was the right moment. He knew he must try.

Sol asked his dad simply, "What if I die?
Will you find a new prince, one more prince to try?
'Cause I think that might happen. I know I can't fly
to escape from your plates as I see them sail by.
I think that someday if I don't duck
you'll need a new son. I'll be out of luck.
That's why I was wondering what you two
would do if I'm killed by a plate you threw?"

King Sol stopped his ranting. He looked at his small son's face.
The love he felt for this little boy he never could replace.
And his son had asked a question that shook him to his core.
King Sol had never considered a thought like this before.
Kings could yell if they wanted... No one could tell them no
but if he hurt his beloved son, he could never stand the blow.

King Sol scooped up Prince Sol and held him to his chest.
Keeping his small son safe and sound was his most heartfelt quest.
He vowed that day to think twice and then to think some more
and try to curb his temper as he'd never done before
...and also, to stop throwing dinner plates to crash upon the floor.

The Queen was quite surprised to see new manners in the King
and Cook began to smile again. It was quite a wondrous thing.

The King, at Prince Sol's suggestion, started talking to the Cook
about seasonings he liked better. That was all it took.
The King and Queen at dinner became happy, once again
and Cook's food got even better than it had ever been.

The New Wave

Spirit watched in secret. New thoughtfulness began
to touch all parts of the Castle. It looked like his Goodness Plan.
No, nothing was perfect in this place but Spirit began to see
that Goodness and kindness were spreading, a hint of what might be.

Fighter stopped haunting the Castle. He had no idea or notion
of what "was wrong" with the Royals, but he heard much less commotion
than he was used to hearing. It decreased year after year.
There was much less Chaos to watch there, less fighting, evil, fear,
but thankfully, he didn't guess that a small Scrap prince was near.

What Chaos could Fighter expect there? "Not much", he concluded.
"But the crazy King is still crazy." This fact was now included
in plans Fighter had for the future. He knew it was fate
that this crazy king would fail someday. He would simply wait
for the Grand Revolt of the People. Someday it would begin
and Fighter's Plan for Chaos would, at long last, win
in a cosmic revolution with blood and People roaring!
Until then, he'd leave the Castle alone. These Royals were just, plain boring.

Lessons

Above all the places Prince Sol liked to be,
was riding in hiding, on His Majesty.
Prince Sol studied the King at his daily affairs,
riding safely among the King's curly beard hairs
or tucked out of sight where his crown firmly rested
or on the King's chest where the Royal Crest was crested.

King Sol was proud. It gave him much pleasure
to show what he knew to his son, his small treasure.
"I must give Sol Royal Lessons and, in return,
he will learn all the skills that a young Prince should learn.
And when he grows older, the whole world will see
that he'll be a strong man and a great King like me.

"It won't take folks long until they realize
that a King is a King! It won't matter his size."

Consciences—and the Legends of The Big Game

So King Sol decided he'd begin on this day,
to instruct his small son on the most proper way
to be a *strong* king. "You must follow my lead
so that one day you will be a *tough King,* indeed."

Prince Sol was excited.

"Thank you much, Father. I'm certain that you
know all the best stuff that a king needs to do.
There's nobody better to learn from than you."

Lesson #1-Politics

"First, as a King, you must know how to lie,"
instructed King Sol with a gleam in his eye.
"You must learn how to trick and connive and be sly,
to not show your hand and give cheating a try!
"You must tell all the People what they want to hear.

Then do as you please, without back-thoughts or fear.
If folks learn the truth and they're ready to fight,
you can just say *they're* lying. It works out just right.

"Come here, my son let's give lying a try!"

Prince Sol looked confused and asked his dad, "Why?"

King Sol replied, a wise look in his eye,
"Because my father taught me what he always knew.
This is one of the ways leaders make People do
just exactly the things that they want them to do.'

"You just take the truth and manipulate it.
Then you give it a spin and recreate it.
Kings tell their own 'facts' and use them to show
the side of the truth they want folks to know.
My lies are the keys to my power, my dear.
I 'create' my own truth that I want folks to hear."

Prince Sol thought this over a minute or two.
"Why don't you just tell folks the stuff that is true?
It seems that would be so much easier to do.
It must take lots of work to remember each lie,
to say high is low and to say low is high.

"With the real truth, you wouldn't have to recall
what was true and what wasn't," suggested Prince Sol.
"And it seems like the People would like the truth, too.
Don't they get mad when they find stuff's not true?
I was wondering, have you, as King, ever tried
just telling the truth when you could have lied?"

"Heck, no," said King Sol with a look of surprise.
"I've always known I rule better with lies."

Consciences—and the Legends of The Big Game

"Lying looks hard, Dad. I can't deny it.
When *I* am the King, as your son, I will try it.
But, if I tell a lie, I don't think folks will buy it.
They will know it's a lie. It will show on my face.
I think, as a liar, I'll be a disgrace.
I seem to have trouble when I tell a lie.
What is the chance we could give truth a try?

"Hmm," mused the King. "This thought is quite new
and a challenge to what I most commonly do.
Now you've brought up a new way to do it.
I hear what you say. I will try to think through it.
It sounds quite unique, but it might just be true
that the truth would be simpler. How novel! Who knew?"

So, King Sol decided to give truth a try
to see what it felt like to not tell a lie.
And he liked it! The truth is it made the King smile.
And King Sol decided (after one or two trials)
that he rather *liked* his new 'truthfulness style.

His lying became an old way of the past.

Then some town folk tried truth, though it didn't spread fast.
Some People decided to try this new way
of working things out. At the end of the day
they liked the truth better and gathered to say,
"We should try, now and then, the King's 'truthfulness' way!"

They would sit down and bargain and look eye to eye
to see how it felt to just not tell a lie.
Some truth became common. It became "the new thing".
Town life was more honest because of the King.

Sample:
"Are these turnips rotten?"

"Some of them are...
Take the ones from the back. They're much fresher, by far."
"Thanks for the tip. I'll buy here again."
"Back at ya. Enjoy those good turnips, my friend."

"Did you hear?" bragged the King. "Folk are trying my trick
of being more honest. They seem to learn quick.
I *never knew* folks would try it, indeed.
You see, my son, how a good leader leads.
I'm glad that we talked," the King said to Prince Sol.
"You must learn things like this to be King, after all."

"I see that," grinned the Prince. "Teach me the rest
of the stuff that you know. What you know works out best!"

Lesson #2-Public Speaking

"What else should I teach him?" The King thought aloud.
What should he learn that will make him stand proud?
"I know! Public speaking: "How to threaten a crowd."

"The first thing, my son, is to learn to yell loud!
I'll shout you a sample. I'm sure you'll do well.
Listen and learn, son, the art of 'The Yell'!"
King Sol puffed his chest way out and delivered a mighty roar,
a display of awesome bellowing that he was famous for.

Sol plugged his ears and asked his dad, "What is 'yelling' for?"

"To impress the crowd", the King said, to show that you're in charge.
Try it yourself! Take a big breath and yell out strong and large!
Shout out all commands you make just as loud as you can.
This will make you sound real tough, and sound like you're a man!
When I yell my loudest, what I want to be done
Is always done quite quickly. Fear rules People, Son!"

Sol wanted to please so he did his best.
Like his Dad, he inhaled and puffed out his chest
to yell very loud. He would *not* fail this test!

King Sol stood back from Prince Sol so that he
could hear what a 'shouter' his young son would be...
"Come on. Yell your loudest! Go ahead! Let me hear!
Shout your fiercest shout at me! Make me quake with
fear!"...............................

Hearing nothing, King Sol called, "Come, Son! Don't be shy."
Still the King heard nothing. Wouldn't Sol even *try*?
King Sol stomped toward his tiny son, intending to know why.

Suddenly he heard a little squeak. It was very faint at first.
Prince Sol was yelling his loudest, as though his lungs would burst!

King Sol finally understood. This was all his son could do.
"Sorry, Dad. I'm not good at this." This was clearly true.

"But Dad, won't People listen to me, if I speak strong but quiet?
I could speak like that, I think. Couldn't we just try it?"

King Sol pondered the question. "He's right. Why do I yell?
I could say quietly what I want. That might work just as well.

"For you, I'll try it," announced King Sol as he thought
this new thought through.
And when he spoke in a quiet voice, he saw what he could do.

"Demanding loudly's a Royal Right, but there might be an occasion
when speaking quietly could produce a new kind of persuasion."

He decided he would try it. It wouldn't hurt to try.
The People listened closely and, right before his eyes,
they did what the King had quietly asked. What a huge surprise!

Why, the King mused thoughtfully, *have I not done this before?*
And he sort of liked the change, himself, so he tried to do it more.

Folks saw these changes and started to say,
"We like this new style. The King's found a new way
to rule with more thought and consideration,
less screaming and yelling and irate frustration,
and we like it, here in The River Nation.

"Maybe we'll try to imitate him.
Of course, we don't want to over-rate him,
but, if the King's style works when he is nice,
we might give it a try for ourselves, once or twice."
So, some People began to speak nicer too.
 It's really quite strange what small changes can do.

Changes

The Scrap King watched as his son progressed
and he realized gratefully that he had been blessed.
King Sol had learned faster than Heart had guessed
would be the case when their Plan had started.

King Sol seemed gentler, more open-hearted.
Heart watched and, in truth, was relieved to see
the outcome Queen Connie had predicted would be
occurring from this sacrifice that they were making,
the painful, yet hopeful, chance they were taking.

Though their young son couldn't yet read or write,
he naturally seemed to know wrong from right.
Like Scraps before him, Sol naturally knew
what was a good or a bad thing to do.

By example he'd made the Royals more content.
King Heart could see now what their sacrifice meant.

King Sol was watching *his* small son as well.
Prince Sol was smart. It was easy to tell.
There was no doubt King Sol was proud of his boy.
He learned everything fast and that gave him much joy.

King Sol now concluded (which was very wise)
that tiny Prince Sol would not have the size
that he had once wished for. He finally knew,
but he remained happy... Surprising but true.

Prince Sol had changed him. He didn't know how
but his days were more joyful and happier now.
Both fathers were happy and most proud to see
that their son was the son that both hoped he would be.

Lesson #3-Etiquette

Now, Queen Luna decided she would now coach her son
in the ways that Royal Etiquette should be done.
She believed that every good Prince should be
prepared to *impress* all society.

So, she taught the Prince what she thought was polite,
but somehow, it didn't seem to work out quite right.

"First", said the Queen, "you must show you don't care
for anyone else in the room that is there.
You must stick up your nose very high in the air.
You must gaze through the room with your most haughty stare.
You must learn to ignore all who want your attention,
showing *you* are the *best*! That should be your intention."

"Now you must practice. I am anxious to see
my handsome son act like true Royalty!"

Prince Sol could not seem to see
why this was the friendliest way to be

in *any* kind of society,
but he knew that his mother thought this was best
so, he poked up his nose and puffed out his chest.
With his most stuck-up look, Prince Sol walked out the door,
doing his best to completely ignore
the Queen who was calling him back once more.

His mother was shocked. She was stunned to the core.
(She had never seen someone *else* act like *her* before!)

"Please, dear. Come back! Please don't treat me this way.
You've made me feel bad. I don't know what to say.
I've never known what it felt like to be
someone *else* watching *me* act like 'true royalty!'

"Now that I see it, I don't think that you
should be learning this style I was teaching to you."

"That's great," said Prince Sol. "With my nose in the air,
it's real hard to see how I'm going to where.
The maids and the servants seem to like it much more
when we all smile a lot. That way, we can chat more."
So, the Queen thought a bit and then quickly chose
to redo her own style and to lower her nose.
With a friendlier smile, she decided to try
to speak to the folks that she met, eye to eye.
And soon she discovered and thereafter would say,
she began to make friends when she acted this way.
She discovered that all that she needed to do
was 'be friendly' to others and 'be nice'. Who knew?

Folks started to visit and stay for a while.
Luna learned how to laugh. She took time to smile.
Her new social calendar soon rearranged.
She was no longer lonely. She was friendly ...*and changed!*
Amazing!

As his Scrap parents watched, they both knew from the start
that their son made these changes by revealing his heart.
In fact, his Scrap parents were so very proud,
that they almost forgot and praised Prince Sol out loud.

And Prince Sol was happy. He could feel their proud glow,
but, of course, where it came from, he couldn't know.

Lesson #4-Sharing

There was one special change that made Scrap parents smile.
Queen Luna next learned a more *generous* style.

The pretty Queen loved finery, gowns above all,
but that was before she "gave birth" to Prince Sol.
Changing her dresses and gowns the day through
was what Luna, the beautiful Queen, liked to do.
But being a mother had caused her to see
how useless and vain all these changes could be.

Caring for Sol was so very much more
important to her than the gowns that she wore.
"What should we do, son?" she asked Sol one day.
"Here hang my gowns, brightly colored and gay.
But I don't need all these. They just get in the way."

Prince Sol grabbed her fingers and gave them a hug.
"You don't need pretty dresses," he said with a shrug.
"You are so pretty that everyone knows
that you really don't need all these great, fancy clothes."

Luna blushed a bit but now thoughtfully knew
that there must be something else that she could do.
"I don't change as often, now that I'm a mother.
I don't need to switch from one dress to another.
Changing wastes time. I can see this is true.
I have ever so many more things now to do."

Prince Sol had a thought that was happy and new...
"I have an idea that you might think is fair.
Why not give some to others...in other words, 'share'?

Sol climbed on her shoulder and sat very near
whispering happily into her ear.
"Sharing is fun. All the ladies will love it.
That's a kind thing to do. What do you think of it?"

"Dearest Sol," said Queen Luna. "It just came to me.
It's a wonderful custom to share, don't you see?
Although this is something that I've never done,
doesn't sharing with others seem like it's fun?"

Prince Sol sort of knew how this plan came about,
but he didn't try hard then to figure it out.

On the very next morning, before break of day,
Queen Luna prepared to give dresses away.
She bundled each one of them onto a cart
and, with a big smile and a generous heart,
she had the whole pile of them hauled into town
and proceeded to give away each precious gown!

To the poorest of ladies, she gave out her best
and to each of her servants, she gave the rest
until, at the end of a very long day,
each woman in town walked happily away
with a beautiful garment tucked under her arm,
thrilled with their gifts and discussing the charm
they'd not seen before from their beautiful Queen.
All remarked, and admired, the great changes they'd seen.

Scrap Royals watched the Queen and again they just smiled
at the "Prince Sol Effect" from their generous child.

Spirit noticed the change in the Queen and he, too,
could see what these wonderful changes could do.
The changes now growing from one small Scrap boy
now helped Spirit look at The Big Game with joy.

As the women walked home with each colorful gift,
Spirit could see a most notable lift
in the feelings of all as they went on their way,
chatting and sharing this wonderful day.
Goodness and happiness walked hand in hand.
This looked like the world that Spirit had planned. (score!)

But,
by chance on this day, Fighter also passed by.
Rumbling through town, this new joy caught his eye.
"I must check this out. I must find out why
River People are smiling. Such smiles are quite rare."

Such happiness caused him to stop cold and to stare.
"These ladies look happy," he growled with a sneer.
"Too much gladness abounds...too much happiness here.
I almost suspect that old Spirit is near
trying to find Good where there is none to find,
trying to score a quick and 'come from behind'.

"But I also know I've not seen Spirit since
the crazy King 'showed' his invisible 'Prince'.
"Spirit's a loser. His team's 'Good' is past.
His chance for a 'come-back' is fading real fast.

If it's not Spirit's doing, this smells like his way
to find something nice just to 'brighten a day'.

"I'll rain on this scene, though I'm not really worrying."
Fighter brought forth a storm. The women went scurrying.
Fighter had used his old trick of bad weather

to ruin the joy of these ladies together
and dampen all signs of their new happiness
as he drizzled some water on every new dress.

Then, thinking he'd wrecked them, he zoomed out of sight.
Spirit knew that old trick, and he *would* make it right.

The ladies all scurried for cover to a large Willow tree,
(a tree standing bold where no Willow should be.)

"How handy that we could suddenly spy
this tree that is here to keep our dresses dry,"
the women announced as the rain flowed around them.
(Had they found The Willow or had The Willow just found them?)

The welcoming Willow gave all time to see
and be thankful for what they held under that tree.
"Thank you, Queen Luna. You are our great Queen,
the most generous monarch that we've ever seen.
We never guessed or supposed you could be
the genderous Queen you have turned out to be."

No one had seen her behave in this way
with the spirit of kindness she had shown them this day.

Spirit watched Fighter leave. He now nodded and smiled.
"Fighter doesn't suspect this joy was caused by a tiny child
who just spoke in the ear of his mother to produce all this gladness.
Goodness has proved that a good word can fight old Fighter's badness.
Just a small act of Goodness that we've all witnessed here
Improved these ladies' thinking. That fact seems quite clear.

"I wonder if that's what the Fireflies propose
for all Scraps in the future someday...who knows."

Spirit was happy as he could be...
though he had some help from the old Willow tree.

Breaking Rules

But all was not happy as time wandered by.
Prince Sol grew more lonely, unchallenged and shy.
His days became boring. His evenings were sad.
King Heart became worried. He knew this was bad.

Though the Prince had more comforts than he'd ever need,
young Sol was a Scrap and a boy of that breed
needed friends he could run with, friends that would play,
someone his age he could play with each day.

How can a young Prince who knows no one, learn to be a man?
Can he learn about friendship with no friends? Is it possible anyone can?
How can he learn to win a race or even catch a ball?
Who can he play hide and seek with when there's no one there at all?
How can a little Scrap boy learn what's right and fair,
when there is *no one* who can challenge him because there's *no one there?*

The Castle servants felt bad for Prince Sol.
They could see Sol was lonely... and bored, above all.
"What he needs is playmates," they would secretly say.
But it wasn't their place to speak up in that way
nor reveal to the town what they saw every day.

Day after day, Sol wandered the Castle halls alone.
He was safe but lonely, *and still* he hadn't grown.
His mother had said he'd grow bigger someday and then he could go outside
but until he could do that safely, that pleasure would be denied.
Queen Connie saw this from her perch on a rafter.
Prince Sol was too quiet. There was not enough laughter.

Connie said this to Heart one sad afternoon.
"Our son is too lonely. This problem will soon
Make our son a hermit. He won't understand
nor finish his training the way we have planned."

Connie, once more, could not stand by. She knew her son's need.
It was up to them, Scrap parents, to help their son succeed.
"He's supposed to bond with humans. That must be his mission,
but our son cannot learn what he needs to learn in this friendless condition."

The Plan was for Sol to know humans and think like them and so
Connie and Heart hadn't wanted their son to meet the mice below.
But desperate times and loneliness called for desperate deeds.
Connie would ask Mouse Spirit Club to fill Sol's friendship needs.

Connie went to Moses Mouse. She had just one plea:
"Could you send some mice to play with our son? He needs some friends see
how to get along with others. He can learn this naturally
the way we all learned in the old days from what we, as friends, all did.
It is time that our son learns these lessons. He must learn to be a kid!"

Training, Mouse Style

Until now, by Mutual Agreement, young mice had been forbidden
to play in plain sight in the Castle. From Prince Sol they'd stayed hidden.
They had watched and listened, but as they were asked, they'd stayed
out of the parts of the Castle where young Prince Sol had played.

Carefully Connie explained her goals and why this need was grave.
This was part of Spirit's Plan that they *all* were trying to save.

The Spirit Club listened thoughtfully and then gave out a cheer.
They had been waiting to join the Game. "We will help now, never fear!"
They gathered up their young ones to answer The Big Game's call.
Their mission was important. It was time to play with Sol!

So, one day, as Sol wandered alone once more,
he heard a small sound he had not heard before.
It seemed to be coming from under the floor.

"Hello?" called Sol toward the squeaking sound. "Is anybody there?"
"Sure, there is", a voice came back. "Bet you can't find out where!"
Prince Sol started searching. He followed the tiny voice,
but the voice kept moving from place to place with a little scampering noise.

At last, before the mysterious voice could make any more escapes,
Sol followed the noise and found 'the voice' behind a set of drapes.
And there, for the first time in his life, the little Prince could see
a fuzzy creature with a tail, about the same size as he.
Sol reached out and touched its nose. The creature did the same.
"I'm a mouse," the creature said. "Tell me. What's your name?

"I'm a Prince. My name is Sol." M0re mice crawled from the cracks.
The first mouse said, "Hello, Prince Sol. My friends just call me Max
and these are a few of my closest friends. We live underneath the floor.
We've watched you for a long time, but we couldn't play before.
You want to play with all of us? If you do, come on! Let's race!"

The mice ran in different directions, a grin on every face.
Sol ran, too. He was not sure why, but it looked like it might be fun.
In this way, Sol met the Castle mice. Great friendships had begun.

Prince Sol was beside himself. He couldn't believe his eyes.
"You guys are the best thing ever. This is such a cool surprise!
And you say that you live in this Castle? Why didn't you let me know?
If I knew you guys were here before, we could've played long ago.
Where have you been all this time? It's so great that you're all here.

"I've been stuck in this Castle, alone, year after year after year!
What else can we do together? Where else can we go?
There are so many things I want to do and so much I want to know."

Sol's new mice friends were happier, too. They'd been cloistered
but now they knew
they could go *anywhere* with Prince Sol. There was so much more to do.

They showed Sol all the passage ways,
where to play tag on rainy days.
They took some twigs and hit a ball
and jumped from rafters without a fall.
They hid from People, played ball with the rats,
swam in milk jugs, climbed into vats.
There was nothing Prince Sol wouldn't do.
Soon he was part of the regular crew.

Now Sol was playing, day after day,
with his friends. Every morning he'd run off and play.
Poor Queen Luna didn't know
what Sol was doing or where he would go
when for hours he'd disappear.
This new habit brought on her usual fear.

One day, Sol stayed too long while he played,
causing Queen Luna to be so afraid

that she sent all the servants to search through each hall.
She started to panic, to run, scream and call
until she was in such a wild, fearful state
that she broke down, convinced of his terrible fate!

Then Sol popped up, laughing, all out of breath,
scaring his trembling mother to death.
"Where have you been?" Luna cried to her son.
Sol answered smugly, "Just having some fun."

Luna picked up her son and gave him a hug.
Sol had a secret. He felt very smug.

Queen Luna said nothing, her energy spent.
She was glad he was safe now, where ever he went.

The Prince was not telling with whom he was playing.
His Mom might say no, so he wasn't saying.
He poked up his chin and stuck out his chest.
He was keeping his secret. (This was not for the best.)

This was not a good Practice and Sol's Scrap mother knew it.
Prince Sol needed training, himself, to undo it.
She must act as his Conscience. Connie stood by this night
to help a young Scrap learn to do what was right.

Prince Sol wasn't perfect. This was *his* turn.
This was a lesson *he* needed to learn.
Connie hid in the shadows above Prince Sol's head.
"You've worried your mother," she quite plainly said.
"She is a good mother. You're a good son and so
a *good* son would tell her what she needs to know.

"Your mom doesn't know mice. It's true she might say
that mice are not creatures with whom you should play.
So you must convince her that your playmates are nice,

how much you like them, how much you like mice.
You must *not* keep your secret. You must say what is true.
This is a good thing and the right thing to do."

Prince Sol was amazed. He was almost struck dumb.
He had heard a voice speaking. Where did it come from?
Time had stood still, his Queen Mother was waiting.
What was the message this weird voice was stating?
Sol heard one thing. "You must say what is true."
Suddenly, Sol knew the right thing to do!

Sol looked at his mother, at her worried face.
He knew he had caused this. He should try to erase
her worries, her fears, do the best that he could.
Why should he do this? He just *knew* that he should.
Sol stood on one foot and then on the other.
This wasn't too easy to say to his mother.

"First,
I need to say I get lonely. I needed some friends, and mice
were the friends I found to play with, friends that were just my size.
I have fun with these mice almost every day. They're as cool as they can be.
With mice as friends, I'm not lonely. Mice are perfect friends for me."

When he had finished, Sol looked at the floor.
Maybe his mother would need to know more.
He had never 'confessed' to his mother before.

Queen Luna was shocked... *her* son, playing with mice?
How could she accept that *mice playmates* were 'nice'?

"Are you trying to be funny? Did I hear what you're saying?
You've been playing with mice? It's with rodents you're playing?"

But she looked at Sol's face and she finally decided
that she was at least grateful her son had confided

and told her the truth about where he had been.
So, she listened and talked, asked more questions and then
they both listened and talked to each other again.

Mice? The Queen couldn't believe her young Prince!
Sol pleaded his case. She was hard to convince.
"They're really great, Mom. They are honest and kind.
There are no better friends that I ever could find!"

Luna listened and thought and at last... changed her mind.
She began to see mice from a new point of view.
Seeing mice as Sol's buddies was completely new,
but little by little, lack of prejudice grew.

She could see Sol was happy, and she had to admit
that the size of these creatures was quite a good fit.
So, she gave her permission for Sol's new-found friends.
(Sometimes that's the way that true honesty ends.)

Queen Luna was okay with Sol playing with mice,
but King Sol wasn't sure that mice were that nice.
When he was told of the friends Sol had chosen,
he scowled at the thought. His approval was frozen.

King Sol didn't think that a plain mouse could be
a fitting role model for young Royalty.
But both King and Queen could quite easily see
that Sol was now happier, as he should be.

King Sol gave in and he left Sol alone
to play with the friends he had found on his own.
(But not quite on his own if the real truth were known.)

Like any young boy, Prince Sol liked to play
with his friends from the floorboards, day after day.
Rats were his big friends, bugs were his small.

Mice were just perfect, the most fun of all.
Prince Sol's best friend, in light of these facts,
was Moses' young grandson, the one they called Max.
They spent time every day, day in and day out
as Sol learned what friendship was really about.

Though they had disagreements, but they made up each day.
Sol would call through the floor boards, "Can Max come and play?"
And Max would squeak back, "No, you must come down here."
Through cracks in the floorboards, Sol would soon disappear.

Together with mice, Prince Sol learned how to share,
how to take turns when needed and how to be fair.
Prince Sol learned a lot with his mice friends, you see,
like the regular Scrap child he was meant to be.
These youthful friendships were a good way, indeed,
for Sol to learn social skills that he would need.

The Game Heats Up

– M. Mouse Observations

Sol learned a great deal from his friendship with mice.
They both shared respect, points of view and advice.
Sol shared ideas that he thought were good.
Max shared ideas, too, as all good friends should.
Both argued their thoughts about wrong and right
with discussions that lasted well into the night.

Little by little Sol started to share
these ideas with his father. They'd discuss and compare
their thoughts about fairness and life in the town
and how to decide when two 'good sides' are found.

This small, would-be leader began to erase
some very flawed thoughts of the King and replace
some unfair decisions he'd made in the past
with better decisions and fairness, at last.

King Sol began seeing the good and the bad
and, of course, right and wrong more than he ever had.
More, every day, King Sol found it wise
to consult with his son and to take his advice.

On these days, with his father, Prince Sol quickly grew
in mind and in heart, but King Sol, by now, knew
that his dreams for Sol *growing* would never come true.

So he had a dilemma. He wanted to show
how smart his son was so his People would know
Sol would be a good king and, of course, he was proud.
King Sol wished to display his bright son to the crowd.

But both Royals were frightened to let People see
how tiny and fragile Sol still seemed to be.
He was only the size of half a string bean,
the tiniest young man they'd ever seen.

"I know that you want to show off the pride
what we have in our son but put pride aside.

"Our People are ruthless. They won't understand
why their Prince is so tiny, more so than we planned.
They will think that his size means 'the crown' is not strong
and plan for rebellion before very long.
Until he is larger, he must stay in our care.
His loss for us both would be too hard to bare."

Now the King had a plan. It would fill his great need
to show to the People that his son could succeed
and some day emerge and show all he could lead!

He may never grow, thought the King in despair
but my son <u>must</u> be known for his insights, so rare,
and his brilliant decisions. Folks won't <u>see</u> him there
but they'll know he's a part of my royal decisions
while not being seen, always quite out of their vision.
He can remain hidden as he's always been
but consult from the shadows where he can't be seen.
So the People will <u>hear</u> but because of this choice,
they will not <u>see</u> his face. They will <u>hear his voice!</u>"

King Sol tried his new plan. He was most proud to say
that now People talked to him more every day.
They seemed to accept what the King had to say
although it was said in this very strange way.

His new style of governing became quite well known
because, in this style now, he wasn't 'alone'.
He seemed to be judging complaints with more care.
He would listen intently, then turn in his chair
and speak to a curtain... but no one was there. (??)

Prince Sol was quite present, but, *in his dad's hair*
where no one could see him. He *surely was there*
and would speak with his dad about all his decisions
with a strong, honest voice, keeping well out of vision.
But nobody heard him. His voice was so small
that most People thought they heard nothing at all.

King Sol explained this bazar 'consulting action'
with some stories that gave no one much satisfaction.
"Can you hear my son? He is smart, through and through
but my son "has a cold" or "My son has the flu
so we don't want to spread it to any of you.
That is why we have both made certain
to keep him out of sight behind this curtain,"

"My son is quite wise with amazing insight.
He helps me decide what is wrong and what's right.
When you get to meet him, you will quickly see
that he'll be good and wise with you all... just like me".

The People all listened and acted polite
though the excuses the King made didn't sound right.

"I think that he's crazy. He's been so ever since
he first tried to tell us he'd fathered a prince."

"He's 'lost it'! He knows that his lie isn't true
but he still keeps pretending. What can we do?"
"He talks to a curtain when no one is there,
but since his decisions are usually fair,
if he talks to a curtain, I really don't care."

However...
The questions continued. "Why does he pretend?"
"How will the King's craziness come to an end?"

"If his son was real, we'd be able to see
what kind of king he will grow up to be."

"If he's real, he'd be big now and almost full grown.
What kind of a king might he be on the throne?"

"But I don't think he's real and I'm not alone."

"Will the King's craziness cause us some day
to be in some danger when he acts this way?"

"If he talks with a person we know isn't there,
can he fight to protect us? Be ready? Prepare?"

"What if we're threatened by forces we fear?

"What if we give him a pass every year,
but then, he's too crazy to really react?

"A King must be ready, then. That's just a fact."

"Until then, don't worry. There's no need to fear
for a King who just talks to nobody that's near."

"Well, we can't be sure, but right now I don't care
as long as his judgements and rulings are fair,
he can talk all he wants to a son that's not there."

So, to humor the King, folks continued to say,
"How is your son, Prince Sol, doing today?"

"He's on top of his game," Sol would casually say.
"He is thoughtful, indeed and gets smarter each day.
He's as smart as a whip. He just blows me away.
He wanted to meet all of you here today,
but he had an appointment so he couldn't stay."

The town folk just snickered and went on their way.

Fighter's Stance

Fighter now laughed. "Those excuses get old.
All know the King's crazy. When this story is told,
King Sol will just die and fall off of his chair,
and no son will be found so he won't have an heir.
There isn't a prince since this King is a fool,
so the King will just die leaving no one to rule.

"All true fans of Chaos, should now have no fears.
Violence was growing, more so through the years.

CONSCIENCES—AND THE LEGENDS OF THE BIG GAME

The town folk now say the King's more fair each day,
but that weakness just shows that he's fading away.

"The King's getting soft. If I thought this would last,
I would just kill him off. I've done such in the past.
But I would much rather his death be organic.
There's no need to rush. There is no need to panic.
His death *from his* People will be the best thing.
My Game Plan grows hot and just ripe for the picking

"A riot of some kind is what this Game needs
with a strong, final drive as my Chaos proceeds.
This Game will be mine. I now live for the day
when a true revolt grows and blows all Good away!

"But I'll need the right players to handle my plan.
I'll find natural leaders with a talent for greed.
Inborn evil is good. That is just what I'll need.

"They will go for my endgame for all the wrong reasons.
I will look for them soon. I am in 'Gaming Season'.
First I run up more yardage to strengthen my cause
Where there are no umpires and no need for laws.
Then I'll set up my win. 'Til then, hold your applause."

Unfortunately...
the "crazy King" gave Fighter incentive
to become more lethal and more inventive.
Fighter hadn't felt such a combat desire
since the night he started the famous 'Great Fire'.

Fighter now coached fights on all sides to increase.
From morning to night, none could find any peace.
Fighter also coached families to fight one another,
father to father and brother to brother.
Folks stole every day with insatiable greed..

No one was safe and no plans could succeed.
What anyone earned was soon stolen away.
Beatings occurred when folks got in their way.
They looked to each other to find the solution,
but of course, they found none. What was their conclusion?

"If something is bad, it can always get worse.
Just get used to mayhem, a regular curse.
Soon anger will eat up the whole universe!"

"This is the way the world's now going to be.
I don't care about you. It all about *me*
and what *I* can get, by hook or by crook.
I will do what I want! Just don't bother to look."

In the marketplace, Fighter put Chaos in charge.
Greed and selfishness grew. He was coming on large.
"Spirit of Good now has no chance to win.
Since the beginning, my cheating and sin
have been winning the Game. That can't be denied.
And Spirit is AWOL. He has run off to hide.

"Spirit gave up, but what more could he do?
He has no defense. That is obviously true.
He has no one to stand up for Good on his side.
I doomed all 'Good' before it could be tried!
No one knows the difference between wrong and right
so Chaos will win without much of a fight."

Pining for Goodness

King Heart became worried and then became sad.
"Earth's People seem worse. They are more than just bad.
Should I inform Spirit? Maybe our son

could help People now, and if he is 'The One,'
maybe he can start sooner. Isn't he almost done?
Our son seems quite ready. Now he helps the King.
Can he now start our Plan? That might be a good thing."

Queen Connie was very troubled, too. "I guess I didn't know
how terribly long it was going to take for our dear son to grow.
How long should we wait, Heart? How much time will it take
to train our slowly growing son, for the changes he must make?
Must we wait much longer? Will the world first fall apart?
When will he be ready? Isn't it time to start?"

Spirit of Good now heard the lament.
With no trouble at all, he felt their discontent.
He felt that way too. As each evening passed,
he wished he could stop Fighter's Chaos, at last.

The world was chaotic, but Spirit thought, No...
Before Sol can lead others, he should probably know
about the real world that he's never seen,
good folks and bad folks and folks in between.
Prince Sol is already quite smart and wise
in spite of his youth but, because of his size,
he must learn more of the world he will meet
or his Goodness will surely go down to defeat.

Though the poor King and Queen of the Scraps were upset,
they tried to be patient. Sol was not ready yet.
But what should they do now? They couldn't see
what more they could do to help their son to be
the man he should be when he took up the reign
as Scrap Leader for real. Such doubts caused them pain.

But, one day, with Scrap Royals so deeply concerned,
they both got the answer for which they now yearned.
High above in the midnight sky, the Fireflies had returned!

The Fireflies were needed, Spirit now knew,
to reassure faith that their Plan would come true.
In response to this need, the Fireflies now flew,
singing, and glowing and circling The Sew
where the Scrap Royals were trying to think these things though.

King Heart and Queen Connie could hear every word
that the Fireflies were singing, and they knew that they heard
a sweet reassurance they would not ignore.
They would have, in good time, that which they waited for.

"When he is ready, your son, will indeed
become a great champion and be ready to lead
and help all the People in the ways that they need.
The earth will find Goodness, though the time seems delayed.
Scraps will reach the goal soon for which all Scraps were made."

"We know preparation has taken its toll
on you and all Scraps before they take their role.
But that time has been needed and soon you will see
that Scraps will be ready as they need to be
to follow your son. We hope you understand.
You've not suffered in vain for the goal you have planned.

"Patience is needed. One day, Scraps will do
their work for real Goodness. This, in time, will be true."
The small Royals were grateful. All doubts were rejected.
Their plan would continue as Spirit expected.

The Wretcheds

– adapted by Scraps from Scrap Records

As time went on, Scraps had taught the rats about the market places they had developed before the fire and soon *all* tiny creatures began *trading* up and down the stream as well as just transporting. What one rat found and didn't need today might be used in trade for something that a mouse or bug needed tomorrow. Rats became ingenious entrepreneurs.

The Scraps were impressed by the business activity of the rodents. King Heart also felt that he still owed Ramon much in return for the friendship and generosity he and his friends had showed them over the years. With the maturing of Prince Sol taking a longer time than expected, he had a little time on his hands.

Heart discussed the situation with Ramon. Was it possible that *he* could help Ramon with his scavenging? They were both not getting any younger. At first Ramon just dug his toes in the dirt and insisted that nobody owed him anything, but King Heart continued to ask him.

In the end it was decided that Heart could help Ramon *transport* salvage. He and other Scraps would move the items that the rats found up and down the stream, from one destination to another for trading as needed. It seemed like a very reasonable and mutually helpful arrangement for aging rats and Scraps working side by side.

Everyone living along The Sew was quite content, everyone except for a pack of outcast rats. Most said that the outcasts looked like River rats when they saw them lurking about. They were very large. Some even said that there was one who looked exactly like Ramon, but unlike Ramon, he had no desire to work.

These rats had no desire to socialize, either. They were clannish, sticking to themselves most of the time, making friends with no one, not even other rats. No one knew exactly who they were, where they lived or why they would not join with any of their fellow-rats. There were definite trust issues.

Those who lived in The Sew began to refer to these cultish rats as "The Wretcheds" because they never seemed to be happy. They even made those around them unhappy. They did not intend to lower themselves to the day-to-day grind. They preferred to steal what they wanted from those that worked for it. They were the kind of rats that gave rats a bad name.

As the months and the years had gone by in The Sew, Scraps were completely accepted by most of the rats. At the same time that Scraps were gaining in popularity with most, however, they were becoming increasingly despised by The Wretcheds.

The Wretcheds were jealous. That is what the other rats finally decided. Their jealousy boiled up in their small, narrow minds and began to make them not only a nuisance, but dangerous. Jealousy was not healthy. Everyone could feel it. These rats were up to no good.

The Wretcheds often met together in secret for the express purpose of telling each other that the reason for their unhappiness was Scraps and "Scrap lovers", as they called the rats who worked with Scraps on a daily basis.

"It's the fault of them blasted Scraps that The Sew's not like it was afore. Nothin's the same." groused The Wretched leader. "Them Scraps've taken over our housin', livin' right next door to rats and bringin' down the property values. They move them boats up and down the stream and keep such a close eye on everythin' that there's nothin' left over for a true rat that deserves it.

"I say that it's time we fight back. We don't want 'their kind' in The Sew. It's time that we band together with other like-minded rats and drive em out. I don't know what that stupid Ramon thought he was doin', invitin' em here, anyhow. Whadaya say, boys?"

The slimy group squeaked loudly in agreement, their long, yellow teeth flashing in the glow of their tar ball torches. This rat was right. And he ought to know. He was Reardon, Ramon's twin brother.

Reardon had not died in The Great Fire, after all. When the fire started, he had run, leaving behind the rest of his friends and family.

Reardon was a river rat. He was an excellent swimmer. Completely focused on his own wellbeing, he dove into the River and swam out toward the center. From there he had watched as his family and their homes were consumed by smoke and flames.

The memory of the night haunted him still. When the fire finally went out, Reardon, tired and shaking from treading water for almost an hour, had slithered out on the Riverbank and slipped away into the darkness.

Consciences—and the Legends of The Big Game

Ashamed of having left his family and friends to burn, Reardon kept to himself and eventually found the company of other rats that were very much like him. When he discovered that his brother was alive, he had not been able to face him. They had always been somewhat different, but Reardon's guilt and shame made him feel even more disconnected. Only with these other, hostile rodents who were as miserable as he was, was Reardon comfortable. He was sure that Ramon would never want to see him again.

Reardon's misery had grown steadily in the years since The Great Fire. Day after day, he had watched his brother start his life over with the help of the Scraps. Ramon actually seemed happy. The resentment in Reardon grew. It wasn't fair. And it was the fault of the Scraps.

Of all the Scraps, Reardon hated King Heart and Queen Connie the most. To Reardon, these two scrawny, hairless creatures had no reason for living. *And,* they were living next to his own brother, even working with him. They were taking his place. They had to be eliminated.

Driven by this jealousy and hate, Reardon and the other members of The Wretcheds watched King Heart and Queen Connie regularly. They spent all day, every day, 'tailing' them. Soon they could predict with amazing accuracy just where the Scrap royalty would be at any time of the day.

At last their spying was complete enough and their anger was high enough to be ready for action. With no hesitancy or doubt to slow them down, they planned to strike out against these Scraps once and for all and show them they had no place in The Sew.

One evening, just as the work day was starting for the Scraps and the rest of the rats, Reardon and his gang slipped out of their hiding places and began the operation they had been planning for months.

"Make it look like an accident," Reardon hissed to his partners as they parted ways.

Because Reardon knew that he looked exactly like his brother, his was a special part of the plan... the elimination of the little Queen!

Quietly he began climbing up along the dark, dripping aqueduct that led from The Sew toward the main part of the Castle. The others of his group took off toward the stream. Reardon knew all the ways to the main part of the Castle from the thousands of times that he had traveled them with his brother in years past.

He needed no lights and climbed easily and quickly in the darkness. When he came to a particular bend in the passageway which had a broad and shadowy landing, Reardon stopped. He flattened himself against a far wall and waited. His red eyes shone with evil.

He didn't have long to wait. He could hear Queen Connie approaching before he saw her. Her tiny feet tapped along the path and she was singing a children's song. Reardon knew she was on her way to say goodnight to her son.

Connie was carrying one of the tarball torches. Reardon could see the glow on the wall as she came closer. She was almost here. He was almost ready.

"Is that you, Queen Connie?" Reardon asked in a familiar tone. He stepped out of the shadow, directly into Connie's path. He smiled his most friendly smile and waited. What would she say? What would she do?

Connie stopped short and stared. "Why, Ramon! What in the world are you doing here? I thought I left you only a moment ago, paddling down the stream with Heart. However did you get here before me?"

Drat! This was good news and bad news. The good news was that she thought he was Ramon, just the way Reardon had hoped. The bad news was that she knew where Ramon was right now and he couldn't very well be in two places at once. It was something he hadn't thought of. Reardon's mind raced. What was a good reason for him to be there and, how had he done it?

"I know a-a-a shortcut," he stammered. "I knew you'd be comin' this way, so I took a shortcut. In other words, I knew a different way." Reardon was talking very quickly.

How odd, thought Connie. *Ramon always speaks so slowly.*

She had never heard him speak like this. No matter. He seemed to be upset. That was probably why he was speaking strangely. Poor Ramon... What must the problem be?

"Dear, Ramon," Connie said gently. "Is there something wrong? Why did you take the shortcut to find me?" Connie put one of her small hands on Reardon's coarsely furred arm.

Reardon felt trapped. Here he was trying to execute a fiendish plot, and the little Queen was being *nice* to him. How dare she?

Reardon forged ahead. "There was a problem down on the stream. There was a bad accident. A boat tipped over and spilled everythin' into the stream at its deepest part. Everythin' in it went overboard. *Everybody* went overboard, too. So-so-so did King Heart. He sank! He didn't come up. They're out there lookin' fer him now." Reardon blurted. There. He had said it. What would the little Queen do? He waited.

Connie didn't move. She just stood still in the flickering light of her torch and stared at the rat she thought was her friend. Quietly, large tears welled up and spilled from her eyes. She covered her face with her hand.

Reardon watched her. As a rat that no longer liked himself, he refused to feel sorry for this little woman. He was glad that she was shocked. Yes sir! It was about time that this creature knew what it was like to be as miserable as he was. It was way *past* time.

But Reardon had been watching his brother's behavior. He knew what Ramon would do in a situation like this. He could put on an act. That is exactly what he did.

Carefully he reached down and took the torch out of Connie's hand. Easily (he was surprised at just how easily) Reardon picked up the little Queen.

"I will take you to the stream," Reardon stated. Thinking Reardon was Ramon, Connie held on tight to the scruff of his furry neck.

Back at the stream, the second half of The Wretcheds' plot was taking place. Ramon and King Heart were hard at work. Early that morning they had set off downstream in their slipper boat to pick up a load which promised to be very difficult.

It was silverware, heavy, awkward spoons. It was a very rare find and valuable, but also very hard to handle. Clearly, this load would be able to shift quickly and tip over a slipper boat. It was a dangerous mission.

The pair pulled up to the dock at the edge of the stream and hollered for the loading crew. Two very large rats lumbered down to the dock, hands in their pockets and yellow teeth glistening in friendly-appearing grins.

They sauntered over to the boat, giving the impression that they were in no hurry to conduct business this early in the evening. Only their furtive glances from side to side gave away the fact that they were not nearly as casual as they looked.

King Heart was a good judge of character. Something was not right about these two rats, but he couldn't quite put a paw on it.

"Good mornin'," saluted one of the rats in a friendly enough fashion.

"Back at ya," responded Ramon, smiling.

Ramon sees nothing wrong, thought Heart. *Maybe it's just because I don't know these two. I should reserve judgement.*

"I hear you have a pretty big load for us today." King Heart picked up the chatter as he climbed out of the boat.

"Yup. We came upon a whole set of spoons," the biggest rat bragged. "Never seen such a bunch all together like that. And they're real fancy. Word has it that they used ta belong to King Sol at one time years back. We found 'um in a hedge under the Castle window. It was our lucky day."

'I'd say. Let's take a look at 'um and see how many we can take in one load. Where ya got 'um stashed?" asked Ramon. The rats exchanged looks. "Out behind that stack of weeds there," answered the smaller rat. "Why don't you come on back and take a look? We'd like ta move 'um all at once if'n we can."

"Oh, I don't know about that," chuckled Ramon. "Spoons 'r heavy and hard to handle and all we've got is a slipper boat. Let's see what ya got and then we'll decide how many at a time." In his slow, deliberate style, Ramon followed the two strange rats out of sight behind the weeds.

King Heart was still trying to figure out why these rats made him feel uneasy, when the two strangers emerged quickly from behind their stash with concerned looks on their faces.

"Your friend, that big rat, he just had a little accident," they explained to Heart. "He slipped on a hunk 'o slime out back and fell. Looks like he hit his head when he landed. He's out cold."

Heart jumped from the boat and ran to the aid of his friend. Sure enough. There lay Ramon, sprawled out on the mud, unconscious. Heart could see a big goose egg already rising over his left ear.

Heart knelt over him for a closer look. He didn't look badly hurt… just knocked out. Pulling a hanky out of his pocket, Heart wetted it in the cold stream and applied it to Ramon's goose egg. Ramon groaned a little but did not awaken.

"Looks like your friend is going to be out for a while," commented the large rat. "Maybe I should see if I can find another boat for transport. We gotta get this load upstream by noon. We got a buyer waitin'."

King Heart looked at poor Ramon, sprawled out on the mud. He looked at the spoons stacked nearby, glistening in the moonlight. Ramon would be so disappointed to lose this job. He had been planning on this big load. He would be upset when he woke up to find that the business had gone to someone else.

Suddenly King Heart knew what he had to do. He had to take this load, himself. He could do it, but it wouldn't be easy. The spoons were so big and heavy that he was going to have to take them in his slipper boat one at a time. It would take until morning if he started right away but he was sure he could do it. He would do it for Ramon.

Heart made up his mind. "Don't worry about finding another boat," he declared. "I will take the load, myself. I'll have to make many trips, but, if I start right now, I should be able to get the entire cargo there before the sun comes up. I don't want Ramon to lose this load."

This was perfect. It was working out just the way Reardon had said it would. "Great!" grinned the large rat, almost too quickly. And then he added with forced sincerity, "I'll even help ya load and go with ya."

King Heart was grateful. Dipping his hanky in the stream one more time and pressing it to Ramon's head, he reassured himself that he was doing the right thing. Struggling with his end, he helped the big rat load a heavy spoon onto his boat and pushed off toward the center of the stream.

King Heart began poling his boat slowly but steadily upstream, watching for wayward currents. He was so intent on his work, that he didn't notice what the big rat was doing behind him. Living a life with no positive feelings at all had left this rat completely uncaring about anyone other than himself. What he was about to do did not bother him.

Without making a sound, the rat tied the belt sash of King Heart's robe around the end of the spoon that they were transporting. Suddenly the rat stood up in the boat, violently shifting his weight in the little craft!

"What are you doing? What is happening?" Heart yelled as he slid across the boat, landing on his side. But it was too late. The large rat leaned in the way that the boat was tipping. That was all that was needed. Water spilled in over the side of the slipper, allowing the spoon to scoop down into the stream and out of sight, dragging King Heart with it.

The large rat now dove in after the spoon, yelling "Help! Help!" and splashing violently in a make-believe attempt to rescue the little King. The rat did not feel bad, but he was not above acting like he did, just for show.

But, of course, the rat had tied Heart firmly to the spoon and he could safely assume that both were now washing away downstream. With mock sadness and a face full of water that looked very much like tears, the Wretched Rat dragged himself out of the stream and collapsed upon the bank.

"I tried to save 'im, but it all happened so fast." he moaned.

Scraps and rats began diving frantically after King Heart, but, they couldn't find him…not even the spoon, As they raised themselves to the surface and swung onto a larger boot boat that had been brought for the purpose, a revived Ramon staggered crookedly to the shore and wept for King Heart and his own inability to protect the little King.

At the same time, Reardon, intent on his side of the horrible plot, progressed with strange and unexpected emotions toward the upper bank overlooking the stream. He was uncomfortably aware that he was carrying the little Queen to her well-planned doom.

When should I do away with her? Should I do it now? Should I do it at all? His mind tumbled as he was becoming confused. The little Queen was talking in his ear.

"Thank you so much for carrying me so quickly, Ramon. You are such a good friend. Heart and I do not know what we would have done without you over these years. You and your friends have kept Scraps alive to reach their destiny. I only hope that my beloved Heart has been saved and will live to see that day!"

As Reardon reached the edge of the cliff above the stream, it became obvious, even from a distance, that a deep and sorrowful mourning had already begun among the Scraps and rats below. All were gathered together, staring sadly into the gurgling water, hugging each other and sobbing.

"He's gone, isn't he?" Queen Connie murmured as she peered down over the cliff's rim. "My sweet Heart is gone. He will never be able to see his son rise up to help the world."

"How could a stupid little Scrap runt help the world, anyway?"

It just popped out of Reardon's mouth before he knew he had said it. Now, for the first time, Connie turned her tear stained face towards Reardon and really looked at him. Ramon would never have said such a thing. This was not Ramon.

Reardon turned his eyes away. He could not bear to look into the hurt and discovery that he saw reflected in the eyes of the little Queen. When he looked again, she was still staring at him. She didn't blink.

"No," he blurted. "I'm not Ramon! I am Reardon, Ramon's twin." Reardon closed his eyes again, unwilling to see the fury that was sure to be directed at him.

Nothing happened.

He opened his eyes. Queen Connie was still looking at him sadly... and looking through to all his stored up, evil thoughts.

"You poor thing. You have been living alone in the shadows without your brother all this time, haven't you? What was it that kept you apart from Ramon? You must have been so hurt and angry. Come, let us both go down to the stream together to mourn the loss of my dear husband and the love of your brother, lost to you over all these years. Come. We should go together."

The power of the tenderness in that statement was too much for Reardon. He had been ready to *kill* this little Queen. She didn't know that, of course. But *he* knew what his partners in crime had already done to King Heart. How could this tiny woman look into his face with kindness?

Reardon reached down into his soul and released a shriek full of so much pain that it rose above the crying of all the Scraps and rats below.

Howling forth from his huge rat chest came a sound of such total misery that no one could mistake its horrible source. Everyone on the bank of the stream looked up just in time to see Reardon fling *himself* from the cliff to the Riverbank far below.

Everyone was shocked, incredulous and then hushed.

Reardon did not die right away from his fall. He was lying there on the Bank of the stream, mangled and ruined, but he was still awake, as his brother, Ramon, came to his side.

They hadn't seen each other since the fire. Reardon brokenly confessed everything, including how the other Wretcheds had been involved in King Sol's 'accident'. A huge posse of rats took out after them immediately.

Ramon was distraught about what his brother had done. Finding him after all these years, losing him again now as well as losing King Heart... nothing was making sense to him. The huge rat began sobbing. He was ashamed and embarrassed and sad and mad, all at the same time.

Queen Connie walked over to Reardon and Ramon and she got down on the muddy stream bank with them. She was not young any more. It was not easy for her to get down there, but she did it. She picked up one big paw from each of the brothers and they all three cried together.

"Ramon, don't hate your brother," she told him. "Reardon was consumed by hate for himself all these years and had no one to talk it over with. There has been too much hate and violence, already. You brothers need to forgive each other before it is too late. King Heart would have wished it."

Ramon buried his head in his brother's fur and cried. No one stirred.

Then Queen Connie spoke again.

"My wonderful Heart would have wanted us all to forgive Reardon for what he has done. Reardon is truly sorry, aren't you Reardon?" Reardon nodded weakly. He was fading fast.

"We all forgive you, Reardon. You had no one to help you decide right from wrong. It was not completely your fault. And as for you, Ramon, there is nothing to forgive. You are a loyal brother and a true friend."

Fireflies swarmed in the evening sky over the River. The inhabitants of The Sew were in mourning. Spirit, too, arrived to mourn the loss of King Heart, one of the first Scraps he had ever known...and the birth father of the little being he hoped would complete his complex and difficult Plan for Goodness.

In spite of Spirit's un-ending admiration for Scrap abilities, in this moment, a sudden fear crept into his thinking. Queen Connie was alone now. Would Prince Sol's preparation for life as a support for human Goodness be able to continue without both Scrap parents to guide him? He had no idea.

After King Heart

- as recorded by Maximilian Mouse
(The ancient Moses Mouse died peacefully but
passed his recording duties to his grandson.)

It was some time before life in The Sew
returned to the pattern that everyone grew
to expect with the comforting rhythm of regular days
with their regular work and their regular ways.

Queen Connie, now aging, watched over her son,
in the way that she and her husband had done.
She was determined, as mother and wife,
to complete this great task that would honor Heart's life.

And as time went by, what was true remained true.
Sol continued to 'grow up' but, in size, never grew.
As a prince the same size as the tiniest mouse,
he continued the friendships he'd made through the 'house'.

Bugs were still buddies and rodents, good friends,
friendships on which such a small life depends.

Sol also kept friendships with the whole Castle staff.
He learned what they liked and what made them laugh.
And they all learned together about give and take.
Now they all made decisions that one needs to make

and made them with fairness. Each tried to see
what kind of Good person each person could be.

Queen Connie watched and encouraged this turn
of events. She saw that all this would help her son learn.
But, what else did he need? He was a young man.
What would make him most ready to take on the Plan?

Queen Connie thought and thought. Then she suddenly knew
what her grown son lacked still, what experience was due.
She had at last discovered what she had left to do.
Sol had no book learning!

She must take action. The time had now come.
Sol needed more learning than he could get from
his friends. Sol was smart, but he had never quite
sat down to learn how to read or to write.

What?

True!

So, Queen Connie spoke up for her non-reading son.
And delivered a message. (It had to be done.)
She spoke to Queen Luna in her own special way,
concerned but intent upon what she should say.

"Your son has grown up. I know that you've seen
that he's now a young man and as good as he's been,
content to stay here, quite protected from all,
your son must learn more to become a 'King Sol'.

"He must learn of the world. This is what he will need
to become a true leader. He must now learn to read."

Queen Luna listened, though she didn't know it.
She heard Connie's truth. She took no time to show it.

She hitched up her skirts and went straight to King Sol.
(Queens need to grow up, themselves, after all!)

"My dear", she began, "We've protected our boy.
He has given us love. He's our pride and joy.
But I have now noticed, since he's become older,
I believe that it's time for us to get bolder.

"I no longer see, upon further inspection,
that our dear son needs quite so much protection.
He is friends with our staff. They are People of size,
and it may be quite past time that I realize
that he needs a good tutor to teach him to read."

(King Sol had tried several times before
to allow other trainers inside Castle doors,
but fearful Queen Luna had always denied
the admittance of strangers with the Prince to be tried.)

Luna was pleased when King Sol agreed.
At last, *both* King Sol and his Queen saw the need.
It was time for Prince Sol to learn how to read
and learn of the history that he'd surely need
to be a great King and be ready to lead.

King Sol sent his servants to search far and wide
and find that *first stranger to welcome inside*
and give needed instruction to their precious son.
Of course, they must choose the 'most suitable one'.

The Queen said 'just anyone' would surely not suit her.
"Sol needs the *right person*, not just any tutor.
There are few River People who will meet my strict test.
From our River People, we must choose the best."

King Sol contemplated the Queen's change of plan.

What was needed to help his young son be a man?
Just who would I choose if I was Prince Sol,
to be the *'first stranger from outside our wall?*
Since poor Sol has been all his life here alone,
he deserves a *young* tutor and not an old crone.

"For safety, this Castle has been our son's cage,
so he needs a young tutor who is close to his age,
someone with whom he can speak and relate
but... someone who's *safe* to bring inside our gate."

"Aha!" smiled Queen Luna, "I know one to try!
On a day many years ago, she caught my eye.
A lovely young girl who is, if I recall,
just a bit older than our dear son, Sol.

"Her father's a Teacher. I'm quite sure that he
has brought up his daughter to where she could be
a wonderful tutor. At least we should see
what kind of a person she has turned out to be."

King Sol was quite willing to accept this plan.
He knew that his son, to become a real man,
needed book learning. His son should be schooled.
(A king should know more than the People he ruled.)

Learning from someone his own age could be
much less of a chore than most tutors might be.

Queen Connie watched the Royals from her place
in the rafters above Queen Luna's bright face.

"It's amazing," she thought. "how this Queen, King and I
now think quite alike, seem to see eye to eye.
It's almost as though we three are now one
and can truly agree on what needs to be done."

Queen Connie thought back. King Heart had not been
with her that day when she saw the Yesmen
and the Teacher she'd noticed all those years before
who had carried his daughter through the great throne room door
to confront a mad King and to most clearly state
that his love for *his daughter* was why he was late.

It was he that the Yesmen chose then to conspire
and accuse him of starting what was called 'The Great Fire'.
She remembered the father then standing his ground
and how his young daughter on that day had found
Queen Luna's heart and suggest what was right.
Her presence had changed her father's sad plight
Queen Connie wished that her dear King Heart knew
that Queen Luna remembered that sweet history, too.

Connie smiled at the memory.

"I remember that child and her father so well.
He loved his daughter, it was easy to tell.
He was one of the People who had a head start
on the Goodness we wish was in everyone's heart."

"As a Teacher himself, he has cared for the need
to teach River People to learn how to read
as well as his daughter. I also believe
she must have the learning our son should receive."

"Her father was caring. I know that was true.
If he passed on that nature, she'll be caring too.
Of all River People, she may be the one
who has knowledge and heart to work well with our son."

That night, Connie dreamed a good dream of King Heart.
I wish he could be here to be a real part
of this next preparation, this part of the Plan
that our son must receive now to make him a man.

In her dream, Heart agreed. He smiled down to say,
I agree with your judgment. You were most wise today.
Sol must know history. He must understand
how to fight for the right things, planned and unplanned,
how such battles were fought before he becomes King.
Such knowledge as this is an important thing.

In her dream, King Heart seemed to be charmed by the tale
of the young girl whose upbringing might just prevail,
to teach their dear son both to read and to write
and learn from past writings about wrong and right.

Soft, in her dream, she heard that Heart said,
The balance of history must live in his head.
He will learn all of this from the things that he's read.
This knowledge from reading will widen his mind
so we must find this tutor that you wish to find.

Connie dreamed that King Heart smiled and sent out the word.
It was then that a *most* strange occurrence occurred!

Through the cosmos, the Teacher *and* his daughter heard
that the King needed help and without hesitation
the girl walked to the Castle without invitation.

She looked at the guards standing firm at the door
of the Castle that night. She had been here before.
"I believe there is, in this Castle, indeed,
a need for a tutor. Is there such a need?"

Then Connie's dream faded. She smiled, half asleep.
She missed her King Heart with a love true and deep.
But without knowing how, Queen Connie now knew
that the dream she had dreamed would soon become true.

Queen Connie was grateful. She was relieved.
She had done her best, and she now believed
King Heart, too, was happy. They both had been tested.
Queen Connie relaxed. Quite warm now, she rested
with trust in her son, now at peace and content.

The Fireflies were gathering. She knew what that meant.
She would soon be with Heart. They would now send their love
to their young, learning son, from somewhere above.

The very next morning, just before dawn,
Scrap friends looked for Connie, but Connie was gone.

Spirit came by. With true sadness, he knew
how much grateful respect for this Scrap Queen was due.
With his own love and caring, he bid her adieu
as into the cosmos a new Scrap angel flew.

But Spirit feared for the future. Connie's wisdom was prized.
Prince Sol was alone now. Spirit realized
that Sol had now lost all the calm supervision
that Scrap parents had given to his Goodness mission.

How would Sol be guided? He was just a young man.
How would he discover his part in the Goodness Plan?

Then Spirit saw them. He suddenly knew.
Sparkling and dancing above morning dew,
in the warm glow of sunshine, *two* Fireflies flew.

Enter Awake

- by Maximilien Mouse

Before a request could be sent by King Sol,
a guard told Queen Luna that, outside the wall,
a young girl was waiting. She had told them, indeed,
that she was a tutor, the one they might need.

The Queen was surprised and quite shocked to receive
something she wanted but she did not believe
that she had yet asked for. She had no idea how
the tutor she wanted was right there, right now!

But she did not question just how this took place.
She smiled and accepted the young girl with grace.
"Come into the Castle," Luna said with a smile
and offered a seat to the girl with some style.

Queen Luna recognized that this girl, indeed,
was the girl she remembered, the tutor she'd need.

The young girl remembered Queen Luna, as well
...from a family tale that her dad liked to tell.

"My name is Awake. I've been told that you need
a person to teach your young son how to read."

King Sol looked happily at this addition.
For years he had wanted Queen Luna's permission
to widen the world of his treasure, Prince Sol
and prepare him for "Kingship" that someday would call.
This tutor was young and just right for Prince Sol.

"I can do that," she whispered. "When should we begin?
May I meet the Prince?" She tried hard not to grin.

Awake knew well, like the rest of her clan,
that there was no Prince, no *actual* young man.
But she was still willing to at least play her part
and pretend that she saw a real prince from the start.
She believed that there really was no prince at all,
but she felt it her duty to be loyal to King Sol.
(He had not killed her father back then, after all.)

Imagine her shock. The King pointed and said,
"Look here. You will find our small son on my head."

Awake blinked her eyes and then started to stare
for there *was* Prince Sol standing in his dad's hair!

"Speak up! said King Sol. "Let her see that you're there!"
Sol felt shy at first but soon he didn't care.

"Hello. I'm Prince Sol," he said when he was able
as he jumped from his father's head onto the table.
"I know that I'm small but I might be quite smart.
What shall I learn first? Tell me, when can we start?"

Without saying a word, Awake stretched out her hand
with the palm facing up so that Prince Sol could stand
in her palm and Sol jumped there without thinking twice.
He studied her face. Hey...she looked pretty nice.
Raising her hand (and Sol) up to her face,
she smiled. "Do you know of a good reading place?"
she asked as she carried Sol off toward the door.

Sol grinned.
"Space is one thing we have. We've got space galore."
And off went the pair, him riding, her walking.
Nose to nose, down the hall, they could hear the two talking.

Spirit was stunned. He didn't know how
all this had happened, right here and right now.
He remembered this girl from the long-ago day.

How did she know she should come here this way
and offer her services to this Scrap, Prince Sol?

Then Spirit thought, *'Fireflies!'* He knew, after all.

Prince Sol was very, very real! This was Awake's surprise.
At first Awake just stared at him and then she rubbed her eyes.
He looked like River People, a handsome, bright young man,
but he was as small as an insect and could sit upon her hand.

How could she teach a young man of this size?
How fast could he learn things? She must improvise.

So, using the items around Castle halls,
she made unique lessons to use for Prince Sol.

With seeds she taught arithmetic, how to add and multiply.
He swung from a hook to read each book. He looked like he could fly.
Over the page he dangled, tied to the end of a string.
"Give me a push!" young Sol shouted as he began to swing.
Sol enjoyed every moment, sailing like a bird,
but even more surprising, Sol was reading every word.

Awake taught Sol to write next, but his script was too small to read.
She strapped some lead to each of his feet and he learned to skate with speed.
Then he skated his letters onto the page, a new writing style, indeed.
Awake would laugh at the notes he wrote when he left them for her to read.

"What important things are you writing, boy?" She lifted him in her hand.
"I wrote it clear, Awake, my friend. What don't you understand?
And don't call me 'boy'. I am a man. We are almost the same age.
And soon I'll know as much as you. Now, please just turn the page."

He frequently leapt from a table top and landed in her hair.
Awake would laugh at the things Sol did. "Sol, you don't play fair!
I know you are somewhere on my head. I know you're there, but where?"

Sol would jump back down to the printed page
while Awake scowled at him with pretended rage
and before they discovered or either one knew,
while learning and playing, a fine friendship grew.

For hours they read and discussed every thought.
They argued and chatted as all young folks ought
to mature and grow up with ideas of their own
but Sol was still tiny. No, he still hadn't grown.

King Sol and his Queen were pleased to see
that this mismatched pair got along happily.
And, little by little, Awake came to be
much loved and a part of the Royal Family.

But King Sol sighed, "Why does this have to be?
Awake is a wonderful girl, I can see.
She would make a fine wife for a youth of her size,
but I feel Sol's affection for her is not wise.

"She is Sol's Teacher, a tutor, a friend,
but I fear that this 'friendship' may meet a sad end.
There's no way that Sol can be more than a friend.
She may break his heart in a way that won't mend.
"We have accepted his size as a fact,
but that isn't the way that most others react.
What kind of romance can there ever be
for a man who's as tiny and fragile as he?

"He *will* be a king because he is my son
though his rule will be hard and not easily done.
Awake is a beauty. Awake is a catch,
but not for our son. Sol is not a good match.

"How will our son ever look for and find
a girl who is more of his rare, tiny kind."

Queen Luna said, "We must just wait and see.
Things will work out as they're meant to be."
Then Luna smiled. Her feelings were clear.
"Don't worry about our son's love life, my dear."

CONSCIENCES—AND THE LEGENDS OF THE BIG GAME

Lessons progressed and Sol learned very fast,
so happy was he to be reading at last.
Sol loved to discuss every book that he read.
With Awake he would question what every book said.
They read and discussed every good book and bad
until they had read every book the King had.

There were victories and exploits of Kings that had passed,
stories of battles (where the foes came in last),
stories of heroes, (most of them kings),
tales of beheadings and most gruesome things.
There were volumes of intrigue and glorious war
and histories of conquests and bloodshed galore.

Sol stared from the window sill, gazing afar.
"I wonder just what other books that there are.
Our books are all war tales and gruesome, indeed.
I wish there were other books that we could read.

"We've read every book here. We've read them all."
Sol and Awake sat alone in the hall.
They were both very young, but she seemed a bit older.
Sol peered past the gate, quite relaxed on her shoulder.
She had lived in the real world that he'd never known.

"I need to know more. I have been too alone.
I've read the Royal Library," mumbled Prince Sol,
but that's the Royal point of view. I'm sure that's not all.

"Are there other books somewhere that I haven't read,
books with different views instead
of the views of Royals and what their side has said?"

Awake laughed out loud and then nodded her head.
"There are thousands more books in the Kingdom!" she said.

"There are?" exclaimed Sol as he rolled from his seat,
slid down her arm and jumped to his feet.

"If there are, as you say, lots more books to be found,
why are we here, still just sitting around?
Where should we go first? Where should we look?
Let's go on a book-hunt and find some more books!"

"You're right!" said Awake. "That's just what we need.
I should go out and find you some *good* books to read."

Awake began planning what she could do.
"Once a week I will travel the whole Kingdom through,
searching and snooping each cranny and nook
and asking the town folk to loan me *their* books
to bring back to you so that you can learn more.
That's just what a good friend and tutor is for.

"I'll borrow their books so that we can both read.
In this way, we'll have all the books that we need."

"And I will go, too." added Sol with a grin.
"Together we'll find all the books hidden in
every niche in a wall, every book shelf and hole.
We will find every book that there is! That's our goal!"

But Sol's plan was flawed as Sol clearly knew.
This was a plan that Prince Sol couldn't do.
Prince Sol was excited... but then hung his head.
"I'm a prisoner here, aren't I?" he gloomily said.
"It just isn't right and it's no longer fair.
There's a world I don't know about waiting out there.

"I am *a Prince!* Someday I'll be a King!
How can I rule if I don't know a thing
about the big world that is outside this hall?"

He strained to see out, far beyond the rock wall
that surrounded the Castle but saw not much at all.
He only saw clouds and the birds flying by.
He shut his eyes tight and wished *he* could fly.

Awake felt his sadness. She now knew his pain.
Although he was sad now, he wouldn't complain.
He had, all his life, done what he was told,
but his 'over-safe' life had become very old.

Someday, she knew, he would challenge the rule.
There would come a time soon when this cage was too cruel.
She knew that Prince Sol must go out on his own
to explore all the dangers that he'd never known.
He'd then break for freedom. He'd break with his past
and meet outside evils. That future was cast.
She just hoped his first freedom would not be his last.

"You won't take me, will you?" mourned poor Prince Sol.
Awake remained silent, said nothing at all
but shook her head slowly and hid her sad face.
She was only a servant. It was not her place.

The Book Hunter

So, Awake went alone on her excursions,
traveling the countryside, looking for versions
of ideas that Prince Sol had not heard before.
Sol read all the new books and clamored for more.

Good folks of the town had no trouble sharing
the books they had hidden into this tutor's caring.
They knew her father and the Teacher he'd been
so they trusted Awake to bring books back again.

"They're for the Prince, too," was 'the joke' that they heard.
They didn't suspect the real truth of her word.

Sol's lonely life was not perfection
but Awake and her books now gave him a connection
to all River People and what they'd been doing,
thinking and learning...loving and wooing.

He studied their stories, remembering each one,
the hopes that they had had for each daughter and son,
some plans that had worked and some more that had not,
each hope for survival and each counter plot.

Happiness stories were in short supply.
Sol dreamed of ideas that he someday might try.
"If I get a good chance, I think that I could
offer some thoughts that I think might be good.
I would sure like to help folks. I wish that I could."

His thoughts about life were now growing and churning.
With every new book, Prince Sol was learning.

Spirit was watching. To him it was clear.
Sol's time as Scrap Leader might be getting near.
But how would he do it? Was Prince Sol that wise?
Would his knowledge and learning make up for his size?

When should Sol start on his mission in life?
Would the world fall apart first? Was there too much strife?
How would he learn what was planned as his duty
to join The Big Game, Spirit's planet of beauty?

Sol had always been *inside*. How could it be
that he'd find his place in the earth's destiny?
Spirit was worried. He watched close to see
just when or *what* Prince Sol's future would be.

Sol was meant to help humans but he didn't know many.
He was meant to lead Scraps but he'd never met *any*.
He was meant to *share* Goodness but with whom and where?
Poor Spirit wished that Sol's Scrap folks were there
to show him the future that he couldn't see,
what Sol should be doing to achieve destiny.

Queen Connie had known how this job should be done,
to change Sol from his role as 'obedient son'
to a Leader for Goodness. She was the one
who had the vision of intricate ways
to take the next steps. Spirit now spent his days
trying to learn how this sheltered Scrap man
could change to 'Scrap Leader' as had been the Plan.

The Brothers

At a bend in the River, just over the hill,
lived two Storytellers of rather ill will.
They were sons of a Yesman who in earlier times
had been banished down River for undisclosed crimes.
Their family had lived there and scratched out a way
to just stay alive as they could, day to day.

As boys, they'd decided, with their future delayed,
they couldn't be farmers. They would need a new trade.
Storytelling might do for a trade they could share
and eke out a living where no one would care
just where they came from or how they got there.

Fighter discovered them. He had been looking
among outcasts down River to see what was cooking.
He searched among those who felt they had been wronged,
disgruntled rejects who hadn't belonged
to a cohort of Yesmen who would stand up and say
that they were *not guilty* of 'that crime' 'that day'.

Fighter approved of the way these boys lived.
They told gossip and lies. They had hogwash to give.
They were crude and dishonest, which Fighter respected.
Their stories of intrigue were never rejected.
Did they plow or plant, work hard or hustle?
No. They both took great pride in not moving a muscle.

They destroyed reputations much more than they ought,
but they were quite crafty and seldom got caught.
And Fighter applauded the trouble they brought.
These boys have promise, he happily thought.

They would both sit and listen to all they could hear
of tall tales and rumors from both far and near.

Then they would change them, "add to" and "improve"
and work these fake stories right into their groove
to create the wild tales that would make listeners move
and dig into their pockets to pull out a dime
or bring a meal out to them, time after time.

Then they would gleefully act out their story,
with vigor and props just to make it more gory.
Even better, at times, a fake story or lie
stirred up bloody fist fights in listeners nearby.
These boys were recruits now for Fighter to try.

"These are my new players. They could be my best,
the kind of recruits I can put to the test
to rile up the People and unleash the unrest
that might start up violence or even a war,
the Game-winning climax that I've waited for.

With me as their coach, these guys cannot lose.
They already stir battles with only 'fake news'."

The brothers were named "Brother Brood, Brother Grin."
Their names were like labels of what lay within.
Brood was the worst with a 'strong arm' projected.
Grin wore a sweet manner that he had perfected.

Today they were sprawled by the side of road
with a full stash of gossip and lies to unload,
waiting to share all the "news of the day"
with anyone able and willing to pay.

Today was quite slow, with Brother Brood napping.
Fighter hovered above, knowing something might happen
because he had spotted a girl passing by
with a satchel of books. She caught Brother Grin's eye.
This brother was handsome, not allowing to pass
any lady of interest, much less this young lass.

Grin smiled and slicked his hair a bit, a patented approach
that usually scored approval, while Fighter, now 'the Coach',
watched from above, very eager to see
what these scoundrels would do, what their moves might be.

"Hey, hey!" whispered Grin. "I like this one's looks.
I wonder why she has that big load of books."
Now Grin put together his most charming charm
and reached out to tap this sweet thing on the arm.

"Do I know you?" she asked, stepping back from his touch.
She smiled, but she didn't trust men very much.

Her soft little smile made Grin's heart jump for joy.
(It didn't take much to stir up this young boy.)

"Please pardon me, Pretty, for my 'forwardness sin'
and allow me to tell you that my name is Grin.
I call you 'Pretty', for pretty thou art,
but I never intended to give you a start."

Grin tipped his hat and then bowed from the waist.
This sweet, lovely miss was just right to his taste.

(Fighter kicked back now to watch for a while.
"This guy is smooth with a great con-man style.")

"From where do you travel upon this fine morn
with a satchel of books, all alone and forlorn?"

"I return to the Castle. I've been gone half the day.
I'm a tutor by trade. That's how I earn my way."

Grin smiled again broadly. "A tutor, you say?
Where ever did you find a pupil who'd pay?
Most folk nearby plant seeds or grow hay."

Awake knew of reading and numbers and such,
but she didn't know ways of the world very much.
She wanted to show this young man with the smile
that *she* was mature, a young woman of style
who was *not* going to 'just stop and chat for a while'.

"You see, Mr. Grin," she said, straightening her dress,
"I'm employed by the King. I'm 'The Royal Governess'.
Now, if you'd be so kind and if you'd be so good
as to let me pass by, I do wish that you would."

Bingo!

Fighter came to attention. This girl might have dirt
on the lives in the Castle! Fighter now came alert.

This girl lives in the Castle? How could he have missed it?
And she says that she 'works for the King?' Fighter could not resist it.
The Royals had been too quiet. They had been so for years.
Fighter geared up and snuck nearer. He was now all ears.

"The Royal Governess?" Grin smiled, scratching his chin.
"I would like to hear more of the work that you're in,
not to mention the Where and the What and the Who.
Yes, I'm very impressed by the work that you do."

He glanced at his brother who was, of course, near
and now quite awake. He was straining to hear.
Brood came alive with fake yawning and blinking
which was meant to disguise the intrigue he was thinking.

"You say that you're teaching the King how to read?
That's quite fascinating. Tell me, how can he lead?
A king who can't read is a story, indeed."
Brood moved in more closely to pay this girl heed.

He loved to make the Royals a joke.
These stories played well with the commoner folk.
Awake glared at Brood as she moved to pass by,
returning the bold look of Brood, eye to eye.

"How dare you," she sniffed, "even think such a thing?
You haven't the right to make fun of our King!
Of course, the King reads! Please don't be absurd.
And so does his son. The Prince reads every word."

"'His son'?" (Fighter couldn't believe what he heard.)

Awake continued with gusto, looking Brood in the eye.
"Don't insult our King now. I say, don't even try.
King Sol is brilliant as a good King should be.
To imply that he isn't sounds like treason to me."

One might be surprised to hear Awake state
her defense of King Sol in a tone so irate,
but Awake had also, by now, come to feel
love for the Royals that she did not conceal.

With a tone most sincere, she defended her King.
Grin and Brood listened, not 'doubting' a thing.

Brood smirked a bit and then shook his head.
"I'm only repeating the words that you said.
You said you're "Royal Governess." Why am I bold?
I'm only repeating the story *you* told."

"I did not mean 'the King'!" spoke Awake with a shout.
"You, sir, are a cad, an uncivilized lout!"

(Brood shrugged and sneered, but Grin warmly smiled.
Brood often was rude while Grin was more mild.
This was a 'play' each had shared since a child.)

"Brood means nothing bad," said Grin very sweetly.
"I don't think that he understood you completely.
Please, sit for a spell and explain everything
that you wish to make clear for His Honor, the King."

Awake slowly sat, giving Brood a side look.
In her heart she suspected that Brood was a crook,
but Grin was the brother she thought she could trust.
She would speak in defense of her King now. She must.
(She had never been taught to avoid the real dangers
that can suddenly come when you're talking to strangers.)

"Well, you see," she related as she sat prim and tall.
"It isn't the King that I teach. It's Prince Sol."

Fighter was listening and watching it all.
He let out a wind gust that shook nearby trees.
It stirred up the dust. It was not a small breeze.
This was talk of 'the Prince' whom all knew was not real.
What crazy tales would this young girl reveal?

Grin grabbed his hat as it blew off his head.
Fighter crept near to hear all that was said.

"Prince Sol?" hooted Brood. "What lies are you telling?
Your story's a fish and that fish is smelling!
We know of your King. His story is old.
The King's fair but crazy! It's a story we've told
many times, many ways. He thinks he's a father
but your King is a nut! There's *no Prince*, so don't bother
to tell us lies, Governess. Hear what I say!"
And with that, Brood just snickered and then walked away.

"But I'm not telling lies!" Awake almost snorted.
"Have you never heard of the small Prince reported
born to our Kingdom some twenty years past?
I am *that* Prince's tutor!" she blurted at last.

"I've taught him to read! He reads books by the score!
Now I journey the country side, trying to find more.
He's smart and he's nice and he's funny and kind
and he reads and discusses each book I find.
Until the wee hours, he reads every night
and studies to learn what is wrong and what's right.

"These books that I bring, tell what thinkers think.
To the rest of the world, these books are his link.
He's a very real person, just like you and I.
But, in truth, he is only as big as a fly."

The brothers both listened and glanced at each other.
A plot started forming inside of each brother.
And, soaring above, Fighter heard what he sought.
He knew these two boys were concocting a plot.
That was their practice. Yes...that was their style
of tricks and deception. Fighter started to smile.

CONSCIENCES—AND THE LEGENDS OF THE BIG GAME

"Now, now, my dear," said Grin. "Don't be upset.
We believe what you tell us here. That you can bet."
A chaotic evil now settled around
the young Storytellers that Fighter had found.

Brood pulled his brother aside and he said,
"We know of King Sol. He's not right in the head.
He thinks there's a Prince and the town plays along
but this tired old story has gone on too long.

"It looks like this tutor is part of the show.
She *pretends* there's a prince, although why, I don't know.
A kingdom whose king isn't right in the head
must be ripe for the picking. Do you hear what I said?"

Grin whispered back while Brood huddled near,
"I believe that I do see your point, brother dear.
This pretty young lass may just be the key
to a much finer life ahead for you and for me.

"Two men like ourselves, have true wisdom and wit.
For much higher stations in life, we are fit.
It's not really right that fine men such as we
are destined to live in exiled poverty.
Though this prince can't be real, it appears this girl must
live *inside* the Castle and have the King's trust."

Brood nodded. "And I have a plan that's a pearl!
We two, you and I, will make friends with this girl,
a friendship that shows our trustworthy perfection.
We'll waltz into the Castle, no fear of rejection
as this tutor's 'friends'. We'll need no inspection.
And how do we do this?............ We'll offer *protection*!

"*We'll* be her saviors! We'll 'save her' today!
The King will be grateful to us, I must say.

And once in the Castle, we can easily do
whatever our brilliant minds think of to do.

"As 'Fearless Protectors' of this governess,
the King will adore us. We'll be heroes, no less.
And, after we tell our tale of protection,
we can stir up the town folk to grand insurrection!
We'll be in position to lead and to rule!
This plan is great and this girl is our tool!
Wahoo!

Fighter looked down on these two with great pride.
He *loved* all the violence this plot implied.
He blew swirls of evil glee into the skies.
This plot would be perfect! A revolt would arise!

Revolt in the Castle! What a joy to behold!
What Fighter had dreamed of was soon to unfold!
These men were the key for which Fighter was waiting.
This plot was perfect. There was no understating.

The world would erupt from one end to the other.
Chaos would reign. There could be no other
result from this plot if it went as was planned
and Fighter, at long last, would take full command
of all of the cosmos as he had foretold.
Fighter lit up! This Game Plan was pure gold!

Awake sat there innocently, patiently waiting.
She could not suspect the plot they were creating.
Brood beamed with excitement, his eyes bright and wild.
He'd not been this happy since he was a child.

Grin agreed with his brother. He had made up his mind,
but one part of Brood's plan Grin still needed to find.

"Your idea is simple. Indeed, it's perfection,
but *from what* does this governess need our protection?"

"Just watch this!" hissed Brood. "Just watch my style!"
He twisted his face into *almost* a smile.
"Please tell us, dear Governess. Please tell us true.
What does a small prince's governess *do*?
You've convinced us he's real, but you have not said since
why you are traveling so far for your prince.
You may work for a prince that's as small all a rose,
but you shouldn't be traveling alone, goodness knows!"

"Do tell us all," added Grin. "Please confess
why 'book finding' is done by a Royal Governess."

Now Awake flushed with a glow of deep red.
She really liked Grin and she liked what he said.
She felt, from Grin, she had nothing to dread.
She responded, "It's true that there is a Prince Sol
but it's also quite true that he *is* very small.
Although he's almost too tiny to see,
he's smart and he learns very quickly, you see.

"He's stuck in the Castle and cannot go out,
but he wants to learn what the world is about.
So, I bring him books and we read them together,
day time and night time, no matter the weather.
And, when we're through reading, I head for the door
to take the books back and go looking for more.

"The King and the Queen say he must stay inside.
There's risk for my Prince in the large world outside."

Then Awake smiled and she added demurely,
"You don't think *I'm* in danger on this road, now, surely?"

"Not from us," Brood replied with fake indignation.
"You have our respect, as befits your high station.
But I must admit that you cause me to wonder.
Don't *you* fear the dangers you find yourself under?"

"Dangers? What dangers?" said Awake with a gasp,
her fingers beginning to clasp and unclasp.

"Why, the dangers from highwaymen!" offered up Brood.
"Men of pure evil who are ruthless and crude.
They lurk all along these remote hillside passes,
just waiting to pounce on unwary young lasses."

"Oh my!" Awake sputtered. "Good heavens! Oh dear!
I had no idea I had reason to fear!
What do you gentlemen think I should do?
I must travel safe, to and fro, fro and to.
To find Prince Sol's books, I must go far and near
but what you say now really fills me with fear."

Fighter was laughing. "This plot is too rich!
These boys' tale of 'danger's' is an excellent pitch.
Now they'll offer *protection*." Fighter saw it all clear.
"Not one thing works faster or will better endear
these men to this girl than the prospect of fear!"

"To be sure, you shouldn't be traveling alone,"
agreed Brood, with a warning sigh, clear to the bone.
"You *should be* protected, but that's your decision.
Do you need these new books to retain your position?"

"Will the King fire you?" asked Grin. "Do you see
that these books are important to the young King-to-be?
Do these books really matter to him? Do you know?
If there were no books, would it be a great blow?
If there were no books... would they ask you to... go?"

Awake heard these questions and suddenly knew.
Tears came to her eyes. What they both said was true.
If she couldn't get books, then what would she do?
Her job might be gone. And then, what about Sol?
These books were his link to life outside the wall.
Sol would feel deserted if this became true
and her trips to find books were quite suddenly through.

She was not just Sol's tutor. Awake was his friend.
For the sake of their friendship, book trips couldn't end!

Fighter watched for the plotting below to unfold.
He knew there was more of this scheme to be told.

Then suddenly, the way that a sunny day
breaks through the clouds of the stormy gray,
Grin and Brood offered a 'helping hand.'
This scheme was working the way they had planned.

"Don't be sad," offered Grin. "We both understand."
With Grin on one side and Brood on the other,
they offered solution... *two gallant young brothers.*

"What you need is protection. This much is true
but we have a suggestion of what you might do.
We're strong and trustworthy. *We* hereby declare,
if you need protection, *we two* can be there.

"*We* will protect you. *We both* are true-blue.
It will honor us both if you let *us* help you.
As you travel the roads, *we* can be by your side,
routing out bad men where ever they hide."

"Well done'" whispered Fighter. "A most frightening tale.
With these two in charge, it's a scheme that can't fail."

Awake stopped her crying and dabbed at her tears.
Could this be the answer to her sudden new fears?
These 'men of the world' said she could be protected.
What wonderful men they must be, she reflected.

"You are so kind. I don't know what to say.
But what of the work that you both do each day?
Who will do all your work if you travel away?"

Grin and Brood could see that Awake was believing
the clever and masterful plot they were weaving.
Just a couple more threads now were all that they'd need
to knit up their plan in a fine style, indeed.

"We're Storytellers," said Grin. "We find tales and tell them.
People *pay* to hear stories, so you might say, we sell them.
But lately our stories have been sort of boring.
We've noticed that some of our listeners are snoring."

Now Brood assumed a splendid pose.
"But just think, dear Governess, just suppose
how our audiences would be listening,
with mouths wide open and eyeballs glistening,
if we were to tell them in detail gory,
a grand tale of honor, a gallant story
of how you're protected from a horrible fate,
the fate that most probably *does* await
you as you travel around and about.

"Folks will love that story, without a doubt,
a story of men who have no fear
and can rescue fair damsels! It's all very clear.
This kind of tale all the world loves to hear."

"We'll keep you safe as safe can be.
There's no room to doubt it.

And *our* only reward will be telling other folk about it.
A blending of two needs, you see, a solution to adore.
We'll protect you, then tell your tale. Who could ask for more?"

"To you, oh Royal Governess, we offer our protection."
Said Brood to Grin behind his hand, "This plan is *now* perfection!
We'll have access to the King when we tell our story.
We'll be heroes to the Royals, awash in our own glory.
And we will *bow* before the King in a way that does befit him.
Then we will take over his Kingdom! He'll never know what hit him."

Gratefully, Awake agreed to hire the plotting pair,
never once suspecting she was tangled in the lair
of Fighter's evil 'dream plot' that was rotten to the core.
Awake was happy with her new friends and much safer than before.

Fighter nodded his approval as the plot played out below.
He would watch them close the next few days, to see this great plot grow.

"Bravo!" blew Fighter into the dust. "I admire you two, I say!
You boys will win my Game for me in a most creative way!
You players were worth waiting for. At last my time has come.
Soon Goodness tunes will be drowned out by the beat of my victory drum."

Fighter spun up toward the sunset, matching its fiery glow
with dreams of his Plan for violence. "Today, this much I know:
Never underestimate the creativity of greed.
These players have real talent. They are promising, indeed.
Their moves will speed the future of my promised insurrection
with a civil war of Chaos and the crazy King's rejection!

Fighter roared off in a cloud of dust. This encounter had been great.
He could see Spirit's defeat ahead and he could hardly wait.

Fighter's Coaching Scores

Someone else saw Fighter's dust cloud. Spirit was floating by
just in time to see Fighter leave. He wanted to know why.

"Why has Fighter been at this place? What did he stop to see?"
Spirit decided to look below, a bit more carefully.

He waited for Fighter's dust cloud to swirl and then un-swirl.
He suddenly saw the group below. *He actually knew this girl!*

"That's Awake, Sol's tutor. What's she doing here,
out on the road with two raggedy men? Is this something I should fear?
I know I just saw a cloud of dust. I saw Fighter here
and these are two suspicious guys with motives that aren't clear."

He decided to watch more closely, to hear what he could hear.
Awake and Grin set off at once while Brood went on ahead.
"I'm going to check for highwaymen," Brood very bravely said.

Catching a wink from his brother, Grin brought up the rear.
"With my brother and I both on the job, you should have no fear,"
said Grin to Awake with a comforting smile and a very protective air.
"No one will dare attack you. With me here, they wouldn't dare."

So, Awake set out on the road with Grin, feeling quite content.
She didn't see Brood's sneaky wink or suspect his bad intent.
But Spirit watched and saw the wink and wondered what it meant.

Suddenly, from out of the path ahead
jumped a fearsome man with a mask on his head!
He was draped in rags that were far from clean
and only his brows and his eyes could be seen.
He leapt toward Awake and danced about
with a growl and a snarl and a frightening shout!

"Give me your money, your food, your jewels!
You travelers here are a pair of fools
if you thought you could travel without protection.
Give me your satchel for my inspection!"

Spirit watched from behind a tree. He heard the threatening tone.
This robber was bent on violence to these travelers here alone!

The robber grabbed at the satchel and ripped it from Awake.
"You don't have much of value here that I would want to take,"
said the highwayman with a squinty sneer, tossing the books away.
Awake struggled to save them, but there, in the dust, they lay.

"No!" cried Awake. She stooped quickly, trying to retrieve them.
The highwayman grabbed her close and hissed, "Come here, girl!
Just leave them!
Just leave those books there in the dirt! Just leave them there I say!
Come here, my pretty little wench! Let's have a kiss, today!"

He pulled Awake up to his chest with a growl.
Spirit cringed. These gross actions were fowl fowl.

Spirit knew, with shame, he could not interfere.
However, Grin rose to the test without fear.
Spirit thought.
Could it be that this raggedy man is sincere?
With Awake in distress, is he ready to save
her from this highwayman? Was he that brave?

"Unhand her!" cried Grin, a strange look on his face.
He slapped the man hard! The man sprawled in disgrace.
Grin picked up the highwayman, turned him around,
and again, threw the scraggly beast to the ground!

The highwayman sputtered, completely surprised.
This 'highwayman' truly had not realized

that Grin might, in actual fact, knock him down.
Brood's eyes 'neath his mask narrowed into a frown.

"Just what are you doing?" he squawked up at Grin.

"Defending this lady against a most sinful
scoundrel who went for a kiss from this lass.
As a real man, I couldn't let such a thing pass."

"Bravo", said Spirit from behind the tree.
"This man is more brave than I thought he would be."

The highwayman rose, half staggering, half stumbling.
Rubbing his chin, he limped away, grumbling.

Awake stood rooted to the ground.
Her mouth was open, but not a sound
escaped her mouth. She just stood there trembling.
There was something about that bad man resembling
someone that she had met before, but where?
Right now, she didn't know or care.
She was just grateful that Grin was there.

With his arms around her, she felt secure.
No need to fear anything more, she was sure.

"Oh, Grin! You rescued me, quite clearly!
What would I have done? Why, that man nearly
captured me and took me off with him
where I'm sure my future would have been most dim.

"You're my hero! There's no doubt that I
am lucky that you were with me here, nearby!"

Spirit, too, was quite impressed.
He felt this young man had done his best
to protect a young girl that he had just met.
But Spirit, in truth, was not sure just yet.

"Although one young man fought off another,
did the bad one resembled the good one's brother? Hmmm.
I should be sure to not believe
in a *fake* bad guy. That would be naïve.

"But I saw that defense. I am not blind
and the courage he showed is so hard to find
that I must applaud when Good is done.
Maybe Good will grow from this skirmish won.

"My suspicions were probably mistaken
and I really admire the actions taken
to help Awake travel the road today.
I must have been wrong. There's no more to say.
At a time of such bravery, I shouldn't doubt
what bravery like that was all about.
I'm sure that a bad guy was under that mask.
It would be insulting to even ask."

(Spirit had not seen the scheming done,
so he was quite pleased that Grin had won.
How long would it take him to understand
that this "rescue" had been so carefully planned?)

Grin dusted his clothes and picked up the books,
basking in Awake's most grateful looks.

"That's what Brood and I tried to say.
There are evil men all along the way.
You should never travel out alone,"
said Grin with a humble, husky tone.

Awake's admiration for Grin had grown.
"It's true," she sighed. "I'd have never known
until you warned me. I'm so grateful that you
are brave and strong and knew what to do."

Grin was her champion, through and through.

Awake stared at Grin, a most grateful stare.
(There might have been more than just gratitude there.)

And Grin suddenly had a thought most rare...

Awake is a woman for whom I could care.
Why do I feel this way? Grin didn't know.
What was this feeling? Could this feeling grow?
Might this be a woman whose life he could share?
If so...
what he was doing was not right or fair.

But...
because Grin had not had feelings like this before, they were easy to resist.
He was now part of a hideous plot. His feelings left in the mist.

"Come, Governess. We had better go. It will be getting dark soon, you know."

As they walked on, Awake said with concern,
"I fear for your brother and his return."

Grin remembered the sight of Brood retreating,
a 'highwayman' suffering from his beating.
Hand in hand, they walked on their way
as the sun slid down toward the end of day.

Spirit smiled. He liked what he'd seen.
This shows Goodness, he thought as he left the scene.
If this romance blooms and their love is pure,
they will join my Goodness Team, for sure.

Brood Returns

Brood limped up to the pair, at last.
After almost another hour had passed
and they were nearing the Castle gate.

"Oh, Brood!" Awake bubbled. She couldn't wait
to tell Brood all that had taken place.
She smiled up happily into his face.

"You should have seen your brother Grin.
It was such a pickle that we were in!
A highwayman leapt from the side of the road.
He grabbed me and then he grabbed my load
of books as you both predicted he would.

"You should have seen Grin. Grin was so good!
He swung the man 'round and knocked him flat!
Oh, how I wish you could have seen that."

"Oh yes, I wish that I could have seen it."
Brood replied but looked like he didn't mean it.

Grin nudged Brood and winked his eye.
"Yeah, you should have seen me whack the guy."

(Brood let this bragging of Grin go by.
Now was the time to engage their plan.
Later they'd 'have 'a talk', *man to man*.)

The Castle was visible up ahead, the gates locked from behind.
The two men studied the Castle, unsure of what they would find.
Their plan had gone quite well, so far. They knew Awake was a fan
but they couldn't know what the King would think. They had never met
this man.

Would King Sol see right through them? Would he be hard to convince?
But, how could that be hard to do with a King who *imagined* 'a Prince'?

"Please let me in," sighed poor Awake. She was tired and cold.
"The gates were all locked early," she was very quickly told
by the Castle Guards on the other side, standing firm and bold.

"But we will open the gates for you. We know *you*, Awake.
But who are those two other guys? They're roughnecks. That's out take.
And Queen Luna may not like them. She's fussy, as you know.
We will have to ask her if they should stay or go."

The brothers looked at each other. This was not what they expected.
They had thought they would waltz right in. Would they be rejected?

The guards went back to the Castle. It was time to speak to the Queen
to explain the situation to her and tell her what they'd seen.

Grin and Brood just backed away. They didn't know what to expect.
Would the Queen allow them in...accept them or reject?

Awake just waited patiently. She was not offended.........
and somewhere, in the dark of night, the Game's 3rd Quarter ended.

LEGEND IV

The Heroes Arrive

The Castle rose dark in the setting sun.
The Big Game's 4th Quarter had now begun.
Outside Castle gates, new challenges loomed.
Somewhere Fighter whispered, "Goodness is doomed."

Awake now stood at the Castle gates. Would the guards allow her in?
Why were the gates locked, anyway? She usually walked right in.

But, much had changed at the Castle since Awake had first arrived.
New thoughts were tried by everyone. Now everybody strived
to try things they'd not done before, to think and be aware.
If the Prince was learning and growing, these goals all Royals could share.
Awake was getting Sol more books so that he could learn something new.
If Sol was learning new things, his parents would do so,

The Queen had become more social, inviting ladies in
to chat or have a cup of tea and give new tales a spin.
King Sol now journeyed the countryside to subjects far and near
to discuss the problems that *they* had and how crops grew this year.

The Royals had shortchanged these things while watching Sol so close.
They were more engaged with their kingdom now since Sol was nose to nose
with someone that they trusted who was helping him to learn.
He would be the King someday, a position he must earn
but he was working hard on that. They had no concern.

Yet one thing hadn't changed at all. No matter how he tried,
Sol hadn't left the Castle. This freedom was still denied.

Tonight,
King Sol was visiting farmers so Luna was in charge.
To be in charge of the Castle was a challenge she took on *large!*
For safety, she had ordered the gates locked as day turned into night.
When Awake arrived, they'd be opened. The guards knew her by sight.

But Luna watched, too, for young Awake to arrive at the Castle gate.
She was a trifle worried since Awake was very late.

Awake had been traveling weekly to find books that were new
so Luna also watched for her. "That's the least that I can do."

Upstairs, Sol also watched for Awake. She'd been gone all day.
He paced the windowsill again in his lonely, stranded way.
He peered past the gate toward a roadway, too far away to see
and dreamed of the day that he could leave.

I should already be
with the People of the Kingdom. Staying inside is wrong.
I should be out there now, he thought. That's where I belong.
I should be talking with the People, out there among the folk,
hearing them gripe when they get mad or laugh when they tell a joke.

I don't know what makes them happy or even what makes them sad.
How do they decide what's 'good to do' or know when something's 'bad'?
They might talk to a good friend who will listen and talk things through.
That's why Awake is important to me. With her, that's what I do.
But I don't know where she is right now. It's late. I wish I knew.

Sol searched the shadows sadly and paced the sill once more.
Where was Awake? He didn't recall her being this late before.
Didn't she know he was waiting? Didn't she know he would worry?

Just then, his mother bustled in, obviously in a hurry.

"Sol, are you somewhere nearby, dear? I've been looking for you.
You need to help me decide tonight what's *'right for a Queen to do'*.
Awake has arrived at the Castle gate but she has brought two guests.
The guards say they look scruffy. They're 'roughnecks', at their best.
But she's told the guards to let them in. She says that they somehow
rescued her from 'a highwayman', though she hasn't told them how."

Prince Sol was suddenly focused. "Was Awake hurt or harmed?
A *highwayman* attacked her? Our forces must be armed!
Where is Awake at this minute? She's still outside now?...Why?
She should come in right away...but beware those 'rescue guys'."

The Queen heard Sol's reaction, suggestions good and wise
that sounded like something the King would say. That was no surprise.

But she thought,
only a few short months ago, I kept all strangers out.
Though I see myself as braver now, I must think this out.
As the Royal in charge, I must decide if they should they stay or go.
What would King Sol do here? I'm not sure that I know.
I must review my options.

Her thoughts bounced to and fro.

The guards say that Awake is fine although her knees still shake.
But, if she was rescued by these men, would it be a mistake
to send these men away tonight just because the King's not here?
I must make a Royal Decision. I must show no fear.
These men appear to be down and out. The guards say they look needy
but Awake insists that they saved her life. Do we care if they look seedy?

Sol listened to Luna's thinking. (This was a skill quite new.
Sol didn't know that this was rare, a **new skill** he could do.)

He thought her questions over before he began to speak.
He'd decided things with the King before, but this would be unique.
For the first time, he felt like 'the man of the house.' He wondered if he could
help his mom be fair and just, the way his father would.

"I hear you think Awake is fine. We needed to know that first.
Now, think how much *you* trust these two, on a scale of best to worst."
The Prince spoke to his mother but sounded like his dad.

"I'm not quite sure," the Queen replied. "They aren't exactly bad...
but they're not exactly good, either. I really would be glad
if you would take a look at them before they come inside.
But... you *can't* let them see *you!*"

Sol shook his head and sighed.
He needed to see these men, first hand, so he shrugged a bit and said,
"I have a plan that you might like. Let's try this out. Instead
of my standing on your hand and openly consulting,
I'll hide and whisper in your ear to talk to you, resulting
in your *hearing* what I think without anybody knowing
that I am anywhere nearby."

"My confidence is growing,"
smiled the Queen. "Jump here behind my ear.
I'll feel surer of myself, just knowing that you're near."

Together the two swept up one hall, then down the stairs beyond,
out the doors and down the path, past ducks sleeping by the pond,
to the gates locked from inside, so as to 'protect the Castle'.

The Queen heard Brood as she approached...

"Let us in now! What's the hassle?"

"Did you hear that?" the Queen asked. "They sound like a pushy lot."

"You expected these two to be gentlemen?"

"Not really. I suppose not."

The guards stood at the Castle gates, like statues firm and straight.

"Guards,
open the gates," ordered Luna. "The hour is getting late,
and Awake has travelled a long way. We're rude to make her wait."

The heavy gates swung open with the clanking of heavy metal
and the creaking of rusty hinges as doors do when the settle.

There stood Awake in the moonlight. She looked quite alone,
but she sparkled with excitement and related in breathless tone,
"My Queen... I must tell of a wonderful deed.
Two heroes arrived in my hour of need.
I had no defense," she gushed in one breath.
"A highwayman frightened me almost to death!
"He threw down my books and grabbed me up tight.
Never before have I had such a fright!
If it wasn't for Grin, it can truly be said,
my books would be gone now and I would be dead!"

Queen Luna held her arms out and gathered up Awake.
"Oh, my dear, my darling child! Come to me, for goodness sake,
and tell me all that happened. Please tell me right away
of all the dreadful dangers that threatened you today.

"Where are these men, these brave souls who brought you?
I must meet them now....to begin with, I ought to
thank them for their bravery. That's the Royal thing to do.
You said there were two of them? Where are these two?"

From out of the darkness now, Brood appeared.
Grin approached slowly, then gallantly neared,
stepping up toward the Queen with shy looks side to side.

Prince Sol sensed at once they had something to hide.

"My brother Grin, Highness," stated Brood right away,
"was really the hero of record today.
He fought off a man that he knocked to the ground,
...'least that's what I heard, ma'am. I wasn't around."

"These two are the heroes?" said Sol with a sneer,
"I *don't* see heroes, but I have a strong fear

that these 'heroes' who make Awake sparkle and shine
might have rescued Awake on the road 'by design'
with motives less worthy than they seem to be.
They seem to be sneaky and shiftless to me.
Awake is impressed but I don't yet see
that these men are as great as she thinks them to be."

(The Queen smiled but wondered if these heroes so zealous
were possibly making Prince Sol a bit jealous.)

"My Queen, Brood spoke true! It was Grin who fought bravely.
Without thought for himself, he leapt forward to save me!"
offered Awake, gratitude in her voice.
Grin was her champion, her hero of choice.

Brood was not going to be left out.
This Queen needed to hear what was *due*, without doubt.
So he made an announcement, specific and shrewd:

"Please let me explain more. *My* name is Brood.
Your Highness must know we don't wish to intrude...
just because *we* protected this dear girl, Awake...
and went *out of our way a long way* for her sake,
being *the gentlemanly fellows we are*.
We brought her to this Castle...*far from our humble home*,
though we're *both tired and hungry* ...with *a long way* to roam,
we should be struggling off right now, back to our dreary home."

Brood staggered a bit to show he was tired,
an act that conveyed the show he had conspired
to perform for this Royal, one designed to convey
the *extreme*, noble deed they'd performed on this day.

Sol groaned from his perch behind his mother's ear.
"These two are conmen. I see that quite clear."

Brood slowly turned as though starting to leave.

Sol laughed as he watched him from his mother's sleeve.
"Not for one second does this man believe
that you are going to let them leave
and not stop them both from walking away
after 'all of the great hero work' they did today."

Sol scoffed at the acting he saw on display.
"They want us to swoon and be part of their play."

(Sol had been reading. He knew of this ploy.
He thought like a man now, no longer a boy.)

"They're faking this, Mother. It's a plot I can feel.
Though they say the right stuff, these two 'heroes' aren't real.
Don't let them inside of the Castle tonight.
I can tell from their act. They don't know wrong from right."

But, the Queen Mother thought... *Sol may not be fair.*
Awake said they helped her with bravery and care.
Though my son is as small as a young man can be,
he isn't immune to some big jealousy.

(Sol read Luna's thoughts... Though he didn't know,
his Conscience behaviors were starting to show.)

Into her ear now, Sol whispered back:
"I know what you're thinking. That's just a fact.
You think that I'm jealous. Well, this might be true,
but that isn't the reason I say this to you.
They're *after something*. We must be aware.
Awake likes this 'Grin'. We should guard her with care.

"We *should* always thank those who take care of others,
so give a reward to these two suspect brothers,
then send them away. Let them do what they do.
There's something about them that doesn't ring true."

But,
Luna wanted to prove she could make a decision
as a strong female monarch. This was now her mission.
She treasured Awake. She thought she understood
the action required. As 'the Queen' here she would
be quite correct as a strong, *brave* Queen should.

In spite of suspicions conveyed by her son,
Queen Luna would do what *she* felt should be done.

"You mustn't leave now, Mr. Grin, Mr. Brood.
After all that you've done, it would be very rude
for us to repay you by turning you out.
You must stay in the Castle tonight, without doubt."

"Okay, Mom," Sol whispered in his mother's ear.
You must surely do what *is right for you here,*
but *I still* believe they should *not* come inside.

"If you feel their 'bravery' cannot be denied,
then do what you wish. That's for you to decide,
but I have a feeling that something's not right.
To be safe, we should watch them *like hawks* here tonight.

"And,
In view of this caution, I've one request more.
If you let them in, please, *post guards at their door.*"

Success!

They were inside the Castle! This was the key!
This was, at last, where they wanted to be.

"We're in!" snickered Brood and then thought better of it.
"*...in your debt,*" Grin concluded. "Thank you. We would love it."

"Good," said Queen Luna. "Please do come inside.
We'll serve biscuits and gravy with plums on the side.
And while you partake of the dinner we're sharing,
you can tell me some more of your bravery and daring.

"Follow me," Luna ordered with queenly command
as she reached down and took young Awake by the hand.
"Come in, Awake dear, lest you take a chill.
Please warm yourselves, gentlemen."

They answered, "We will."
And...in they paraded through the huge Castle doors.

"Watch them," warned Sol.

The Queen answered, "Of course."

Sol left the Queen's shoulder, sliding swift down her sleeve
with such careful moves, she did not see him leave.

He jumped expertly to Awake and scrambled to her ear.
"Awake, I'm on your shoulder, but don't tell them that I'm here."
Awake made a little squeak of surprise... then smiled that Sol was near.

"Tell my mother everything. *I* want to hear it all
but don't let on that I'm nearby," whispered the watchful Sol.

That night, the Castle was filled with light and the tables piled with food.
No more could they have wished for, the 'heroes', Grin and Brood.
Without much hesitation, they soaked up every pleasure,
the act of gallant gentlemen, entertaining at their leisure.

They told their story grandly, with flourishes for the Queen.
Sol hid out by a candle stick, seeing all, but quite unseen.
Awake would see him now and then, but pretended she did not,
hidden beside a ladle, blending in by the gravy pot.

Brood proudly told of 'the rescue'. Grin modestly looked at the floor …a young man with humility. Who could ask for more?

"That highwayman," asked Luna, "How big a man was he?"
Awake gave Grin an appreciative glance and spoke up gratefully.

"He was as tall as a mountain and as fierce as he could be.
He had scraggly arms and knobby legs and his breath was hot and fowl.
His face was covered with stinking rags, and his eyes held a vicious scowl.
If I see him again, I'll know him," she breathlessly concluded.

Grin glanced at Brood. Brood glanced at Grin. (This thought had quite eluded both of their thinking up to now. What if this were true?
What if Awake discovered what was what and who was who?
If she learned that Brood was the highwayman, their plans would all fall through.)

CONSCIENCES—AND THE LEGENDS OF THE BIG GAME

Sol watched and listened closely from behind a mug of ale.
He looked at both their faces, analyzing each detail
of their twitching noses and darting eyes that snapped from side to side.
He was even more convinced that the pair had much to hide.

To cover his discomfort, Brood built upon his story.
"The highwayman was huge, alright! He'd have made a gory
mess of Awake and then of me if it weren't for my brother.
Of course, I had gone way on ahead to scout out any other
dangers lurking down the road. Imagine my surprise
when I returned to check on them. It was then I realized
that a highwayman had come and gone...off in a cloud of dust,
driven away by my brother, Grin, a man of grit and trust!"

"These two cannot be trusted," Sol whispered again to his mother.
"Don't forget the guards at their room tonight. Tell each guard to watch
a brother."

"I'll remind the guards to watch them," Luna thought without knowing why.
She was having suspicions, too, so she said with a tired sigh,
"I've been most impressed tonight by all that you have done,
the evil you fought for our Awake and the battle that was won.
But, you have had an eventful day. I am sure you must be tired,
so, I've had your room prepared for you. It is time that I retired.

"Tomorrow the King of this Castle will thankfully be returning.
I imagine he will have much to ask. He will be intent on learning
just *exactly* what you did and how you saved Awake.
If highwaymen are on our roads, there are measures he will take."

The brothers heard this prediction. They felt a pang of dread,
but they smiled and thanked their hostess and made their way to bed.

Because the boys knew how well they'd lied,
they went to their room, fairly satisfied
that at least the women believed their tale.

But the King might be different. Could they possibly fail
to convince the man that ruled this land?
A way to convince him should be planned.

"Don't worry, Brother," Brood counseled aloud.
"Our smart plan design will make both of us proud.
Remember, this King is not very bright.
Remember the stories we've heard left and right.
He talks to a son that just isn't there.

He'll believe every story that we have to share.
We will play to his weakness and when that is done,
we'll take over the Castle. Our goal will be won."

Their beds held piles of welcoming quilts. How could they ask for more?
They were too content to notice there were guards outside their door.

Confrontation

As Awake climbed up the stairs herself, Sol balanced on her shoulder,
then jumped to where he could see her face, perched on her candle holder.

"You really had me worried when you came home so late.
I'm very glad you were rescued from a 'dreadful and dangerous fate,'
but there's something weird about these guys. I don't think that they're that great."

"I've never been so frightened, Sol." Awake chattered as she went.
"That highwayman just grabbed me! Mr. Grin was heaven sent."

Sol saw Awake in front of him. In the candle light, she shone.
He *was really* jealous now, a feeling he'd never known.
He saw the face of Awake, his friend, but Awake, the woman, too,
a beautiful, full sized woman, and, himself, just an inch or two.

For the hundredth time in recent months, he was forced to realize
that he couldn't do what he wanted to do because of his tiny size.
He stood up 'tall' before her. He had to speak his mind.
His thoughts came tumbling forward. Tortured words weren't hard to find.

"Look at me. I'm a *man*, Awake, though I know I'm small in size.
But I care as much as a big man. You know this. You are wise.
If only I could leave this place, in fresh air, I might grow.
Then *I* could be your protector, defeat evil with one blow.

"With size, the things I dream of might suddenly come true.
For you, I would banish *all evil*, not a highwayman or two.

"I could lead men into battle, just like the books we've read.
I would be a man of Goodness, but now I am, instead,
a man who can't even help a friend who has given me such joy,
a woman who has helped me change to a grown man from a boy.

"My growth is all inside me, not visible, it's true,
but I'm as big as a mountain in the way I care for you.
I'm a man who wants nothing more than to love you and be strong,
but I see now that it's size you need. As a small man, I'm just... wrong."

Sol stared at the candle beside him. How stupid he must look
to a girl who could hold him in her hand the way she would a book.
His situation galled him. Why did he have to be
too small for her to love him as he'd dreamed that it should be?

Awake stared at Sol in wonder. She had known him for a year,
but she'd not suspected *these* feelings. This was sadly clear.
He was her 'little brother'. Her love for him was great,
but never as a boyfriend or a lover... or a mate.
He was *her* little buddy. He was *her* little friend.
But now she saw him as a *man*, afraid that he might spend
his life locked in a Castle, too small and alone.

He loved her as a woman, the first young love he'd known.

How could I have been so blind? she thought. *Why have I never seen
the longing that shines now in his eyes? How could I have been
so ignorant of his feelings? Why did I never see
that the feelings that I have for him aren't the same as his for me?
The times we've spent together are the best I have ever known.
How cruel it is for both of us that he has never grown.*

Awake was filled with sadness. What should she do now?
She had to make it up to Sol, but she couldn't think of how.

Sol stared up into her face. Her pain was clear to see.
Then he closed his eyes. He had said too much. *What must she think of me?
She likes Grin more than she likes me. Why not, goodness knows?
Of course! She wants a full-sized man more than one who never grows.
I'm a flea, a fly, a termite! I am nothing in her eyes!
How stupid of me to take this long to finally realize.*

Sol felt sorry for himself. He angrily stared at the floor
and silently cursed his tiny size. *What am I living for?
Now, at last, I get it. How useless I must seem,
waiting for her in this Castle, locked in a childish dream.
I'm a stupid, little, tiny runt! And what else could I be?
She wants a man to protect her, a much bigger man than me.*

Slowly Sol collected himself and looked her in the eye.
"I guess you were really lucky that those fellows happened by.
I wouldn't have been too useful, not much larger than a fly.
You need a man who can save you...a much better man than I."

Sol jumped to a potted plant and slid behind a leaf.
He was through with confessions, too proud to show more grief.
Awake just stood in the hallway in total disbelief.

"Sol, I don't believe you! Sol! Where did you go?
Are you mad at me b ecause y ou're s mall? We're *still* best friends, you know."

No response.

"You're smart and strong! I know this. You have a *huge* heart inside.
Come back and stop your pouting! You know you that you can't hide.
I know how to find you," she teased. "I know you're in that plant.
You think that you can hide from me, but you ought to know you can't!"

Awake pulled several leaves aside, revealing a tiny ball.
Only Awake would have ever guessed that the tiny ball was Sol.

"What good is a big heart?" Sol mumbled, "if I can't take it outside?
My heart, if I have one, will die without being tried.
A man who is small and protected is worse than a doll on a shelf.
I could *never* rescue you. I can't even rescue *myself!*"

Sol shook his head in misery. "I'll just plant myself in this pot.
Maybe by morning I'll grow huge... Ha! My guess is, I will *not*.
I know now that I'm worthless. I'm no better than a boy,
just an amusing plaything, a unique but useless toy."

Awake stood back and looked at Sol. What was happening here?
He had never been one for self-pity, always strong, his thinking clear.
She saw his slumping shoulders and they made her want to cry.
He was hurt and angry. This was painful...and she knew why.

All at once, Awake remembered. *Sol really is a prince!*

"A prince must be treated with respect".

Old instructions made her wince.

I should not have teased him. I was speaking out of turn.
*I accused **a prince** of pouting.* Her face began to burn.
I am a common village girl, my behavior's a disgrace.
What gave me the right to speak that way? I must know my place.

"I'm sorry I was rude," she said. "I really need to remember
that I am only your tutor. I am not a family member.

I will take my leave, tonight, Sir. Tomorrow's another day.
I'll remember then that I must speak in a more respectful way."

Sol was lost in his own thoughts. He didn't hear a word.
He was focused on his misery. None of this was heard.

"Do you want to meet in the morning, Sir?" Nothing she said seemed right.
Sol said nothing and looked away.

"Please excuse me, then. Goodnight."

She went to her room and closed the door. She was gone and out of sight.
Sol heard the door close and looked up but Awake was no longer there.
Her "goodnight" echoed down the hall. Sol was sure she didn't care.

With hopeless, deep frustration, Sol groaned, "Life isn't fair."
He obviously had no future. He had dreamed of so much before.
He had dreamed he would someday discover just what his life was for
and maybe grow to a manly size, to someone she'd adore.

From the reading of his many books, he had seen a world in need
of knowledge, truth and Goodness. These were noble goals, indeed,
but what could *he* do about such things when he was so very small?

Nothing! That was the answer. Why had he been born at all?

The Plot Thickens

Sol climbed down from the potted plant and trudged off toward his room,
passing the room where 'the heroes' slept. His heart was full of gloom.

Suddenly Sol heard voices as they drifted across the floor.
He could see the glow of a candle's light from under the brothers' door.
The two guards dozing at their posts had just begun to snore.

At first Sol could just hear mumbling, but he now heard something more.

"It's all been going as we planned." The voice belonged to Grin.
"We wanted to get into the Castle and, just like that, we're in.
They appear to be a trusting lot. They believe everything we say.

"But don't forget, when the King returns, he may not feel that way,"
said Brood with a warning whisper. "He might see right through us.
If he guesses that *I* was the highwayman, what will he do to us?"

My suspicions were right! Sol thought with a jolt. *Now I must learn much more.
I suspect there is a greater plot.* He rolled in under their door.

"Don't worry about the King," said Grin. "I'm sure he'll believe us, too.
Remember, this King isn't right in the head. Fooling him won't be hard to do."

Sol was listening from under the bed. He couldn't believe his ears.
He had feared that these brothers were crooked. This verified his fears.
But why did they have no fear of the King? What were the words they said?
...something about his father, the King, not being "right in the head."

Sol scrambled up the bed curtains and snuck to the dresser top.
He hoped to hear more about their scheme before their chatter stopped.

"Did you see how they believed 'the rescue of Awake'?
Grin kicked off his boots and britches and gave his covers a shake.

"Awake confirmed everything we said. That added a special flare.
The Queen was hanging on every word, just like she was there.
Awake's our 'secret weapon' so what we say rings true.
It's clear that the Queen has no idea that the highwayman was you."

"Yeah. I made an impressive highwayman. When Awake described her fear,
the Queen just soaked up every word. She couldn't wait to hear."

From his hiding place beside the bed, Sol fumed at what he heard.
Awake had helped sell this pack of lies and his mother believed each word.

Their inspiring tale of recue, "the rescue of Awake",
the 'heroism' they displayed was nothing but a fake.

What was the reason for their lies? What could be their goal?
Sol needed to find more answers before they took their toll.

Now Sol remembered the treachery he had seen in the books he'd read
...Gory thoughts of intrigue began running through his head.

Awake is part of everything. She said she was my friend
but, since she is part of this evil scheme, our friendship's at an end.
Awake is in the middle of unbelievable betrayal.
When did she start to plan this out? When did our friendship fail?

Sol could not believe it, but he felt he surely must
give up his feelings for her now...She had lost his trust trust.

Grin snuggled down in the feather quilts, his pillow beneath his head.
Brood offered Grin a question from his side of the bed.

"Have you noticed we haven't seen 'a prince' the whole time we've been here?
This goes along with our theory. There *is* no prince. That's clear!"

"I'm sure you're right, my brother. There was no 'Prince' in sight
from the time that we entered the Castle 'til we came to bed tonight.

This must be a game they play when the crazy King is near.
Tomorrow, when King Sol returns, a 'Prince Sol' should *'appear'.*"

Brood doubled up with laughter that almost shook the bed.
Grin chuckled, too, with a knowing snort at what his brother said.

"We'll play 'The Prince Game'" added Grin, "if that is what it takes.
We have no trouble acting. We're pros at being fakes!"

"Yeah," said Brood. "We'll play along. It won't be hard to do.
When the King says that *he* sees the Prince, we'll say that we do, too.

And soon the King will trust us both. He'll love us, me and you!
Then we can take over the Castle! *We* will run the show.
We'll be in charge of everything and the crazy King will ....go!"

So, they plan to take over the Castle! Sol thought with sudden fear.
I need to warn my father of what they're plotting here!
They think the King is crazy. They think I don't exist.
They plan to rule the Kingdom before anyone can resist.
Can't they see that my dad is good, see this is unfair?
I must thwart their plan, somehow. How should I fight this pair?

(Sadly, Sol didn't know yet. Here, in this midnight hour,
he didn't know what a Conscience could do or understand his power.)

Now,
Brood sat up straight and sneered. 'I think I'll become an Earl.
If I have an important title, I'll impress that governess girl.
But she might fancy you, Grin, before I've even tried."

"I hope so since I like her, too," the smiling Grin replied.
"And soon the King might think of me as though I am a son.
You be an Earl if you want to, but *I'll* be his Number One!
Soon he'll forget his 'invisible prince'. Our battle will be won!"

Brood yawned.
"We will both see quick enough who wins the fair Awake.
Now blow out the candle and go to sleep. It's late, for goodness sake.

"Tomorrow, we're *Storytellers*. We'll tell the town our tale.
When we 'sell' the folks our story, we will *really* 'make the sale!'
To the town folk we'll be heroes, but that's not the only thing.
If we get the town to help us, we can overthrow this King!"

Sol now knew the whole, sick plot, and Awake was in on the scheme.
The town folk would be easily fooled. This was like a horrible dream.
I must warn my mom, right now, Sol silently declared.

*We can no longer trust Awake. Mother must be prepared
to warn my dad of the evil plot that these lying three have dared
to set up against our family. Such plotters won't be spared!"*

But, even as Sol made his solemn vow, his heart broke in his chest.
How could his own dear friend, Awake, be as evil as the rest?

The Drawer

Grin shuffled toward the table where the candle (and Sol) now stood.
Quickly Sol jumped into a drawer to hide as fast as he could.

Grin blew out the candle and... bumped into the drawer.

"Dang," said Grin as the drawer slammed it shut.
"What'd you leave that open for?"

"Leave what open?" mumbled Brood. (Sol was now *trapped* in that drawer!)

Grin rubbed his leg and lay down, yawning long and wide.
(He never could have guessed that Sol was now locked tight inside.)

Sol couldn't believe it. How easily he'd been caught,
without one word of protest, without one battle fought.
He looked at his situation. He must get out a warning
to prepare his mother and the King of these traitors before morning.

But, how stupid could one person be? How stupid and how small?
How could Sol warn his mother now? He could do no good at all.
These men were plotting treason. Sol knew he couldn't wait.
By dawn their plot would be under way. The morning would be too late.

These two were determined to end the reign of a king they didn't know.
Why did they want to do him harm, much less, to overthrow?

This question paraded through Prince Sol's mind as he struggled in the gloom.
Why did this question never touch these brothers in the room?

The answer is very simple. It cannot be denied:
Evil destroys good questions when no Conscience is there to guide.
Fighter had coached these two boys to be Players in the Game.
Now they were a part of his evil team. Yes, Fighter was to blame.

Sol sat alone in the darkness. This was sure a mess.
He was trapped inside a dresser drawer, a prisoner, nothing less.
His family was in danger and his only friend had turned
into a friend of his enemies. How her betrayal burned.

This is what happens, Sol thought to himself, when you're puny and protected.
You don't know enough about People to expect the unexpected.
And I have no clue who I can trust... Sol felt useless, trapped, rejected.

But...slowly, this man that was born a Scrap got his head back in the game.
"I won't take this lying down, a looser without shame.
I won't let this defeat me. I know that I am smart.
I must fight for my dad and my family. I must summon up the heart!"

Sol scrambled around inside the drawer, in search of a quick way out.
He climbed and fell and climbed again." I can do this, without doubt!"

All night he worked on his prison. Every trick that he tried failed.
He scraped and clawed all the edges... but by morning, he was still jailed.
He was alone in the darkness. Again, self-doubt prevailed.

"I'm too small to do anything. This prison drawer has shown
that there is no use for a man like me, a fact I should have known.
Now I'm *sure* that I'm useless, no matter what I do.
Why did it take me all my life to accept that this is true?"

The doubts he had had with Awake before depressed him through and through.
At last, as the sun was coming up, Sol crumpled in a heap
and, racked by nightmares of failure, he sank to a heavy sleep.

The Glory Story

As morning dawned, Prince Sol slept on, locked in the dresser drawer.
His nightmares were filled with the awful scheme he had heard the night before.

But, for Storytellers, Grin and Brood, it was quite another story.
They had dreamed all through the night of ways to win their glory.

Grin and Brood were out of bed before the sun was up.
They laughed while passing the nodding guards, still sleeping standing up.
Up the hall and down the stairs, they headed out the door,
leaving a note on a table top. "Back by evening or before."
They were on their way to the market. They could hardly wait.
They needed to find a place to perform before it was too late.

In the streets, there was already fighting, a usual market day
...cheaters and hustlers in action...greed and thievery on display.
Each shouted that their goods were best, telling lies by the score.
"My goods are "the greatest!"
"These ought to sell for more!"

There were battles on every corner, name calling, a bloody nose.
Everyone was cheating everyone else and would 'til the market closed.
Fighter drifted overhead, enjoying the unrest.
These times of marketplace Chaos were some times that he liked best.

And his new recruits were approaching. He could see them down the road,
on their way to the marketplace with their story to unload.
This would be a momentous day, Fighter definitely knew.
His final drive to win the Game would be started by these two.

The brothers knew these markets. They expected fights and yelling.
The two now entered the town square where the folk were buying and selling
and jumped with gusto onto the scene to set up their 'storytelling'.

First, they found an enormous rock. Brood climbed up to its crest.
Grin herded the town folk toward the rock proclaiming themselves "the best
Storytellers in the land!" Folks soon gathered there.
"Here ye, River Kingdom," Brood announced with great fanfare.
"My name is Brood. I'm a teller of tales! This is my brother, Grin.
We bring you exciting news today. Treachery…violence…sin!

"There's nothing like news flashes to brighten up your day,
and oh, do we have some whoppers! **One** will take your breath away.
You *need* to hear this news, my friends. You *must* hear it. Am I right?
You must never miss the 'breaking news'! Don't miss one grim delight!"

Fighter nudged a large man next to him who didn't look too bright.
"Well, tell it!" the large man rumbled. "Make it somethin' *I* want to hear.
Let's hear about guts and glory where somebody hacks off an ear."
The People laughed and came closer, dropped their wares and scrambled near.
Violence, hate and lots of blood were always great to hear.

"I want to hear about heroes! Some sin and sex would be nice,"
gushed a chubby, rubbery woman, in the mood for a little vice.

Fighter mingled with the crowd in a manner sly and bold.
He couldn't wait for the story that would make *his* plan unfold.
He remembered well the plotting he'd encouraged the day before.
These boys would fire up the final drive that *his* plan was waiting for.

Brother Brood stood on the rock, looking down at the crowd below.
They were primed and ready. He could see that this was so.
He needed to make his performance strong. He wanted all to know
that *everything he said was true*, the real reason for this show.

(If he stirred this crowd up right, he knew where this could go.)

The Big Sell

Brood began with head held high. His arms spread open wide.
Then he gazed out over the gathering crowd with excitement he couldn't hide.
"I will tell you first of a lovely lass with brains as well as beauty.
She was *gorgeous*, a sweet young thing, and attentive to her duty."

"Where is the part about blood and guts?" the big man bellowed loud.

"Yeah! We don't want love and romance!" grumbled other men in the crowd.

"Patience," replied the haughty Brood. "I know this tale will score
enough blood and guts for everyone... bravery, sin and more!
Just listen close to this news, my man, and all it has in store.

"This lass, you see, she had a job. She was working for the King.
She said she was a tutor for a teeny, tiny thing
that the King and Queen say, to this day, is a real-life human being.
But this was 'a teeny, tiny Prince', that no one's ever seen.
And that's because there *is no Prince*. You all know what I mean."

With this, Brood winked and looked around at the eager River Folk.
All nodded and nudged each other. They all knew this joke.
They remembered Awake when she asked for books. They all began to cheer.
They knew the People in this tale! *This* they would love to hear.

"Heck, he's talkin' about our King and Queen. He's talkin' about Awake."

"The news he brings us must be true, then. It's real. It can't be fake."

"Tell us the gruesome details," the crowd began to shout.

"We know the People yer talkin' about. What's *this* story all about?"

Now handsome Grin climbed on the rock. It was time to do his part.
He smiled down at the crowd below. He knew just how to start.

He blew kisses to the ladies and winked a roving eye.
He had their complete attention. He didn't have to try.

"Here we go!" said Fighter to himself. "Now we're under way.
The King's days are surely numbered by what this guy will say!"

Grin began with gusto, the crowd now in his sway.
"One day this beautiful tutor went looking for some books.
She had nothing to protect her...but sweetness and good looks.
Little did she realize that, lurking along the way
was a monstrous, evil highwayman, looking to make his day
by stealing the beautiful tutor and pirating her away!"

The rubbery woman smacked her lips. Her eyes were getting wide
with romantic anticipation. In a high-pitched voice, she cried,
"Oh, can't you just imagine...? This story is so good!
A big, ol' man was attackin' her! I know *I* never *could*
defend *myself* against the likes of a great big, ruthless man!
Tell us all what he was like. Was he tall... and strong... and tan?"
She wobbled slightly, feeling faint while her girlfriends fiercely fanned.

"Tell about blood and guts now!" Farmers shouted their command
and the men all jostled closer. Women panted. Children scuffled.
Grin just raised an eyebrow, a dramatic pause, unruffled.

Brood thought of himself as an actor. He loved to hear folks cheer.
So, he jumped down and grabbed a girl! She shrieked with joyful fear.

Brood stalked with her in a circle, hissing threats for all to hear.
The young girl screamed and giggled as Brood kept up his hold.
All held their breath and waited for the story to unfold.

Grin, a Teller of talent, had a good performer's sense.
He now took up the 'play by play', building the suspense.
From the top of the rock, he narrated, his dialogue intense:

"The tutor was at his mercy. 'Unhand me now,' she cried.
He held her tight against him. He would not be denied.
'I'll take you home!' growled the highwayman, showing no remorse.
'I'll lock you in my dungeon, and imprison you, of course,
and you'll be *mine*. You'll be a slave to my brutal acts of force!'"

Brood now acted Grin's story out with the young girl from the town...

"Come with me, my pretty wench. I will have you for my own.
I will do the vilest things to you that the world has ever known.
I *am* the mighty highwayman! My muscles are so strong
that I can force you to my will. You won't know right from wrong."

The young girl wiggled and giggled in a satisfactory way.
The rubbery woman sighed and smiled... fainting blissfully away.
The rest of the folk leaned in to hear the climax of the play.

Fighter was fascinated at the tale told in this way.
"These boys are really talented," observed the excited Fighter.
"They can tell lies *that sound like news*. My Chaos is getting brighter!"

Brood was in his element. He'd quite forgotten Grin
but Grin leapt into the circle to present 'the hero's' spin.

Grin stood tall and handsome, now the hero of the play.
"But a hero came to the rescue! As that hero now, I say,
'Unhand that wench, you scurvy knave! I'm here to make you pay!
I'll defend this damsel in distress! *I* will save her, come what may!'"

Grin hurled himself into battle, grabbing his brother, Brood.
With the town folk wildly cheering, the actors 'fight' ensued.

The brothers hollered and struggled, tossed each other around
and grunted manly noises, just the way a fight should sound.
Then Grin grabbed Brood by the hair on his head and threw him to the ground,
placing a foot on his brother's chest. There were great cheers all around.

"In this way," shouted Grin with pride, "the hero saved the day,
beat the highwayman to a pulp and, with brute force, made him pay!"

Bowing with graceful modesty, Grin concluded his narration.
As the hero of the play, Grin received a grand ovation.

Brood got up and hissed at Grin, brushing off the dirt,
"I'm all for 'realistic,' man, but *yanking hair does* hurt.

I always get the worst of things. Look! You ripped my only shirt.
Just for that, I'll tell all that's *you're* the highwayman."

Grin grinned,
"Shoot off your mouth if you want to, but you will wreck our plan."

The shouts and cheers now faded as the crowd began to leave,
dropping tokens onto a cloth for the story they'd loved to believe.

"But wait! There's more!" Brood shouted. The crowd turned back again.
What *more* cool stories might there be from the mouths of these two men?

Brood climbed up on the rock once more. Again, his arms spread wide.
"Listen to me, one and all!" (Something wonderful was implied.)

"I must take this time to tell you. I'm as proud as I can be.
The *real* hero of our story is standing here with me!
Observe, if you will, my brother Grin, in all his humble glory.
Grin, you see, is a hero, *the real hero of our story!*"

Grin looked at the ground and smiled a bit and tried to look quite shy.
The women buzzed and giggled and tried to catch his eye.
The men all mumbled, "I'll be darned. He must be quite a guy."
They slapped Grin's back and shook his hand, the first 'hero' they'd ever met.
"Something to tell my buddies and my grandkids, you can bet!"

"How true," Brood continued. "He's a wonder through and through.
And, of course, as his older brother, I taught him all I knew."

The Storytellers could do no wrong as the heroes of their creation.
The morning built momentum and increasing admiration.
They told their story many times and every time it *grew*.
Instead of just one highwayman, the next time, there were *two!*

Soon the story was multiplied from *two to eight to ten*,
and before it could be doubted, an *army of highway men!*

Grin and Brood were center stage. Big frogs in a little puddle,
they told the story more and more, encouraging the muddle.
This was what they'd wanted. They were heroes of the day.
They were the darlings of the crowd, in charge in every way.

But Fighter was getting restless. Too many folks were smiling.
Fighter moved in and coached the crowd, whispering, beguiling,
seducing them with thoughts and fears. It was now his dark intention,
to set folks against their Royalty...with *rebellion* a subtle mention.

Soon, the plan developed and the mood began to change.
The brothers felt it changing and their focus rearranged.

Grin now asked in a sly way, "What should King Sol do
about this threat of the highwaymen who threaten me and you?"

Brood brought out more questions to another gaggle there.
"What do you expect from King Sol? Do you think he'll even care?
Or will he be busy with his Prince, a prince who isn't there?"

The crowd began to grumble. The boys had expressed the fears,
and questions they had always asked for over twenty years.
They liked their crazy King now, but this had come up before.
'Would he, *could* he lead them, if they had to fight a war?'

'Was he too crazy to defend their travel, folk and land?'
Their King *did* have an imagined son. Was he fit to command?

These questions caused more questions...which Fighter had always planned.

Now,
little by little, the happy crowd became an angry mob.
With no Consciences to help them think, old doubts did their job.
The People forgot the good things they knew their King had done.
They only thought of his 'craziness' and 'non-existent son'.

"Why doesn't the King protect us?"

"It's like these two guys say!"

"He's too crazy to protect us! We must find a better way!"

"It's time we get new leadership to set things straight again!"

"And the leadership we think we need... might just be these two men!"

"These guys seem to know the score. They saw bad dudes and then they fought those guys and beat 'em!"

"They seem to have the nerve
to save us all from highwaymen and that's what we deserve!"

"King Sol is through! He must step down! His time to rule is done!

"We cannot trust our crazy King! In twenty years, no one
has seen a prince or heard a prince. His son is just pretend!"

"We need a king who can lead us, be strong, protect, defend!
"We'll follow these men into battle...there and back again!"

Through the day the crowd grew larger, intent upon its mission.
They were going to remove the King! They had come to their decision!

The brothers watched and listened. They stood aside, content
to watch the town get excited. *They* knew what that meant.
The People would stir *themselves* up to do what they wanted to do.
Then *they*, the plotters behind the scenes, could make *their* dreams come true.

Fighter drew back with pleasure. He eagerly understood
the ideas that the boys had planted would result in *nothing Good!*
He wound his way among the crowd. "How easy it will be
to defeat the King *and* Spirit of Good...with Chaos endlessly!

"Spirit has no defense, I'm sure. He doesn't suspect or know
that these two Storytellers will deliver my mortal blow.
All Goodness will be ended as town anger catches fire.
Chaos will rule the universe, my ultimate desire."

Where is Spirit?

Spirit was blissfully unaware of the evil plot now growing.
How could all this be happening without Spirit even knowing?

And he was not at the market. He never wanted to go.
River People were greedy there. He didn't like that show.
He seldom went to the marketplace, especially on market day.
He wasn't proud to watch humans when their faults were on display.

He knew Storytellers would be there but he didn't need to hear
the stories they were telling, their usual lies and fear.

But he *did* wonder how Grin was. Grin had defended Awake.
Grin *had* defended a stranger. That was 'Goodness for Goodness sake'.
Spirit thought Grin had promise. He might join the 'Team for Good'.
Grin had defended young Awake as a man of Goodness should.

Grin's defense of sweet Awake had been beautiful to see.
Spirit dreamed that someday, a true romance might be
growing between these two young folk. Awake deserved the best.
In the future, Spirit would watch Grin to see if he passed the test
...the test of the *lasting* Goodness of People who had *some* heart.
Grin's gallantry wasn't everything, but, at least it was a start.

Meanwhile, Back at the Castle

The Queen awakened early. Awake was already awake,
alone at a throne room table, poking at creamed wheat cake.

Luna quietly joined her, sinking into a chair nearby.
She nodded her head but she didn't smile. She didn't even try.

"Where is The Prince?" the Queen asked. She had spent a restless night.
"I am glad our guests aren't up yet. To me, they don't seem right.
I need to talk to Sol again to see what he suggests.
I should have listened last night. I now think that he knew best."

"Yes, I suppose," sighed Awake, at last. She hadn't touched her food.
She didn't want to talk, either, but she didn't want to be rude.
"Grin and Brood left early as soon as they were able.
I'm not sure why they left so soon. Here's their note left on the table."

"A note? How strange," replied the Queen. "But actually, that's okay.
I want to see what Sol thinks of what they had to say.
Do you think a reward of some kind is something we should do?
I'm sure we should do something, due to 'what they did for you'.
If we should, what should we give them? I haven't got a clue.
What do you think, my dearest? You must have an opinion, too.

"And where is my sleepy son now? He shouldn't stay abed.
His father is arriving home soon. That's something that I dread
unless I have my thoughts in place and all worked out ahead.
Sol seemed to doubt your two friends. At least, that's what he said."

The Queen continued chattering. Awake was 'lost in space',
a worried and depressed look reflected on her face.
She and Sol had had a fight. The night had ended wrong.
She needed to say she was sorry. They had always got along.

What had possessed her to talk to him in such a familiar way?
She wanted to explain herself. She had so much to say
as soon as she could find him. What was taking him so long?
He usually came down early. Was there something wrong?

Awake now grew impatient. "My Queen," she simply said,
"I'll go wake Sol up for you. He's such a sleepyhead."

She dashed away from the table and then flew up the stairs,
tapping hard on his bedroom door. "Prince Sol... Are you there?"

She tried again. Nothing happened. If he wasn't there, then where?
Now Awake was more worried. This was not his style.
She heard no sound from inside his room. She decided to wait for a while.

Awake sat down on the top of the stairs, her chin resting on her knee.
A lonely, empty, Castle hall was all that she could see.
It wasn't like Sol to disappear, but, then, where could he be?

Oh...
Could he have left with Grin and Brood? She knew he was upset
at being confined to the Castle like an over-protected pet.
She knew he wanted to be a man...as he already was.
She should have spoken up for him when freedom was his cause.

Awake thought some more.
I know he wants to see the world. He's sick of being inside.
He wants to meet River People. He doesn't want to hide.
He wants to obey his parents, but his patience has been tried.
Now, I'm sure he's gone off with them, refusing to be denied.

Slowly Awake went down the stairs to stand and face the Queen.

"I knocked and shouted for your son. He's nowhere to be seen.
But I had some thoughts about this. These thoughts will make you frown,
but I'm guessing he went with Grin and Brood when they went into town."

Awake expected anger. She expected the Queen to rage
at the thought of Sol escaping at last, from his safe 'Castle cage',
but, instead, Queen Luna closed her eyes. Then she nodded slightly.

"I think you may be right, my dear. I've protected Sol too tightly.
I've thought about this for a while now and I should have let him know.
I know that he's a man now. It's past time to let him go
...but the world is so big and he's so small and I do love him so."

Spirit slipped in to the Castle. He could hardly wait to see
the classroom chats that he always watched... 'Awake and the King-to-be'.
These were signs of coming leadership that would add to Spirit's score.
The Prince was nearing the place and time that his Plan was waiting for,
and Fighter didn't have a clue. What a huge surprise
it would be when Prince Sol took his place. How Goodness scores would rise!

But something didn't seem quite right. Spirit circled the throne and hall.
There was no sign of study time, no sign of Prince Sol.
Awake and the Queen appeared worried. This was not like them at all.

Now, from outside the Castle gates, a commotion could be heard.
"Oh, my goodness! The King is home! Nobody say a word!"
whispered the Queen. "*I* must tell him about the Prince
and the two men *and* your rescue *and* what has happened since.
Oh, how I wish I had more time to think through everything."
And off she bustled to the door to welcome home the King.

Spirit drew back to a corner to watch. What was happening?

A few short minutes later, the King walked through the door
wearing a look of sadness Spirit had never seen before.
He looked like he had aged a year or maybe even more.

Queen Luna followed slowly, wringing her hands with worry.
She had told King Sol everything she knew. She was too upset to hurry.

King Sol looked around him. He saw the empty hall.
Sadly, he walked from room to room and touched each empty wall.
His son was not in any room. Sol was gone, and that was all.

"The Queen has told me that Sol left. I heard the words she said,
but I'm having trouble believing them. They won't stay in my head.
For the first time in twenty years I've not come home to Sol.
I knew he was going to leave some day, but he's not prepared at all.
He hasn't seen the outside world... and I've been in denial.
We kept him close to shield him so he's had no worldly trial.

"Now he's out there and in danger. This is all my fault.
I should have exposed him earlier, not locked him in this vault!"

Spirit couldn't believe it. What had the King just said?

Sol was gone? Could this be true? Spirit was filled with dread.
He knew that Sol had been restless and needing to take his place,
but was he ready to meet the world alone and face to face?

Without waiting another moment, Spirit headed straight outside.
This wasn't a time to hesitate. This wasn't a time for pride.
He had to search for Prince Sol. He must find him now, today!
Prince Sol was key to earth's future. He must find him right away.
How could he be missing? Had he just run away?

Or,
had he been stolen by Fighter? Had Fighter learned of his Plan?
Fighter had always ruined things ever since the world began.
Spirit must find the Fireflies and find out if they knew
that Sol had gone to the outside world. Could this be really true?
Spirit hoped that the Fireflies knew and could tell him what to do.

Awake just listened to the King. She could understand it all.
She wished she had spoken up earlier and given a "wake up call".
The little Prince had become a man. A million times he'd shown it.

For years he'd wanted to leave the nest. All of them had known it.
Now he was gone from the Castle. Now he was on his own,
an inexperienced, tiny Prince, out in the world alone.

Slowly the servants gathered. Soon, they were all aware
that the little Prince they had always known was now no longer there.
He was out where he knew no one, how to navigate to where.
The servants were all worried, too. They had also learned to care.

Stranded

Of course,
Prince Sol wasn't gone from the Castle, but none in the throne room knew
to go up the stairs and down the hall. (That was all they needed to do
to find their 'missing prince' at once, but, too bad. Nobody knew.)
Sol awoke with a panicked jolt. He couldn't see a thing.
Where *was* he? Had he been asleep? He began remembering...

He was in the room of Grin and Brood, locked inside a drawer.
Slowly it all came flooding back, events of the night before.
Sol's frustration and anger boiled up in him once more.

Self-pity overwhelmed him. Again, he cursed his size.
"There's no future for me. It's time I realized...
No one came to find me. I'm still stranded here.
I'll probably die in this dresser drawer and no one will shed a tear."

Suddenly, tiny lights appeared at the corner of the drawer.
There were now two Fireflies inside the drawer. What were *they* here for?
They darted swiftly about the space as though checking that all was clear.
Then, they drifted slowly down to Sol and floated very near.
Next, gentle, hopeful music was all that Sol could hear.

Sol stared at the Fireflies. Amazingly, he could see
that the Fireflies were tiny figures, smiling tenderly,

tiny people with glistening wings, and about them, such a glow
that Sol, now blinded by their light, could not see enough to know
who the creatures looked like. Somehow, he didn't care,
but he felt a loving aura warming the darkness there.

One flew toward Sol directly, until she was very near.
Hovering there, she sang to Sol in a voice both sweet and clear.
"You are the Prince of two kingdoms, one big and one that's small.
Your destiny is to help them both, as a Prince who cares for all.

"You have learned of River People through Queen Luna and King Sol.
You have learned how humans live and think and you've learned to love them, too.
The Queen and King have prepared you, through the time they've spent with you,
to understand human thinking, why People do what they do.

"*You* naturally understand 'right and wrong'. You have helped them learn that, too.
You were made to help humans. For this you were designed.
You are made of **Special Clay** with a special heart and mind.
You'll return this Clay to humans. To this goal, you're assigned."

"Do I know you?" stammered Prince Sol. "I somehow feel I do."
Both Fireflies glowed brightly overhead. Sol felt they knew him too.

The second Firefly hovered low, as if he wished to stay,
but pulled back with reluctance as he said what he had to say.
"Think of us when times are hard. We have loved you every day.
Remember how much you were always loved." That was all he had to say
and then, like magic, they disappeared, simply floating away.

Sol didn't know what he had seen or maybe it was 'who'.
What message had they given him? What was he supposed to do?

Suddenly, from under the drawer, Sol heard a scratching sound.
Was this the sound of his mouse friends? Had he at last been found?

The scratching sound was welcome. The sound gave Sol some cheer.
Finally, there was someone real who knew that he was here.

"Hello," Sol whispered softly. "I'm here. I am Prince Sol."
He listened for more scratching but heard no more at all.

"I know that you can hear me. Come on! Don't be afraid.
We used to play in the old days. Remember when we played?"

Again, there was just silence. There wasn't a single sound.
Again, poor Sol felt lonely. He thought that he'd been found.
First there were Fireflies, then scratching. Now, what should he do?
Then Sol heard some squeaking. *This* was a sound he knew.

"I hear you, friend," Sol whispered. "Where are you... and who?
Since Sol had been studying with Awake, he had not recently played
at all with the mice and rats and bugs, the small friends he had made.

He had been focused on Awake, reading, discussing, growing,
trying to learn from every book, the knowledge he *needed* knowing.
As time had passed, Sol had missed his friends but he had been intent
on studying People's writings and what their lives had meant.

Were his small friends mad at him since he had left them alone?
Had he not shown enough gratitude for the friendship they had shown?

(Sol had never met an old mouse, and so he never knew
that mice matured more quickly while he so slowly grew.
While Sol had been reading with Awake, what he hadn't known
was that his old friends were not kids any more. They had children of
their own.)

From another corner of the drawer, Sol heard that chewing sound.
He made his way to that corner, crawled closer and felt around.

"Max, is that you?" Sol felt the floor until he found a hole
and then he felt a furry nose poking up like a mole.

"No, I'm not Max," came the squeaking voice, a very tiny one.
"My name is Harry, Harry Mouse. I'm Max's oldest son.
You must be Sol. I've heard of you. My father used to tell
all us kids about you. He said he knew you well.
He says you guys were buddies and used to run and chase.
He said that we can trust you, unlike the larger race."

"How *is* Max? Where is he now? It's been more than a year."
Harry continued chewing the hole. Now Sol could see his ear
as the hole got larger. "He's doing well these days,
but he can't chew like us younger guys. He's slowed his chewing ways.

"But he still keeps his eye on you. To be honest, so do we all.
We're ready to help when we're needed. We're a Spirit Club, on call.
In a way, we feel like we know you. You're our dad's best friend, Prince Sol."

Sol smiled, thinking of the past and the fun had with his friend.
He liked the games he played as a child. Too bad they had to end.
Why had those happy days gone away? Now here he was in a drawer
with no idea what to do next or what his life was for.

While Sol was remembering, Harry chewed. Then Harry chewed some more.
"A couple more chomps," grinned Harry now, "and I'll have you out of
this drawer."

Sol began pacing back and forth. "I can't believe I've been trapped
inside this drawer for hours. I don't know how long I napped,
but the guys in this room are just no good. I heard it from *their* own lips."

"That's why we came to find you," said Harry, spitting chips.
"They're planning a revolution. We could hear them through the wall.
For starters, they don't think you exist. We don't like that, at all.

"They think the King is crazy, that he should lose his crown.
They want to control or replace the King. They're riling up the town.
We know the King isn't perfect, though he's better in recent years.
But the town is ready to revolt. It's enough to curl your ears!

"Who knows what Chaos Fighter will cause. Fighter will come up large!
The Big Game will be lost for sure if King Sol is not in charge."

"What's "The Big Game'? questioned Sol. And who is this 'Fighter' guy?
If he's making trouble for my dad, I need to find out why."

Harry explained as he chewed.
"<u>The Book</u> says The Big Game began before time. Mouse ancestors played a part.
A spirit named Fighter cheated, wrecking Spirit's human hearts
that needed human Goodness to bring happiness to the earth.

"Then Fighter charged to earth himself, spreading evil for all he was worth.
Fighter has fought The Big Game since with the Chaos he can spread.
Spirit's Game has been for Goodness with better hearts, instead.

"We're about to battle on Spirit's side with our Goodness Flags unfurled!
We'll be fighting to defeat Fighter's Chaos and make a better world!"

"You don't say..."
"I *do say!* It was forecast in <u>The Book</u>, soon after the world began.
When *my* father consulted with Fireflies today, he gave us *their* command.
He declared that this was *our* time and mice must take a stand!

"When we heard my father's message, we gathered all our troops.
We've called on mice, rats, bugs and Scraps, all active Spirit groups.

"Then, boom! We saw two Fireflies! We heard them sing to you.
They told you that *your* time had come. What Fireflies say is true.
So, now we're here to free you. This is our big mission.
Next, we'll follow where *you* lead. That will be *your* decision."

"We've heard that you have a future that you may not suspect.
I don't know much about it or just what to expect,
but your old friends have come here. They wait below the floor.
There's an army of bugs and rats and mice, but it's *you* they're waiting for."

Sol didn't understand at all. The mice had seen Fireflies, too.
Maybe Fireflies held the secret of something he should do.
If Fireflies saw his future, that was something new.
Right now, he just felt stupid, with a future no one knew.

Sol peered down through the hole in the drawer, down to the floor below.
There were hundreds of creatures staring up and milling to and fro!

Sol squeezed through and dropped down. Finally, he saw Max.
The floor was alive with all his friends! Sol had to know more facts.

Max looked like he had looked before, though his teeth were a bit more yellow.
His eyes were bright, and his mind was sharp. He was still the same good fellow
who had played with Sol when he was a boy. They gave each other a hug,
but they were soon interrupted by a rat and a pincher bug.

"'Scuse me, Sir," saluted the rat in a military way.
Right away Sol saluted back, (though why, he couldn't say.)

"Me and Bug, we just got back from our recon into town.
We followed those Storytellers. We followed 'em all around.
They stirred up a fuss in the marketplace. It's writ in our report.
They're riot-ready and headed here. The time is getting short.
They're comin' this way with the town folk. The town is actin' mean.
It's the worst uprisin' of town folk that we have ever seen."

Sol just stared in amazement. The last time he'd seen this rat
they had been playing 'Bat the Pea', using a straw for a bat.
And this rat, "Junior" was very large. At last Sol understood
that Junior and Max were grown men now. This was new…but very good.

"I hear you, Rat," responded Sol. "If I hear what you say,
these town folk should be headed off, but I'm not sure there's a way
that we small guys can do that. Look around you. We're so small,
that even an army of all of us couldn't do much at all."

Bug now came to attention. "Come with me, Prince Sol, if you please.
There's a hole in this wall where we all can fit without too tight a squeeze.
Just follow me, Your Highness. It's important that you should.
There's some information waiting that might show you 'small is good'."

Bug led the way across the floor and skittered into a hole.
Sol and the others followed, not leaving a single soul.
Through the wallboards, they scurried, through spaces small and tight,
disappearing without a trace, a whole army, out of sight.

But what could Sol do with this army that said they were waiting for him?
They were all too small for a battle. They must know that their chance was slim.

Roots and Revelation

Sol followed Bug to a window. Bug's army backed away.
They expected something from him. But what? They didn't say.

Sol stood alone on the windowsill and surveyed the scene below.
Town folk were gathering near the gate. A mob was beginning to grow.
The crowd was shouting and angry, but why? He didn't know

Sol's family was in danger. This crowd was looking mean.
Sol hung his head and closed his eyes upon the angry scene.
Once again, he was too small. No solution could be seen.

"What do you all expect of me?" he growled out, course and low.
"There's no way *I* can help my family from those gathering down below.
I see town folk at the Castle gates and there's no one there to defend
the Castle against that angry mob. Ha! What do *you* intend?

"Could *I* help if I went down there? Why am I even here?
As a puny man, I have no size to protect those I hold dear.
I'm a useless man with no value. That truth is very clear."

Sol now shouted his fury. His frustration took the lead.
"I don't want to see this! This is nothing that I need!
Do you show me this to let me know of a battle I can't wage?
Do you want to *prove* how I haven't grown while locked up in this cage?

"How do you think this makes me feel when I see that a crowd advances
and I can't do a thing to help! I'm a small man with no chances
to help the People that I love. That's very clear to me.
I couldn't even warn them of these dangers we now see.
Did you need to show me this horror that I already know?
How much lower in misery do you want me to go?"

Sol crouched upon the window sill, alone in his despair.
If there were others watching, he didn't know or care.

A throat was cleared behind him. Sol started and turned around.
His old friend Max, was standing near, scarcely making a sound.

Sol moaned,
"Why have you followed me here, Max? Why do you watch and wait?
There's nothing here for you to see. I'm a nothing. That's my fate."

Sol slumped down by Max and said, "I'm surprised you're still my friend.
I feel my whole life is broken in a way that I can't mend.
Last night my mother and Awake made friends with two rotten guys.
They were taken into this Castle. I watched *with my own eyes*...
I was missing and nobody looked for me. They didn't even care."

Max Mouse smiled at his long-time friend. "Do you think you're being fair?
King Sol has been very good to you. Queen Luna has done her best.
If you want to judge this fairly, it's time that you know the rest."

"The rest of what?" Sol muttered. "What else is there to know?
My Mom and Dad had a tiny son and he never grew up...so?"

"Your human parents had one son. That much is true, so far,
but that is only one part of it. That's not *all* you really are.
It's time for me to tell you the story of your birth
and why you have more value than you think your life is worth."

Max now scratched his whiskers as Grandpa Mose had done.
"First, I want to tell you of a day when a child was born,
about the size of a peanut, or perhaps a piece of corn.
His parents were not shocked at all when they saw his tiny size
for they were as small as he was. He was perfect in their eyes."

Max waited for a moment. He looked close at Prince Sol.
Max knew what he was about to say was confusing, after all.
Sol still sulked in sadness, his mind not really clearing.
"What is so important from this story that I am hearing?"

"Well,
these parents" Max continued "were the tiny King and Queen
of a very tiny Kingdom, almost too small to be seen.

Their Kingdom was sheltered in grasses on the side of the Riverbank.
It is these unselfish parents that someday you will thank.

"What they have to do with you, you can't guess, perhaps,
but these folk were the tiny rulers of a Kingdom known as Scraps."

Sol began to listen more closely. He could easily empathize
with a little tiny kingdom filled with folk of a tiny size.

"These Scraps were made of Special Clay with the knowledge of right and wrong.
Special Clay was meant for human hearts. That's where it belonged.
But that Clay was dropped from human hearts. Human Goodness was impaired
but no one knew what the problem was. Only Spirit of Goodness cared.

"But the Fireflies watched and thought they knew how human hearts could be mended.
Special Clay was needed back in hearts as Spirit of Good intended.
Scraps were made of the Special Clay, so Scraps would be the key.
The King and Queen of Scraps were the ones who learned what had to be.
Scraps would need to help humans. It was their destiny.

"But their plan for Scraps to help People could not be begun
until one Scrap was ready. They needed a 'Chosen One'.
This Scrap would live with humans to learn what could be done.
Scrap Royals obeyed the Fireflies. Their *son* was the Chosen One.

"The Scrap Queen chose Queen Luna to teach the humans' ways
to her son without even knowing a Plan was taking place.
King Sol and Queen Luna raised that child. They raised him with *human* love,
while his *first* Scrap parents watched over him from above.

"Theirs was an awesome sacrifice, the gift of their only son
to learn to care for humans. Sol, *you* were that "Chosen One.

"Me?"

"Yes, *you* were the Chosen One, Sol. What you now need to see
is how important *you* were *then* and very soon *will* be.
There's this Game we call 'The Big Game' and we all play a part.
We play the Game for Spirit of Good. He gave our world its start.
He has watched us through the years. He knows each Player's worth.
The goal of his Game is Goodness for the humans of the earth.

"Fighter for Chaos coaches the team that took the other side.
His Chaos is what you see below with new Players being tried.
Fighter thinks they will win this Game and they can't be denied.
These men are powerful Players, so Good's defense can't wait.
If Fighter wins, the earth will lose and Chaos will be its fate.

"The Game has gone on for centuries, but we're in its final Quarter.
The fate of the world is at stake today and time is getting shorter
Since the prize for the winner of the Game was declared at the Game's beginning,
the Game has been fought for Earth's control and Chaos has been winning.

"Since Scraps were made from lost Special Clay, humans have lived without it.
None of them know about right and wrong. None of *us* can doubt it.
Chaos is gaining as you can see. It's more serious than before.
It's about control of the earth today, not just *a* winning score.
You are a Scrap of that Goodness, but now that you've learned more,
we need you to use your Scrap Special Clay for what it's intended for."

Sol sat down quick on the windowsill. He wasn't sure he could stand.
This was too much to think about, too much to understand.

Max quietly continued. His sympathy was there
for his friend and his old playmate. This was much for him to bare.

"All this was foretold by my Grandpa Mose. I relate it now to you.
My Grandpa placed *you* at Queen Luna's side, as he was asked to do.
Queen Luna became your mother, raising you as her little Prince.
She loved you when she first saw you. She has loved you each day since.

"Mice have known you were special, although we couldn't see
how we could help with your mission, your unique destiny
but, as the Fireflies requested today, this reveal was left to me.

"The Queen of the Scraps is gone now and so is her little King,
but their dream for you is still alive and their love is continuing.
You were raised by two sets of parents, a truly remarkable thing.
As the son of that Scrap Royalty, you are now the new Scrap King!"

Sol was completely dumfounded, undone, confused, and perplexed.
He couldn't grasp who he was now, nor what he should do next.

Max waited for the things he said to sink into Sol's understanding.
He could see that Sol's mind was tumbling, unsure where it was landing.

Max, however, was serious and bowed at Prince Sol's feet.
Prince Sol was now Scrap Royalty. He was now the Royal Elite.
"Yes, *you* are the *Scrap King*, Your Highness." You have been so for over a year.
Your Scrap father and mother died then. They are still mourned far and near.
But their love has always been with you. This I know is true.
In life they stayed near and still in death. They have always been with you."

Sol thought of the Fireflies he had seen. He now knew this, too.

Max next produced a tiny scroll and placed it in Sol's hand.
Sol's mind was full of questions he was trying to understand.
Max was almost finished. His heart went out to Sol.
How could this tiny, sheltered prince understand his awesome role?
Sol read:

"Dear Son,

We wish you could hear us. We hope that you will see the reasons for the decisions that we thought should be. We shared you with the humans so that you could learn their way, but we loved you more than anything. This we need to say.

Your human parents have loved you. Your role was unsuspected. We, too, have been watching and loving you, hidden and undetected. You have been learning to do the job for which you were created. Scrap Kingdom is ready to serve Mankind.

For many years they've waited. You are a Scrap, now King of the Consciences. You know right from wrong. This is what is needed by humans. To do this, you must be strong. We know that you have read many books to help you understand a world you have never seen yourself, and this learning has been grand. Use this knowledge you have gained by completing Spirit's plan.

You must lead your fellow Scraps. They wait to do as you say, but they don't know about humans. You will have to lead the way. Scraps were born for The Big Game to be Consciences to others. You will show Scraps their future. Lead your sisters and your brothers!

By the time you read this letter, you will be on your own, but all our love goes with you. You will never be alone. You are ready now to lead the way, far better than any other. You are a Scrap,.. King of the Consciences!

Love,
Your Scrap Father and Mother

Sol was feeling dizzy. His legs couldn't move or bend.
This letter from his 'parents'. It was too much to comprehend.
He wasn't a king. How could he be? What else did his friend, Max, know?
His other friends were waiting. There were enemies below.
And what about this 'Big Game'? Questions rolled and churned.
What in the world should *he* do now with all that he'd just learned?

Trouble at the Gate

Meanwhile,
Spirit returned to the Castle. He was nervous and full of fear.
He hadn't found the Fireflies, though he'd looked far and near.
He hoped against hope the Prince was back, and he'd magically re-appear!
Poor Spirit was sad. He had no idea that Sol was actually near
and watching town folk approaching, surrounded by bugs and mice.
Spirit feared the Prince would not be found and his life would be the price.

Spirit was devastated. He was worried about his Plan,
but more than that, he worried for Sol, a tiny, vulnerable man,
a small Prince that was out there in a world he didn't know.
How could he have let this happen? He had waited for Sol to grow,
but had he waited too long? This he didn't know.

Spirit withdrew to a corner, worried, confused, perplexed.
Without Sol, he had no Plan at all and no thought of what was next.
King Sol and Queen Luna sat quietly on their thrones.
Though surrounded by servants, they felt quite alone.
Had their run off without a trace or had he been taken?
Both fear and sadness gripped the Royals, all happiness forsaken.

Awake now wanted to comfort them. She tried to speak cheerfully.
"I'm sure the Prince will be home soon. He's probably having fun,
perhaps his first adventure! He'll come home when he's done."

At least Awake is hopeful, Spirit thought alone.
"At least she's thinking positive," Spirit sighed in a mournful tone.

Queen Luna tried to smile at Awake, hoping her words were true.
King Sol also nodded, not knowing what else to do.

Awake now stared out the window, praying for Sol's return.
She hoped that Grin would bring Sol back. Grin was also her concern.
She thought that Grin was a good man. (Some love is slow to learn.)

Gradually, all became aware of noises outside the gate.
Could that be Sol returning home? No one was willing to wait.
Awake jumped up and ran to the door. So did the King and Queen.
The servants saw them running, (something they'd never seen.
'A King and Queen simply do not run.' Whatever did this mean?)

Who was coming to their gates that both Royals wanted to see?
Spirit also watched the door. What could these noises be?

Guards opened the gates with caution, revealing *no* Grin or Brood,
but a mass of angry town folk in a mean and threatening mood.
The King's eyes searched the crowd for Sol, but he kept his Kingly state.

"What's the meaning of all this noise? Why are you at my gate?"
He motioned to his Castle Guards to stand and block the way.
Never, *ever*, in recent years had town folk behaved this way,
howling like an angry mob. What had they come to say?

One man stepped to the front of the crowd. He checked from side to side.
He had the backing of his friends. His chest was puffed with pride.

Grin and Brood stepped back to the sidelines where they could quietly lurk.
Camouflaged in the background, they observed their handy work.

And Fighter stayed in the shadows, too. He wasn't in a rush.
He could watch this crowd fight on its own. He didn't need to push.

The spokesman spoke up.
"We've all got some questions, Sire, and me, I've been selected
ta speak these questions at ya. Ya might say I was *elected*
ta ask ya what yer gonna do to fix dangers here about.
So, what're ya gonna do, Sire?" We want action now, no doubt!"

"Hundreds of highwaymen wait now to murder us on our roads!
They're gonna steal our women, and what's worse, our wagon loads!
Ya gotta send yer Castle Guard to round up them rotten men!

We won't dare to travel none 'til our roads are safe again!"
Now King Sol whispered to the Queen, "What's this all about?
You told me about *one* highwayman. Did you leave something out?"

"Why no, dear. I told you everything. I told you all I knew.
I only heard of two highwaymen. What has caused *this*, I've no clue."

Spirit was listening carefully to what the town would say.
When Spirit heard the word, "highwaymen," he remembered yesterday.
Did Grin's 'rescue of Awake' *then* have something to do with today?

King Sol spoke with authority. "What danger are you in?
What kind of help do you want from me? And stop this ungodly din!"

The town folk quieted just a bit. The spokesman spoke again.
"We're not worried 'bout *one* highwayman, Sire, but *hundreds* of highwaymen.
Hundreds are hidin' along our roads, sneakin' through hillside passes,
set to attack our wagon loads and the town folk's innocent lasses.
You have to call up the Castle Guards! *You* gotta defend the town!
Declare war on all highwaymen! You must beat those rotters down!"

King Sol was astonished at the outrage that he was hearing.
There was no threat that he had heard like that which they were fearing.
The spokesman nodded snidely and stepped back into the clearing.

"You look surprised about highwaymen but *we* know why that's so.
If you were doin' yer duty, then probably you'd know.
But you haven't been payin' attention. *You've* been focused on your 'Prince'!"

The reference to his missing son caused poor King Sol to wince.

What in the world is happening? Spirit thought with a groan.
This kind of anger at the King, has not recently been shown.
The King has grown more generous. The King has grown more fair.
Prince Sol has shown both the King and Queen new ways to show they care.
Why do River People now have this feeling of distrust?
This sounds like something Fighter would start. I'll check. That's a must.

(And, indeed Fighter was right there, sneaking along the side,
cheering on the anger that the townsfolk didn't hide.)

The growling crowd surged forward with growing disapproval.
King Sol signaled his Castle Guard to get ready for crowd removal.

But King Sol had a second thought. *A King must take a stand.*
It's time for me to speak up strong. It's time I take command.

"Harrumph," said King Sol. "I see now how fearful you must be
if there is danger on our roads that's something I did not see.
So, I intend to investigate and do so immediately!
I will not tolerate terror. Our roads must be kept clear.
I will meet with you People tomorrow. All Yesmen must be here.

"At that time, my plans, if needed, will impressively appear.
A King *must* protect his People from *all* peril far and near
and I will definitely do so. Do I make myself quite clear?"

The King spoke firm with a confidence he knew that they could hear.

The town folk looked at each other, surprised at what they'd heard.
The King looked strong, like a man in charge. Though shocked, they took his word.

It was hard to give up a good fight, but, on the other hand,
the King was sounding pretty stout and they could understand
the solution he had suggested. Tomorrow they would see
if he was full of hogwash or as strong as he seemed to be.

The King had passed his first test. The town backed off and then
bowed to their King but announced with a growl, "We'll be back again!"

Brood and Grin were blown away. This King had sounded good.
He didn't fold under pressure the way they thought he would.
Quickly they huddled together to plan what they should do.
Plan One had sort-of fizzled. They would need to try Plan Two.

Fighter was astounded. "The King looked strong today.
I'll have to go back to the drawing board and find a stronger way
to counteract what Spirit used to make the King sound smart.
He didn't fade like I thought he would, but this was just a start."

Spirit had heard the ruckus. He was quite impressed
with the King's very kingly performance when put to such a test.
King Sol had resisted violence and, though his response was strong,
he had shown respect for the Peoples' fears. Respect was never wrong.

Prince Sol had changed his father. The evidence was plain,
but where *was* the little Prince now? No one had yet explained.
One crisis had been dodged today but Spirit's fears remained.

Now Spirit saw some stragglers as the town folk moved away.
Two characters from the side of the crowd looked like they might stay.

Spirit realized he knew one...'the hero' from yesterday.
He remembered that encounter. He had admired the way
Grin had rescued the young Awake from a fearsome-looking crook.
Did the fellow that was with him now have a familiar look? Hmm...6+

Spirit had liked Grin's style at the time, but perception slightly cleared...
Had that 'rescue' been as gallant then as it had first appeared?

And....no one had spoken of highway men until these two arrived....
And...now the town was angry. Had their anger been contrived?

The town folk were drifting back to town. Grin now stepped up to the King.
He smiled and bowed his friendly best and spoke with a humble ring.

"We're honored to meet you, Your Majesty. I am Grin and this is Brood.
We would have said something earlier, but we didn't want to intrude
on 'discussions' happening with the town outside your Castle door.
Neither of us understood, of course, just what that crowd was for.

"We're just friends of your girl, Awake. We met her yesterday
and defended her from a highwayman in a pretty awesome way.
You might say we're the reason that she's still alive today."

They bowed as low as they could go, displaying no aggression.
They employed their practiced acting skills to make a good impression.

The Queen had told the King, of course, about the young men's deed
and how the two had intervened in Awake's hour of need.
The King stopped now and listened to what these two might say.
But more important than anything that the King might do today
was finding Sol, his missing son. *These men might know a way.*

Spirit decided to watch this. He was not completely convinced
that these two were either good or bad, *but…* could they know about the Prince?

"You saved Awake," the King began. "Thank you for what you've done,
but I must ask before anything else, have you seen my son?
Did you take him with you into town, perhaps to 'have some fun?'

"Our son has never been to town. That world for him is new.
The Queen and I are worried, so we must know what's true.
Please tell us. We won't be angry. You have seen him, haven't you?"

Spirit leaned in for the answer. Was there something that they knew?

Whoa!
There it was! The evidence Brood and Grin were looking for...
the proof that the King was as crazy as they had heard before.
This King *did have an imagined son. He really was insane!*
They would have no trouble fooling him. This result was plain.
Plan Two began to take shape now. The King had assured their gain.

Brood first seized the moment as it was presented,
and, on the spot, he confessed a 'truth' that he had just invented.

"We're sorry to have to tell you for we see you love your son,
but we believe that he's run off to 'seek his place in the sun'.
He left with us. Yes, this is true. We arrived at the market place
and started to tell our stories with our usual style and grace.

"When we turned around, your son was gone. He left without a trace
except for a little note that said, 'Please tell my Mom and Dad,
thanks for bringing me up so far. It's a good life that I had,
but I must go and see the world one time before I die.
Tell my folks I'm gone for good. Tell everyone, goodbye.'"

"Goodbye?" Spirit heard this.... "'Goodbye?' This can't be true.
Prince Sol wouldn't leave his home for good. That is *not* what Sol would do.
He is too kind and thoughtful." Spirit knew that this was true.
He wouldn't leave his parents to go out on his own.
He wouldn't have left them to worry with a frightening fate unknown,
...unless he was *really* frustrated in a way he'd never shown...

Spirit cringed. Maybe...

The King looked mortally wounded. His face turned putty gray.
Awake and Luna held his arms, afraid he would faint away.
They helped him into the Castle, crying as they went in,
followed by the servants... and after them, Brood and Grin.

CONSCIENCES—AND THE LEGENDS OF THE BIG GAME

The Castle servants were silent much like Awake and the Queen,
but the King regained his strength and said, "Please tell me all you've seen.
As you know, our son is small. We have kept him so protected
that he knows nothing of the world or evils to be expected.
We must try to find him. There's no time to wait.
He's too inexperienced to be outside the Castle gate."

Grin continued his 'acting job', and respectfully he said,
"Your Majesties, we're sorry for the part in this we played.
We didn't know your son shouldn't go when he asked to go to town.

"You, Queen Luna, took us in. In return, we let you down.
We feel it is our duty to go back to the market place.
If we don't find your little son, we'll leave here in disgrace."

Grin and Brood were very smooth, sincerity on each face.
The King was touched by their offer. So were the Queen and Awake.
This most appealing offer was one that they would take.

The Queen was first to answer. "Thank you both so much.
You don't even know our son. This is such a generous touch.
And the two of you might be able to locate him quite fast
because it is the two of you who probably saw him last."

The King began to brighten. He rose up from his chair.
"Yes!" he said. "Go back to town and search for my son there.
Perhaps you can rally the town folk. They can *all* look high and low!
You can ask everybody that you see. Surely someone will know
where my son is now and when, at last, my son is found,
you two can bring him home to us, unharmed, safe and sound!"

Awake had been crying quietly as Sol seemed hopelessly gone,
but when she heard Grin's proposal, a light of hope turned on.

"He's so small. He's in grave danger. Please find him if you can.
Do you really think you can find him? He's such a special man."

She took Grin's hands in her hands and held them to her face.
Grin saw the love shining from her eyes that her tears could not erase,
and from somewhere deep inside Grin came a feeling warm and kind.
He wanted to help her all he could. He even wanted to find
this imaginary little prince that she declared was real.
He wanted to stop and ask her, "Do you feel as I feel?"
But these feelings were new to Grin, feelings he must conceal.

Spirit watched and felt some hope. Grin's feelings seemed quite real.
Perhaps Grin would really look for Sol to bring him home and then
Prince Sol could complete the Plan for earth as it had always been.

"Come, Grin," said Brood. "This mystery can be solved.
We will talk to all the town folk to get each one involved.
We'll search the village high and low. We know what to do
and when we have found the little Prince, we will bring him back to you."

This sounds good, thought Spirit. Perhaps their pledge is true.

Back in Town

The Story Tellers left for town with their promise to search and find
the son of the desperate King and Queen. Spirit followed behind.

Searching above, he scanned *over them*, hoping the two could find
the Prince as they had promised, but soon, poor Spirit knew
that searching for a missing Prince was the *last* thing they would do.
There was no doubt that Grin and Brood weren't looking for Prince Sol.
The moment they left the Castle and were outside the Castle wall,
they hurried back to the marketplace to issue a battle call.

Spirit followed closely and now was shocked...surprised.
The market place was still teeming. At once he realized
that the crowd was not dispersing. He saw the truth at last.
"Fighter must be in charge of this. The 'riot dye's cast".

Fighter's spell was upon them. They laughed at the King and Queen.
They sneered at the thought of 'the tiny Prince' who never had been seen.
They were more ready for Chaos now than they had ever been.

Spirit spotted Fighter. He was horrified and surprised
at the size and the quickness of the plan that Fighter had devised.
Why had he not sensed earlier that Fighter was in command?
Why had it taken him so long to finally understand
that the 'rescue of Awake' he'd seen had obviously been pre-planned.

Fighter blew swirling, whirling blasts to whip the retreating crowd.
This wasn't time for them to go home. "Tomorrow" was not allowed.
The brothers must get back to it, regrouping strong and loud.
Coach Fighter knew the time was ripe. No slacking for this crowd.

The brothers immediately rejoined the crowd. "Folks, don't think us rude,
but we don't trust your King at all!" announced the plotting Brood.
"We just talked with your crazy king. He's not worried about you.
He's worried about an invisible kid! Do you know what he wants us to do?

"He wants *us* to find his invisible brat and, if he can find a minute,
he *might* also look for your highwaymen, but his heart's not really in it'"
"Our King has always been like that," the town folk answered back."

"We've always wondered what he would do if we had a real attack."

"He's been a good King in other ways, but we wondered what would be done
if we needed him to *fight for us* 'cause he ain't got no son."

Now Grin glanced from man to man and focused a knowing stare.
"When he's needed to fight the highwaymen, there'll be no one there.
If he thinks his son is missing, he won't have time to care
as the highwaymen destroy you, take your women and your food...
but... we have another answer," crowed the Players, Grin and Brood.
The town folk snarled and listened. Right now they were ready to hear
anything about the King that would fortify their fear.

Sensing the mood of the restless crowd, the boys knew the time was right.
"Why should we wait for tomorrow? We can conquer the King tonight!"
shouted Grin and Brood to the roiling group. "Are you ready for such a fight?

"We'll eliminate your foolish King! Surprise will be on our side.
We're the leaders who can do this! We will not be denied!"

Fighter for Chaos listened. His smile grew dark and wide.
They had stirred the folks up, once again. Men gathered up their tools
to march against the King and Queen whom they now dismissed as fools.

"I knew I could trust these two guys," sneered Fighter with a grin.
They're ready to storm the King, *right now!* That 'll ensure my win.
The Big Game can be mine tonight! Spirit won't have a chance.
Goodness on earth will be destroyed without even a backward glance."

The Big Game was in its 4th Quarter. What could Spirit do?
Fighter would soon be on the move. That was obviously true.
Without a sudden miracle, earth's Goodness would be through.
And poor Prince Sol was still missing. Where was he? No one knew.

Spirit was desperate to find Prince Sol, but he didn't know where to look.
He *must* find Prince Sol to save the King, no matter what it took.
Prince Sol was the key to his Game for Good, but did the Prince even know?
Had Prince Sol ever been shown his task that was planned so long ago?

Who was there to tell him? He was probably never told
that he had been training to save mankind! Spirit's blood ran cold.

He needed help from the Fireflies. A battle was drawing near
and if Prince Sol wasn't there to help, the outcome was too clear.
He needed an Army of Goodness. There had to be a way.
Spirit couldn't give up his beautiful earth! He would not give up today!

"If the world turns into cinders, *today won't* be the reason!
I pledge once more to the cosmos! Today will be Goodness Season!

I *will* find the Fireflies. It's the least that I can do.
It's *their* Plan that's in jeopardy. They *must* know what to do.
Listen to me, Fighter. Hear *my* battle cry!
You are ahead in the Game right now, but it's time for 'do-or-die!'"

With the fate of the world hanging on him, Spirit stormed into the sky.

Prince Sol and the Hall

From upstairs in the Castle, Prince Sol had seen the crowd
shouting and screaming earlier, angry, fierce and loud.
But then they had seemed to turn and leave. Sol had watched them go.
Just why the crowd had come and gone, he had no way to know.

Sol looked again at Max Mouse who had shown him what he'd learned.
He might not be needed down there today, but questions tossed and churned.

"What should I do with what you've said? My life is overturned.
You say that I'm "The King of Scraps", but I don't understand.
Where are these Scraps that I'm king of? Who do I command?

"I can't be someone else's king. To *this* Castle I am bound.
I'm loyal to my human father and his challenge from this town.
A minute ago, they were down there and wanted to take *his* crown."

"They'll be back again, believe me," said Max with a knowing frown.
"But soon you'll know what you should do. Come... We can't let down."

Sol slowly rolled his tiny scroll and stuck it inside his blouse.
He squared his shoulders, smoothed his hair, and turned to the patient mouse.

"Thank you, Max, for all you have done... your Grandpa and Harry, too.
I know that you mice are all my friends, and your counsel is wise and true.
What is it now, my faithful friend, *you* think that I should do?"

"Come," said Maximilien Mouse. "There's something you must be shown.
Your destiny awaits you. You must see that you're not alone."

Max led Sol down through the Castle, to the space known as the Hall.
Sol had played here as a youth. This place was known to Sol,
but today it looked much different, with a serious tone reflected
in a set up for a meeting, somber, dark, protected.

"We've been meeting here for a year" said Max. "You have been expected.
Rodents, Bugs and Whole Scraps have gathered here to plan
how to work together *and*... how to *live* with Man.

"To this brave group of leaders, the members were elected.
From here we mice now govern our world, safe and undetected.

"The human world is raging. Fighter has taken command.
So it's time for small creatures of the world to rise up and take a stand.
Rodents, Bugs and Whole Scraps have joined in this situation.
But now they're waiting for you, alone, with great anticipation."

"How does anyone know about me? They've never met me before."

Max smiled.

"We have all been watching you through the cracks in the Castle floor,
and many of us *are* your old friends from when we played before.
We've all been waiting for you to grow up. We *know* what your life is for.

"Your parents taught Scraps about People as they watched what you were learning.
Now they are ready to follow your lead in a way for which they're yearning."

Max sat down at a table which was made from a dinner plate.
He motioned for Sol to sit down, too. They wouldn't have long to wait.
Rodents and Bugs began filing in. Each took a place at the table,
looking solemn and dignified...as much as the Bugs were able.

A fly, some ants and a cockroach came to complete the group.
Around the room, standing near the walls, Mouse Spirit Club formed a troop.

With a solemn air of purpose, Max addressed the group:
"We have come together this afternoon to join our friend, Prince Sol,
and put destiny into practice and answer the future's call.

"In the days of Michael Angelo, a solemn vow was sealed,
to help Scraps fulfill their destiny at a time to be revealed.
Now that time is upon us. The moment is at hand.
We are pledged to you, oh King of Scraps. We follow your command."

Sol looked around the table. All there looked ready for war,
but he knew in his heart that violence was not what they were for.

Sol stood up and looked around. In a way he had not expected,
he squared his shoulders and countered with confidence projected.

"Thank you, Max, for all you have done and all you are ready to do.
Your family has always been friends with mine, much more than I ever knew.
I know now that King Sol and his Queen were not my first father and mother,
but they have loved me all my life. I have never known another.

"King Sol and Queen Luna are the parents I've always known.
I can't desert these parents now and leave them on their own."

Sol spoke with determination that he had never known.
"I'm told I'm to be 'a Conscience', whatever that might be.
I am told that *I'm already* one, though I know I'm only 'me'.

I see that People need Consciences. I understand that now,
but my human parents' must come first. This is my solemn vow.
I will take my place as a Conscience, but please don't think me rude.
I *must* help my human parents now from two men called Grin and Brood."

Max looked at Sol and smiled again, his expression, wise and keen.
"You *will* help them *as you know you must*. This requirement has been seen
by everyone around you. Soon you'll know what I mean."

Before Sol could ask more questions, a sight froze him to his chair.
He looked down to the end of the room at *new* creatures entering there.
These creatures weren't more bugs or mice advancing to their places,
but tiny people, just his size with big smiles on their faces.

Sol tried to show some dignity, much more than he actually felt.
He was determined to do his best with surprises he'd been dealt
but these were tiny people, entering one by one. They sat down at the table.
Prince Sol wanted to run to greet them, but, in fact, he wasn't able.
He couldn't move a muscle. His feet seemed attached to the floor.
These little folk were just like him! (He had never seen Scraps before.)

"Where did these people come from?" he finally managed to croak.
The tiny Scraps smiled back at him like they knew a private joke.

And Sol noticed one above the rest, a young woman, soft and fair.
She radiated gentleness and a beauty beyond compare.
Her warm eyes seemed to reach for Sol's and hold a connection there.

"I am Moon," Sol heard her say. Her presence held him fast.
He felt that she could read his thoughts and his dreams from first to last.

"You are our leader, Sol," she said. "*Your* destiny is cast.
We are Scraps like your parents, the ones that you never knew.
We are all your subjects. We've arrived here from The Sew.
And you are our King, as your father was. We are here to follow you."

Sol wanted to say something. He tried very hard to speak,
but the only noise he could utter was sort of a gurgling squeak.

Max was watching closely. He chuckled and nodded his head.
Then he smiled his all-knowing smile. To Sol he gently said,
"These are *your* people Sol, my friend. What Moon has said is true.

Moon knew you would need them. She has brought them here, indeed
because King Sol is in danger. She knew you would feel his need,
so she brought these Scraps to you today to begin what has been decreed."

Sol stopped to think for a moment, then stepped forward with hesitation.
He stood up straight, took a giant breath and spoke without reservation.
Sol's gaze took in every single Scrap. With surprise, he heard himself say,
"Thank *you* all for coming here to be with me today.
Thank you, my new-found brothers and wonderful sisters, too.
You tell me now that I am your King. This is something new
so *I am* just your humble servant. I am proud to be one of you.

"Scraps, I'm told, must be Consciences. I am not sure how that will be.
I just discovered that *I* am a Scrap and that this is my destiny.
I hear we were made to help People, though I, for one, never knew it
and I see that People *need* help, of course, if we figure out how to do it.

"I know that folks need to think things through. I hear that it's our role
to help them decide between right and wrong. That is a lofty goal.
How we can help them do that, I'm not really sure,
but I hear we were made out of Special Clay that will keep our motives pure.

"I don't know about Clay *or* Consciences, I must honestly say
but, if Goodness is what we're created for, that's a Game I'm ready to play
to play.

"I've seen Goodness grow in humans. If, as Consciences, Scraps can share
what they know of love and kindness, maybe humans can learn to care."

Sol suddenly thought about Grin and Brood. Were they too bad to repair?
Some humans might be too bad to help. Might they be too much to ask?
And how could Scraps get close enough to accomplish such a task?
Wasn't this what Scraps believed all Scraps could somehow do?
Sol owed it to his *Scrap* parents to try to see this through.

But how should this goal be accomplished? He was ready now to go
do what was expected of him but that's what he didn't know.

The Scraps began jabbering at once while Sol, in a happy daze
continued to greet each one of them and absorb each happy gaze
on their many joyful faces, and their friendly, Scrap-like ways.

Confronting Misery

Then, into the midst of this blissful scene, sad sounds came from above.
Prince Sol stopped and listened. These were People that he loved.

King Sol was groaning with loneliness, the sign of a breaking heart.
"What on earth, do I do now? Where do I even start?
My son is missing. My Kingdom is torn. My world is falling apart.

"Tomorrow the town folk will return. I must think things through.
What would my son advise me? *He* would know what to do
...but he's not here beside me. I miss him and I fear,
while I don't know *where or how* he is, nothing else is clear.

"If only I could discuss this and hold him in my hand,
he could whisper in my ear. I know I would understand
what to do for my People and why they're so upset.
Why do they fear *many* highwaymen? I don't understand that yet.
And why did my son run off to town with two men he'd never met?"

Below, the assembled listened, too. One thing was very clear.
This father really loved his son. Sol wiped away a tear.
Sol could hear in his father's tone, that he was very sad
and he knew *he* was part of the reason that his father felt so bad.

But something else had happened. Something more was on his mind.
"My father is in a crisis. Why is that? I'm way behind.
I was locked up in a dresser drawer. I don't know what's going on.
I saw crowds of People come and go. What's happened since I was gone?"

The rats and mice all spoke at once, each telling what he knew.

Max held up a paw to the jumble, boiling words down to a few.
"Two guys stirred up the town folk, Sol, and set them against the King.
Now, the town thinks they're in danger and King Sol won't do a thing.
They think their King is too busy thinking about his son,
a son that *they have never seen so...they think there isn't one.*

"The town thinks these guys are heroes and so do Awake and the Queen.
They don't know they're just liars, the smoothest ever seen.

"They are Fighter's new Players. We can see it in their eyes.
This is the *huge* crisis today but I hope you will realize
that the only move that will beat them must be of a *smaller size.*"

"What?"

"That's right. Our play must be a smaller play to capture Fighter's prize,
to win The Big Game for Spirit and give Fighter a big surprise,"
declared Max with great conviction...and a twinkle in his eyes.

Sol heard that Awake was not a part of the plot. He was thrilled to understand
that she was not part of the evil scheme that these two brothers planned.
But who was 'smaller, not bigger'. Was that special person here?
And who was this guy named 'Fighter'? Was he someone Sol should fear?
Was he a mouse or a human? This was quite unclear.

Max explained...
"Fighter's that evil spirit that I told you about before."
He's the guy who's been fighting for Chaos for centuries and more.
Spirit just wants more Goodness to be in the universe.
Fighter sees his 'Chaos' as a **big**, earth-ending curse!

"He's called 'Fighter for Chaos', 'cause Chaos is all he's got.
But Spirit has **small** *Consciences now*. These are something he *has not!*
Scraps are here and ready to fight this upcoming War.
Scraps are Spirit's secret weapon and Goodness they're fighting for."

Prince Sol was paying attention. Bugs and rats gathered around.
All watched Sol for direction. They listened, not making a sound.

Quietly, the lovely Moon stepped purposefully to the fore.
Beside her stood a male Scrap that Sol hadn't noticed before.
The pair looked like they were ready, but what were they ready for?

The male Scrap spoke with confidence respectfully to Prince Sol.
"You are now our Conscience Leader, Sire. We answer to your call.
You have lived with People. What do you suggest?
We are here to follow you. What will help your People best?

"I'm Moon's brother, Shaver. I've been watching you for years.
I know that you can lead us, in spite of your current fears.
The men of whom Max speaks now are evil through and through.
They want to take over the Kingdom, and they're set to do it, too.

"I've watched you with your parents. They have been good to you.
I watched *them* grow in Goodness and that was because of you.
You know now how to help People. I can testify that's true.
Just help us do *what you know* and that's what *we* will do."

Shaver straightened up his back as though ready for a fight.
He looked like a Scrap you could count on to help things turn out right.
Sol looked from him into Moon's dark eyes. Her eyes were full of care.
She was ready to be a Conscience, too. He saw the Goodness there.
These Scraps were ready for him to lead, but how...and who...and where?

The Conscience Army

Prince Sol tried to think clearly, seeing all gathering near.
They say that this is my destiny, but I wish my path was clear.
How can 'a Conscience' stop Grin and Brood when they are on their way?
My Scrap parents hoped I'd learn some skills to use on such a day
but what have I learned? If they were here, what would those parents say?'

Now Sol glanced up to the rafters. Two Fireflies were soaring high.
A gentle breeze seemed to kiss his cheek as two Fireflies floated by.
Like that, what he needed came to Sol. Listening closely, he heard more.
The Fireflies were singing strait to him as they had done before.

"If you just *talk* to People, they might think instead of fight."
People need to hear the truth to learn what's wrong or right.
With Consciences, folks might think things through and react honestly.
"Small Consciences will help People think so Consciences need to be...
near enough to speak in Peoples' ears about what is good and true.

You have done this with your parents. You know what to do.
Show these Scraps how to do this, and the will do it, too.

"The town is getting ready. They will soon come marching back,
to overthrow your father, their King. They are ready for attack.
You will need a *Conscience Army* to stand up good and strong
to give People another option and suggest why they might be wrong.
These Scraps are made of Special Clay. They will answer this request.
They have volunteered to be Consciences. Just show them the rest."

"I get it, now!" Prince Sol proclaimed. "I didn't know before
but we Scraps must join The Big Game, though this Game *is* like war.
Chaos won't win against Good thoughts. That's what Consciences are for."

Sol pulled the Scraps around him, a 'General in the making',
and explained the way he came and went with humans without taking
risks or being seen, when only his voice should be heard.
Humans could do what they chose to do though they understood each word.
This would be the free agency that every human had.
He told the Scraps just what he did when he talked to his Mom and Dad.

"I just try to explain what I think about things, what I think is good or bad.
It must be my own Special Clay that provided me a guide.
I never knew I had Special Clay since its somewhere down inside.
If all Scraps are made of Special Clay, all Scraps can do this too.
We can just speak up for our Special Clay. That's all we have to do."

Sol sat down at the dinner plate and sketched out a simple plan,
the Plan that was always intended, ever since the earth began.
Soon all understood the Conscience role of each Scrap woman and man.

"We must return to the hearts of Man, so that Man can tell wrong from right.
We were born to live in human hearts, so that's where we must fight.
We'll go back to where we started and if we do, who knows?
The People may learn to think about things, instead of throwing blows.
They may understand that my dad is Good and the Storytellers have lied.
If they listen to their Consciences, that truth won't be denied.

"It's like I said, gloated Max Mouse. "At last I'm understood.
Now you can believe me, Sol, my friend. 'Being small can be good.

"But... don't let People see you. That's what I suggest.
People should *hear* their Consciences. Not seeing them is best.
They must decide things for themselves. I have come to this conclusion.
Your Special Clay will be in their hearts. To see you will cause confusion."

Shaver was first to answer the call. "Please let me lead," he cried.
"I have watched you do this many times. It's high time that I tried."

"Let Shaver ride on me!" a rat offered. "Junior is my name.
My Grandpa Ramon always liked your folks and he said they felt the same.
If you give me the honor, I'll be Shaver's steed.
We rats are eager to do our part, and very proud indeed."

"Thanks, Junior! I remember you. You're just the guy we need."
So, Shaver rode off on Junior with a proud, courageous heart.
More Scraps and rodents scampered away, intent on doing their part
to try the Plan that Sol described. They were more than ready to start.
The Scraps clung to their Rodent friends, riding inside the wall,
and on to find River People, on orders from *Scrap King Sol!*

The New Plan

A few were chosen to stay with Sol for special work at the Hall.
Sol drew strategies from the books he'd read to flesh out his battle call.
He also asked Moon to stay behind and choose three "special others".
Moon chose her fair-haired sister and two good natured brothers.
Sol had particular plans for them that were different from the others.

They sat cross-legged beneath a grate. They, too were ready to go.
Their faces glowed with excitement, but first Sol wanted to know,

"What are your names, my new Scrap friends? We haven't met before.
Moon chose you for your special skills. Has she told you what they're for?
You will be my advance team, ahead of all the rest.
Thank you for being willing. She knows what you do best."

The first to respond were the brothers. They worked as a pair.
"We are Left and Right. We are twin Scraps. We try hard to be fair
by looking at both sides of things for results both sides can share."

"My name is Daybreak", Moon's sister declared. "I look for the brighter side.
Each sun rise brings a new day with new thoughts to be tried.
I'll try to find the good in folks, where ever it might hide."
The dark-haired Moon was last to speak. For a moment she hesitated.
She shyly glanced at her new King, the one for whom they'd waited.
Now she was sitting here with him. What did she want to say?
She felt suddenly strange and shy. Why did she feel this way?

"You already know that my name is Moon. I'm not special in any way,
but I see things in my dreams at night that can't be seen by day.
That's how I knew it was your time to take your place as our King.
Though you felt lost in a dresser drawer, you heard the Fireflies sing.
You didn't know your destiny or what your parents planned,
so I asked the mice to talk to you to help you understand.

"We Scraps have awaited your special call to come and take our place
as Consciences to humans and help the human race.
I dreamed that you asked the question, "What is my life for?"
We came to answer that question with one thousand Scraps and more."

Sol was fascinated. When his future had seemed most dim
Moon had seen him in her dreams and brought these Scraps to him.
And now they were working together. She was part of his future, he knew.
Sol took Moon's hands in his hands. Old dreams were coming true.

For a moment they saw each other as all young people do
when strong feelings come upon them and romantic thoughts are new,
but Sol couldn't savor the moment. This much the young King knew.

"You were meant to hear me in your dream. We'll work together, Moon.
I want to know more about you, and I will do that soon.
But I need to help my father now with the crisis that I see.
Will you join me in the Castle? For you, I've a special plea.
If you could help my mother, it would mean a lot to me."

Moon nodded and took her place in line, ready to join the fight.
She was anxious to join the battle and she knew this was right.

Frustration

For Spirit, Sol was still missing. He had no way of knowing
what was happening in the Hall because nothing was yet showing.

Sol and the Scraps had met at last, but poor Spirit didn't know.
But he *did* know the town was ready to fight. Would this war be the blow
that would finally lose The Big Game? To a hillside he retreated.
The Game was in its 4th Quarter and Goodness was being defeated.

Spirit racked his brain for a backup plan, something to save the day,
but hard as he tried, he couldn't seem to see decent way
to make up for all he had done wrong from creation through to today.

He had made a pledge that was full of pride, and then he had dropped the Clay.
And when he had another chance, he had thrown it all away
by ignoring the Scraps of Goodness that might have saved the day.
He had no one to blame but himself. Now his humans would have to pay.

What good was the Fireflies' Plan? Where could their Plan be leading?
He had misread both Grin and Brood. It was Fireflies he was needing
to save him from all his mis-ques. As a spirit, he was a flop,
from his blindness with Storytellers, way back to that fatal "Drop."
And couldn't find the Fireflies. His morale continued sliding.
They had always helped him in the past. Where could they be hiding?

And worst, he had lost his precious Sol before Sol even knew
of the destiny he was made for and what his skills could do.
How could he face the Fireflies? How could he show his face?
He had failed to find his missing Prince. He was a pure disgrace
to all that he had hoped for. He knew he had betrayed
all the sacrifices with their son that the little Royals had made.

The world would dissolve into Chaos. Fighter's victory would erase
any hope for Good in the universe. Say goodbye to the human race.

Spirit lay in the grass of the hillside, wallowing in sadness and fear.
He didn't look up to notice that Fireflies were suddenly near.
But gradually he raised his head. Fireflies began to sing.
They were singing songs about Consciences, the most inspiring thing
that Spirit of Good had ever heard. Their singing soothed his fears.
"The Big Game is on," sang the Fireflies. He couldn't believe His ears.

The Fireflies were singing about Prince Sol. 'The Prince was lost no more.
Two special Fireflies had just brought word so now they knew the score.'
They sang that the Prince had a new Game Plan that hadn't been used before.

Spirit was stunned by this wondrous news. He begged them to tell him more.
So they sang that Prince Sol had been joined by Scraps. How had this occurred?
Scraps were going to be Consciences. Spirit relished every word.

Sol was home. He had been found. Just where, they didn't say
but Sol was safe and involved in the Plan... *The 4th Quarter was still in play!*

The Fireflies glowed with excitement. Spirit knew their song was true.
He must see this miracle himself. Was there something he could do
to help Prince Sol and his Consciences? These Consciences would be new.
Who on earth had prepared them to know what they should do?

Spirit must see these 'Consciences' and learn what they were doing.
Prince Sol would be trying to win this Game while a Castle attack was brewing.

"Can he and the Scraps really help King Sol *while* learning their new skill?
But the Fireflies think this shows promise. If I can help, I will."

With gratitude to the Fireflies, Spirit quickly made his way
to the Castle to see things for himself. He would not delay.

Still tension grew within him. The Big Game would end today.

Where are They?

Spirit arrived at the Castle with hope and fear in tow.
What he thought he'd find there, he didn't really know
but he saw no joy in the throne room. Worry still filled the air.

What?

If the Prince was there in the throne room, Spirit wondered, where.

The Castle Guard stood alert at the doors. This time they were not asleep.
Queen Luna was still consumed by fear. She again began to weep.

Spirit grew impatient, filled with anxiety.
He looked around for Consciences. There were none that he could see.
And no sign of Prince Sol, either. Where in the heck was *he?*

Where are all these Consciences? They're needed now, right here
to help these Royals feel better, but all I see is fear.
The Fireflies said there were Consciences. When will they appear?

Patience had never been his strength, and today that fact was clear.

To be fair,
Spirit had no idea at all what was happening down below.
The Goodness Plan was under way, but of course he didn't know.

Bugs were building ladders to get up to the Castle floor
where King Sol was pacing back and forth as he'd often done before.
Scraps were climbing those ladders. They didn't want to wait.
"We are on our way," called Left and Right. They didn't hesitate.
The little Scrap men had been working out so they climbed at a rapid rate
on the ladder made of web and hair that led up from the grate.

Sol and the sisters followed. They squeezed tight through a groove
and hid behind a table leg, to determine their next move.

Sol and Moon left Daybreak and climbed to the table top.
While King Sol paced, Queen Luna sobbed as though she would never stop.

Sol watched Moon travel silently, moving with special care.
She crept to Luna's shoulder and nestled in her hair.
As Max Mouse had instructed, Moon took a position where
Sol's mother could hear what Moon said without seeing she was there.

"Don't cry, Queen," whispered gentle Moon. "Your dear son has been found.
He's *here* inside the Castle. He's home now, safe and sound.
And he's ready for the future. You have raised him well, you see.
He'll share his Goodness with all Mankind. This is his destiny."

The Queen's face suddenly lifted and she looked around the room.
Everything looked brighter, no longer filled with gloom.
Moon smiled down and waved at Sol who whispered back to Moon,
"You are going to be great at this! Here's my Father! See you soon."

Sol jumped to the King as he paced by. It was good to be there again.
He felt at home in his father's beard, where he'd ridden since he was ten.
But he couldn't just ride and listen the way he used to do.
"Hello, Father," he whispered quietly. I am back again with you."
King Sol stopped short in his pacing and froze for a second there.
Then a warm smile bloomed on his worried face, clear down to the tips of his hair.
He raised his hand gently to his ear and softly patted there.

The Queen was looking around the room. Moon spoke again with care
and whispered very softly so as not to raise alarm,
"I assured you that your son is safe, nearby and free from harm.
Now, he's with his father, although he can't be seen.
Just look at the smile on your husband's face and you'll see what I mean."

The good Queen looked at her husband and saw what she wanted to see.
King Sol was no longer frowning but grinning happily.
Queen Luna laughed like a young girl. She forgot about her grief
and rose to take her husband's hand and squeezed it in relief.
The pair just looked at each other. What each had heard was true.
The Queen glanced at King Sol's beard and saw there what she knew.

Prince Sol spoke to his father. "I am back with you once more.
I'm sorry that I frightened you when I seemed lost before.
I will tell you everything... I wish I could say more,
but the River People are headed here and they're fired up for war.

"They've been stirred to insurrection like you've never seen before.
I hope we can talk them out of this invasion that's arriving at our door.

"I want to try a new Plan that has not been tried before.
Because of you I have learned the skills that I want to try today.
You have taught me about People and to work in this special way.
I hope you'll try this with me. Please, Dad...what do you say?"

King Sol listened to his son who'd been gone for just one day.
He was relieved and thankful to hear his son speak this way
but what special plan did he have in mind? He must have more to say.
He listened very carefully to see what that might be.

"Your subjects are marching up the road. I'm hoping we can see
a way to calm them down some and do so peacefully.
I'm hoping for no bloodshed. I hope that you agree."

"This might be good," agreed King Sol. "to try the approach you say,
but I've never known the town folk to revolt in such a way."

King Sol thought of his options as he listened to his son.
If war could be avoided and a peaceful outcome won,
this was certainly worth a try but, how could this be done?

King Sol paced the throne room and thought for one more minute.
But he wasn't sure what Sol's plan would do so he wasn't completely in it.

"We'll work this out together," came his answer to his son.
"But I'll alert the Castle Guard if invasion is begun.
We'll protect your mother and Awake. The stakes are very high,
but I will try it your way first. We'll give your plan a try"

Spirit heard King Sol speaking. Who was he speaking to?
He surveyed the room from end to end, but he saw no one new.
Could it be a Conscience? He began to circle near.
Suddenly he heard a familiar voice, a tiny voice, but clear.
He hovered closer to the sound to hear what he could hear.

Sol continued to his dad. "First, you need to understand
that the two men that you trusted did not help you as you planned.
The town was stirred up by those two. The town has been misled
by these two liars, Grin and Brood and their tales of fear and dread.

"Our Awake seems to like them, though, so she might play a part
in changing these players from bad guys into players with a heart."

King Sol plunked down upon his throne. He needed time to think.
He heard folks closing the distance. They would be here in a wink.

Spirit breathed a grateful sigh. He was hearing Prince Sol he knew,
and the Prince spoke like a Conscience should. His Plan was coming true.

Spirit couldn't sit still. He continued to hover low.
Now he saw some other Scraps skittering to and fro.
Daybreak had the farthest to run. She raced to Awake in a flash.
Next, she climbed up on Awake's arm from her place at the window sash.

Daybreak whispered in Awake's ear, "I see that you care for Grin.
You have opened up your trust and let this Grin come in.
But don't forget your loyalty to the King and Queen and Sol.
They've treated you like family. They *must* be your first call.
The trust of love is sometimes blind, not seeing imperfection.
But loyalty does not change sides without a close inspection.

"Grin and Brood are not *all bad*, but they're acting badly now.
Just Stay loyal to the Royals and Sol. I will show you how."

"That was beautiful," Spirit sighed. "She's a Conscience without training and yet she knows what is right to say." But his joy began quickly waning.

The town folk were back at the Castle gate and displaying a terrible mood.
They were shouting Fighter's curses now in voices loud and crude.
And, cheering them from a distance, were the brothers, Grin and Brood.

"I hear Grin," Awake murmured, trying to be optimistic.
She hoped against hope that Grin would be good. (hopeful, not realistic.)
But she had listened to Daybreak whose Conscience voice rang true.
If it came to a choice between Grin and Prince Sol, she knew what she must do.

Awake didn't know Prince Sol was back. She thought Grin possibly knew where her beloved Sol was and he might tell her, too!

"Grin and Brood have returned at last! Maybe they've found Prince Sol!" She ran at once to the Castle doors to let them into the hall.

Prince Sol tugged on King Sol's beard. "No! That's not safe," he cried. "Grin and Brood can't be trusted at all. Don't let them come inside."

"Halt, child!" King Sol commanded. Awake stopped at the door.
Why was King Sol shouting at her? He had not done that before.

"Come back here, now, you reckless girl! Can't you see what's happening here? Your 'heroes' are not heroes at all. At last I see this clear."

Sol spoke again as a Conscience. "You just made Awake too sad.
Awake *thinks* Grin is her hero. She still hopes that he's not bad.
Awake is our friend who loves us. Don't yell because *you're* mad."

Sol whispered this like a Conscience. His father heard and reflected.
Now, what was his father going to say? It worked better than Sol expected.

"I'm sorry, Awake. This isn't your fault. It's not right that I blame you.
I'm sorry I yelled like a banshee. I know you're worried, too."

Awake looked at King Sol in confusion, unsure of what she should do.
Daybreak, Awake's little Conscience, sat unnoticed beside Awake's ear.
She whispered reassurance that only Awake could hear.
"You know that King Sol loves you. It's just that he's concerned.
It's time to await his direction with the trust your King has earned."

"You are right," Awake replied. "I'll hold off until we find
what Grin has to say about Prince Sol." Her words were soft and kind.
And Daybreak, from Awake's soft shoulder, smiled her shiniest smile.
She had helped Awake say the right thing, and she'd done it "Conscience Style".

Outside, the two brother Consciences went to work, focused on a Castle guard.
These guards now raced to the Castle gates from their posts in the Castle yard.
The two small Consciences, Left and Right, rode them to the stone wall's doors
and climbed to their human shoulders (which they'd never done before.)

Each Scrap found a position, an invisible place to hide.
A collar and a hat brim were the places that they tried.

The young guards came to attention beside the gate's huge doors.
The guards were a little bit nervous. They had never fought before.

The poor men looked at the other. They each had a stomachache.
An angry crowd was approaching. What direction should they take?

Their knees were knocking together. Must they protect their King?
They would have to fight their friends from town. Could they do such a thing?
Maybe it was time to run. Maybe they could just go...
Their King and Queen weren't watching. They would never know.

Left and Right, their Consciences, could feel the young men shaking.
They, too, could hear the angry mob, a riot in the making.

"Stay calm," said the Consciences to each guard. "You've seen these folk before.
Two guys just got them all riled up, but they're not bad to the core.
Be patient. Await your King's orders. He knows what he's about.
Until then, don't do anything. Stand your guard and let folks shout."

The guards relaxed and seemed content that their King would work
things out.

Left and Right looked at each other from the spots where they were lurking.
They grinned and shared a "thumbs up" sign. This 'Conscience Thing'
was working.

Spirit noticed and he was pleased as the Consciences did their best,
but soon the crowd would storm those gates. That would be a greater test.

The Big Game is On—or is it War?

Now the noise from the growing horde rose to a mighty din.
Town folk began beating on the gates, demanding to get in.

"Where's the King? Is he hidin'? Make 'im open this gate!"

"We're takin' over this Castle. We're not in the mood to wait."

"Come out, King Sol, where ever you are. We know that yer in there."

"Stop talkin' to yer invisible son. He's nothin' but thin air!"

"Grin and Brood will take yer place. They know just what to do."

"Grin and Brood can defend us. We can't depend on you."

What should I do? the King thought, (a thought heard by Prince Sol.)
The town is afraid of highwaymen. I don't blame them at all.
If there are highwaymen out there, my only course, of course is
to face those bandits fiercely by sending out my forces.

I shall martial my militia! I will drag them down like dogs,
where those highwaymen have been hiding, in forests, fields or bogs!"

"Do you really think there are highwaymen?" asked Prince Sol in King Sol's ear.
"Before Storytellers came to town, folks never had this fear.
The Storytellers were lying when they said they saved Awake.
She doesn't know yet, they were lying, but their rescue was a fake.
Your town folk have all been riled up by listening to those brothers.
Those two made up one highwayman, then invented many others."

King Sol thought about this carefully and at last he understood.
Outside he could hear both Grin and Brood, stirring folks up good.
They shouted out with gusto. "This King offers no protection
against hundreds of highwaymen out there! It's time for insurrection!"

"There aren't any highwaymen", whispered Prince Sol.
"Theirs has always been a lie. We must help your subjects learn the truth.
That's the plan I want to try."

"I should corral those con men." muttered King Sol. "I should clap them in the clink!"

"But the town folk won't understand that. They'll be angry, don't you think?"

King Sol responded to his son, whispering low and quiet.
"But, if I do nothing, Sol, my son, those rascals will cause a riot!

They'll continue to lie about highwaymen and continue corrupting the crowd."

Although King Sol didn't know it, he was speaking his thoughts out loud.

"Don't throw them in the dungeon, Sire!" Awake now stood up tall,
although she now heard both Grin and Brood in the crowd outside the wall.
"I hear them causing trouble now, not my heroes, after all.
I thought Grin was a good man, but now I understand
that they weren't trying to help us. I see now that they've planned
to turn the town against us. For that, they should meet their fate.
But there might still be *some* good in them. I beg you, Sire. Please wait.

"Don't throw them in your dungeon, at least not right away.
They *might* regret the harm they've done if they learn a better way."

Daybreak was speaking in her ear, although nobody knew it.
Maybe Awake could save her Grin. She had to try to do it.

Prince Sol could see a chance right now to change what was in store
and make a move that just might help to win a "Conscience War."

But, before Sol could say anything, the King smiled at Awake.
He took her little hands in his and gave them a gentle shake.

"You really like those brothers, don't you, my little friend?
They must have some hidden good in them for you to so defend.
But I can't ignore their evil scheme. Just look at what they are doing.
Because of them, I'm under siege. A real war might be brewing!"

Sol spoke up in his father's ear. "What if it's not too late"
What if we try a more peaceful way? Why not negotiate?
We know these men are liars. They started this whole fight,
but there are some other tactics that might make this work out right."

Now Sol jumped to his father's hand so he was in plain sight.
Awake saw Prince Sol for the first time and started jumping about.

"You're back! You're found! You're alive and well!" she began to dance shout.
"Where have you been, my dearest friend? I was worried half to death!"

Awake grabbed Sol and held him close. He could feel her warm, sweet breath.

"I have missed you, too, Awake. I've just been... 'away'.
And many things have happened in only one night and day.
I want to tell you everything, but now, don't think me rude,
but we have a crisis on our hands which was caused by Grin and Brood."

Awake held Sol up on the palm of her hand. "What do you want me to do?
Sol looked carefully at Awake. He could see her heart was true.

"Excuse us, Sire", interrupted the guards. "The crowd is at the wall!
Do you wish to call up the rest of the guard? Is it time for a battle call?

The River People are charging the gates! What would you have us do?
They're climbing up the Castle Wall, to come over around and through!
The town is going crazy. Their mission is pretty clear.
They're gonna storm the Castle! Our gates won't last, we fear!"

Insurrection- the Final Play

Sol now spoke to his father in a way that was 'man to man'.
"We must stop Grin and Brood right now, without violence, if we can.
The way the town is yelling, they are looking for somebody's head.
But Awake thinks the rogues are worth saving. I think that's what she said.

"Isn't that what you said, Awake?" Awake was turning red.

"So, if we can find their good side, perhaps no blood will be shed.
Let's just see if that is true. Do they have a better side?
Right now, I don't see it, but we won't know until we've tried."

Awake's smile was thin and anxious but she couldn't ask for more.
King Sol nodded bravely and strode across the floor.
The two guards followed King Sol's lead and grandly opened the door.

The King stood tall in the doorway, behind him, Awake and the Queen.
Sol slid in back of the King's left ear so that he could not be seen.

Storm clouds grew in the distance as if to make it known
that Fighter had come to supervise this rebellion that was his own.
Sharp winds were stabbing through the trees. It was very clear
that he'd come for a final battle. That's why he was here.

Thunder rolled over the hillsides as Fighter growled with bliss.
"I knew we would finally get here. The Big Game has come down to this:

*A King with a son who is nowhere and never did exist.

*A war between Good and Chaos, where Chaos just can't miss,

"I, Fighter, will win The Big Game today. There's no force here to resist."

Spirit slid forward in silence and invisibly took his place.
He was here to stand for the Goodness that Chaos could not erase
and Consciences that could win this Game as was planned so long ago,
But could this be their last battle? How a few Consciences know
what to do with all these humans? The crowd continued to grow.
There was nothing Spirit could do now. It was time to start the show.

Fighter took a stand as well, for this fight both old and new.
"Get on with it", Fighter hissed loudly as the blustery gaggle grew.
"Storm the Castle and kill the King! That's what you're here to do!"

The town folk barged toward the courtyard, but the King now took command.
(Grin and Brood hid outside the gate to enjoy what they had planned.)

King Sol calmly stepped forward and held up a warning hand.

"There are Storytellers among you," he declared in a kingly tone.
"I charge them now to come forward and speak with me on their own.
If they have a history with highwaymen, I demand that they tell their story,
without dropping one detail, no matter how gross or gory."

Grin and Brood fairly flew to the front. They were ready for more glory.
Brood began to tell the tale, but just as he started the story,
both brothers were grabbed by the Castle Guard, pre-ordered by their King!
This was so unexpected, the two couldn't do a thing.

(But while each guard was holding a man, the Consciences, Left and Right,
jumped from their guards to Brood and Grin and scooted out of sight.)

The Consciences started their pressure. They began their Conscience chatter.
Though Grin and Brood tried not to listen, it didn't seem to matter.
The Consciences asked them about 'faking' and 'pretending to be a hero'.

CONSCIENCES—AND THE LEGENDS OF THE BIG GAME

They asked about liars' stories where the *real truth* equaled a zero.
Prince Sol had told them of the problem and the chaos they had planned.
Could these two get the point across? Would these two understand?

Both boys were hearing something. What was going wrong?
The story the boys had told all day no longer sounded strong.

Hogwash! What a stupid thought! Why should we feel that way?
We are these People's heroes, and they have come to play,
no matter what we are hearing. Who cares what 'some voices' say?

"Hey! Listen up" yelled Brood to the King. "I thought you wanted to hear."

"Indeed, he does!" Awake chimed in. "Tell the truth to our King, Grin dear."

Grin started to tell his famous tale, but he suddenly heard in his ear,
"Just look at the trusting face of Awake. She's in love with you, that's clear."

Grin looked around to see who spoke. He could see no one.
Grin was hearing his Conscience and his Conscience was having fun
but the love that shone from Awake's sweet face was brighter than the sun.

Grin's Conscience spoke from his hiding place. "You can change now if you try.
Awake will be proud if you decide to be a better guy!"

Grin saw that Awake waited hopefully. She loved him. That was true.
He looked at the King standing strong and proud. What was he going to do?

"Tell the truth," his Conscience coached again. "Maybe it's not too late.
Awake loves you for a start right now, but she needs an honest mate.
You can't expect her love for you to ever grow much higher
if she finds out that the man she loves won't stop being liar."

For the first time, Grin could tell right from wrong.
Grin suddenly 'got it'. He would choose to be strong.
He would try what his Conscience suggested, instead of just going along.

"You can do it!" whispered Right to Grin. "You must do it for Awake.
You love her and she loves you. Tell the truth, for goodness sake!
You know that you've been rotten, but you have a better side.
Awake, with love, sees the Good in you, that you've always managed to hide.
You'll never know what the truth can do if the truth has not been tried."

Grin stood up and squared his back, then suddenly felt quite queasy.
(Telling the truth when you've always lied is anything but easy.)

"I regret to say, Your Highness--" Grin started out to say.
"I don't know how to say this--" He tried another way.

King Sol scowled down at the trembling Grin. "Say what you're going to say!"

"Hush, dear. Give the boy some time. Let him do this his own way,"
said Queen Luna with confidence. "He will say what he needs to say.
Why don't you go inside, Grin dear, and tell Awake what's true?

I believe there's *much* you must explain so she'll trust again in you.
And, though the truth will be hard to tell, you'll feel better when you do."

(Luna's Conscience, little Moon, was encouraging her this way.
Grin's Conscience, Right, now waved at Moon. Each Conscience had had
their say.)

Grin and Awake, now hand and hand, entered the Castle door.
Grin begged for forgiveness, on his knees on the Castle floor.
Grin's weight of lies began lifting. He had not felt this before.

Their Consciences sat back to watch. They could not ask for more.

Spirit watched the whole thing and knew he had a score.
Fighter swirled like a tornado. "What just happened here?
Grin was my stud player. This score cannot be fair!"

Fighter suspected Spirit. He stormed through the crowd to see
proof of what he was thinking. Where could Spirit be?
He knew Spirit must be somewhere, sabotaging *his* war,
(but he didn't suspect Scrap Consciences that he'd never seen before.)

A ray of sun peeked over a bush as if Spirit was there to say
that Goodness was stronger than Fighter thought and Goodness was here
to stay.

Fighter blew hard through the bushes as though trying to shred the sun
but the sun kept shining brighter. One small battle had been won.

"Prepare for doom, Spirit of Good!" A gale from Fighter blew,
increasing the town folks' anger, pushing them fro and to.
"Show yourself, you loser! I know that you are here,
even though, for years of *my* scoring, you've chosen to disappear.

"But you will *not* succeed today with the nonsense you have planned.
Go find some other Game to play that you might understand!"

Spirit winced and shook his head for he could not deny
that he'd been quiet for too long. This was not a lie.
But his sun kept shining brightly invading Fighter's sky
as Awake and Grin kept talking, trying to see eye to eye.

The Goodness Plan was coming alive. Spirit stretched to see
if other Consciences were here yet as he was sure they'd be.

Brood looked around the courtyard. Quite suddenly, he was alone.
He was now the crowd's only leader. He was panicked to the bone.
But the crowd was still ready for violence. His feet grew cold as stone.

He just couldn't believe it. His brother was wimping out
right when they were ready to score... but the town folk figured it out.
The crowd began to grumble and complain to one another.
"We had two brothers leading our fight. Now we've lost one brother."

"We see what the King is doing. He's divided up the pair."

"Divide and conquer, that's his game. He's not playing fair."

The People felt they'd been messed with. They were gathering for attack.
They wanted to storm the Castle. Their mood was raw and black.
But they wanted a leader that would lead, not fail and hold them back!

Fighter delivered an evil curse as his storm continued brewing.
"Brood! Stop your stalling and strike the King! Never mind what Grin is doing."

Brood stood forth in readiness. It wouldn't be the same
without his brother with him, but now he was back in the Game.

"Stand back!" crowed Brood, recovering. "Now, I know the score.
Grin is too love-sick to lead this fight. I should have known before.
Now *I* will make all the decisions with great power from my core!
I'll kill the King and take his throne!" Brood was ready for a score!

"Follow me, River People! *Watch me* lead the way!
The King will kneel before *me. I will be your King today!*

The crowd broke out in a lusty cheer! "The crazy King must go!"

"Let's storm the Castle and kill the King! Let's get on with the show!"

"If Grin can't kill the King," yelled Brood, "Step aside and let me do it.
Like the highwayman that attacked Awake, I'll dispatch him! Nothin' to it.
And I will be your King tonight!"

The crowd let out a cheer!
"Long live Brother, Brood!" they yelled. "He will keep our roadways clear!"

Fighter thundered with excitement. Things were back as he had planned.
Grin was down but Brood was up and he was in command.
Chaos was in charge again. New violence would appear!

But Left, the other Conscience, whispered softly in Brood's ear.
"Don't you wish the folks were cheering for something that wasn't a lie?
Look at the brave King standing there. He looks like an okay guy.
Does he deserve to be overthrown? Why not give the peace a try?

"And besides, how long is it going to take for Awake to realize
that *you* look like the highwayman? She will see it in your eyes.
Then everyone will see right through your very weak disguise."

"Who said that?" Brood hissed, half frightened. He looked this way and that.

"I did. I'm your Conscience, Left... I'm here, underneath your hat."

"What the heck is a Conscience? Take that, and that, and that!"
Brood took off his hat and shook it. Then he dropped it and stomped it flat.

That man just heard his Conscience speak, thought Spirit quietly.
Can this rogue be changed for the better? We'll have to wait and see.

Now more Castle Guard appeared, arriving by the score.
King Sol had already summoned them in case he needed more.
Their look was grim. They had spears and swords, a full-fledged fighting Corp.
The Guard stood shoulder to shoulder with axes and swords and more.

Brood looked up at King Sol, himself, as he stood strong at the door.
"This King is smarter that I thought. He has already taken a stand.
Whether the King has a son or not, he is definitely in command
and this plan I thought would be easy may not work out as planned."

"That's because you were always wrong!" His Conscience spoke out loud.
"You *know* there was never a highwayman, so why did you rile this crowd?
What has this King ever done to you? Has he harmed you in any way?
Why did you convince this gullible town to start a war today?
You don't really have a reason to cause this King such grief
so why not call a stop to this. It will bring you some relief.

"Try being truthful for a change. Now, that's a noble goal.
I've heard that 'true confession' does much good for the soul."

Brood heard his mouthy Conscience. He tried hard to decide
how to keep him quiet. His stomach churned inside.
"I can't give this whole thing up. I'm ready for the fight
but I must admit I'm not sure now just what is wrong or right."

Brood's Conscience had his work cut out but Left was smart and keen.
The Castle Guard inched forward and they were looking mean...
The town folk pushed from the other side. *Brood was in between.*

"You have no choice," said Left to Brood. "Do you see what I mean?
When you're left with mud on your face, it's best that you 'come clean'.
You have made this mess today. *You've* gone above and beyond.
Because of your lies, folks want a war, and there's no magic wand.
Because of your lies, this King may die, but so will Awake and Grin.
Because of your lies, *you may* die, too! Don't you want to save your skin?

"*And...* you haven't got the slightest clue what to do if you are King.
So this is the time to do what's right. You must stop this whole dang thing."

Brood hung his head. His shoulders drooped. His Conscience had finally won.
At last Brood understood his guilt. He knew what must be done.
With hat in hand he opened his mouth. A confession had now begun:

"I've told stories all my life," Brood told the King and crowd,
"without caring if they were true or not. 'Made-up' stories were allowed.
In fact, the more I made stories up, the more I drew a crowd.
"Grin and I 'invented' the highwaymen and acted them out as well.
We did such a good acting job that Awake couldn't even tell
what was something to be afraid of and maybe what was not.
We told lies about you, too, King Sol. It was an ingenious plot.

"We wanted to overthrow you and use town folk to do it!
And Grin and I might have done that, too, if you had not seen through it.
Grin and I are sorry. That's what I need to say.
We didn't know it would go this far. We just got carried away."

Brood knelt down in the courtyard, exhausted through and through.
(When you first confess what you've done wrong, it's pretty tough to do.)
Left whispered firmly in Brood's ear, "That was good. You should be proud."

But that was not the thought at all that was streaming through the crowd.

Brood's confession was unexpected. His words made Spirit smile.
He hadn't seen such humility in a very, long, long while.

The King looked down in wonder as Brood knelt on the ground.
Prince Sol cheered from his father's head. He was jumping up and down.
He was cheering for his Consciences as he swung from his father's crown.

"That was great! Did you see that, Dad? Brood's Conscience made him change
from a lying monster to a guy who wants to rearrange
this stupid fight into something good. I thought we were doomed to war,
but it looks like Consciences *can* change m inds. T hat's w hat t hey're needed for."

The King listened to Brood with dignity and an air of Royal reserve.
"Thank you, young man, for what you said. That confession took some nerve.
Rise up and let me give to you the credit you deserve.
A man who is willing, in public, to admit when he is wrong
is of value to us all. Such actions make one strong."

Now the King smiled at Prince Sol.
"But, tell me my son, what's 'a Conscience'? Is that a special trick
that you have learned from reading books? You must teach this to me quick!"

Prince Sol knew he needed to explain this phenomenon to his dad,
but this was not the time or place. Things could still go bad.
Prince Sol searched the horizon. He began to tense with worry.
Would the rest of his Conscience Army arrive? He prayed that they would hurry.

For a moment the crowd stayed quiet. For the moment they were in shock.
But they started thinking things over and they began taking stock
of the fact that they had been lied to and made to look like fools.
Soon their shock would turn to anger and that anger might have no rules.

Prince Sol was anxious to preserve this fragile, peaceful state.
The rest of his Plan was a good one, but would it begin too late?
More Consciences should be coming, but all Sol could do was wait.

"What on earth just happened?" Fighter howled in frustrated rage.
"Brood was another star player. Now he sings like a bird in a cage
with tweets of junk and gibberish that keep falling from his mouth.
This Game was ready to be won. Now the whole thing's going South!
Come on, People! Do your thing! I know you want to fight!
You didn't come here for nothing! We're out for war tonight!"

At first the crowd just milled about. Then they began to roar.
They were growing twice as angry as they had been before.

They turned on Brood as he knelt there. They were swarming, snarling, fuming!
They had been tricked and lied to. Their fury was resuming.

"How dare you two make fools of us!"

"Let me beat you with my fist!"

"Let me whack you into a bloody pulp!"

"Let me sock you! I insist!"

"You and your brother should be hung high and left in the wind to twist!"

The crowd surged toward Brood in a violent mass. "Let's hang him from the gate!"
They pulled Brood up and slammed him down, as though he had no weight. They tugged and yanked at his arms and legs. They screamed and pulled his hair.
Brood covered his head and rolled up in a ball, a picture of despair.

The crowd appeared to be out for blood, even more than they were before.

They stormed over the walls toward the Castle! *Again*, they were ready for war!
"Right on!" shouted Fighter. "This is what I've been waiting for!"

Prince Sol looked out at the turmoil that Brood's confession had brought.
The crowd was ready to kill Brood though he struggled and squirmed and fought.

I can't let that happen, the new 'Conscience King' now thought.
The People are ready for vengeance. Brood groaned and began to cry.
Brood deserves to be punished, but he doesn't deserve to die.

Sol scrambled from his father's ear and charged into the crowd.
He was meant to be a Conscience! He must be one, strong and proud!

Sol couldn't wait for the others. He leapt out, bold and spry,
onto the head of the biggest man with a loud and determined cry!
"I must do my job, now, Father! At least I have to try!"

Down to the big man's shoulder Sol scurried without fear.
Bravely, he scrambled to his neck, coming close to his giant ear.

"Why are you beating on this man? All he did was tell a lie.
Haven't *you* ever lied before? Do you think that he should die?
Just forgive him for being stupid. That might be worth a try."

Sol jumped to the head of another man with swift and invisible skill.
"*You* believed what the brothers told you. Why are you ready to kill?
Give Brood a chance to do better. There is a small chance that he will,
and, if you die in the battle to come, there will be *big shoes to fill.*"

"Please," begged Brood. "Don't kill me! Give me a chance to change!"
What happened next was sudden. You might even call it strange.

Doomsday Begins

Spirit watched in horror. The Royals were fearful. too.
They had no way of predicting what this angry mob would do.
The crowd had been pushed to its limit. Real thinking now was through.

And where was Prince Sol? Was he alright? No one had seen him since
he had jumped into this angry crowd! Where was the little Prince?
The crowd kept surging forward. Many had breached the wall.
The Castle Guard drew their weapons, awaiting their battle call.

Prince Sol jumped from man to man, trying to tell each one
to give poor Brood another chance to undo what he had done.
If the other Consciences didn't come, Sol would have to do his best
alone to change the People's minds...This might be his last test...

Spirit couldn't see him... Spirit expected the worst!
Fearing the surging violence, he felt all Goodness cursed.
He shot through the crowds like an arrow. He searched from above the gate.
He had to rescue his little Prince! Would he be too late?

"Prince Sol can't fight this fight alone! Winning the Game can wait!
The boy is brave but outnumbered! He will meet a deadly fate!
And I don't know what *I* can do to change this tragic scene.
Once again, he thought of the Fireflies. Maybe *they* could intervene.

"But what if they don't arrive in time to stop this mass assault.
Prince Sol may meet his doom today and it will be my fault.
I should have prepared him better. I should have stayed by his side."
Spirit of Good spun into the clouds with self-doubt his only guide.

Fighter saw Spirit sail away. He sneered with satisfaction.
"I guess he knows it's over. This crowd is out for action.
People have always loved to fight. They don't need a reason.
They've made my victory easy. Now it's killing season.

Soon the Castle Royals will die. The earth will be mine to take.
And I will control the universe... Chaos for Chaos' sake!"

The world *was* headed for doomsday. The last surge had begun.
Chaos was at the goal line! The Big Game would soon be won!
The thrill of final victory now swelled inside of Fighter.
He could hardly wait to watch blood flow... deeper, redder, brighter!

The Goal Line Stand

- recorded on site by Max Mouse

Suddenly the town folk stopped, like trees rooted to the ground.
They cocked their heads as though listening to an unfamiliar sound.
They looked around and halted. They were hearing something new
in the uproar of their battle. They stopped what they planned to do.

They shook their fists and hollered, still angry and frustrated
but then their anger seemed to fade. They stopped, and thought, and waited.

Folks began to look uneasy with the fury they had cast
on the King and the Storytellers. Now a change came very fast.

They dropped poor Brood flat on the ground and he slowly crept away.
They asked, "Do you hear something?" A change was under way.

Spirit glanced back and saw a sight he had not expected to see.
The crowd he had last seen charging the gates, froze unexpectedly,
lowered their shovels and axes and started milling around,
looking from side to side as though hearing some sort of sound.

Spirit sailed back to the Castle. Though he couldn't identify
for sure just what had caused this change, he hoped he might know why.
Slowly he circled the battle field from his overview in the sky.

As Spirit observed the People below, he perceived a different feeling.
Instead of the anger he'd seen before, each human face was revealing
what looked like thoughtful wonder, some questioning, some just staring.
They seemed to be looking for reasons for the fury they'd been sharing.

Something seemed to be happening in each River Person's heart.
There was not, as yet, a complete change in folks, but more of a fragile start.
They couldn't know what they were hearing. Only Prince Sol could tell.
The 'Conscience Army' had arrived! ...Could it really work this well?

Could little beings just like him change how People act?
The Scrap Queen, his own Scrap mother, had believed this was a fact.
She had dreamed that this was Scrap destiny, what Scraps were meant to do.
She knew Scraps were meant to be Consciences. Could her dream be
coming true?

This could be their true destiny... a destiny so sweet...
Now they were working *with* People...no longer "under their feet."

Prince Sol couldn't believe it. Scraps were acting out his Plan.
He hadn't known if it would work until the Plan began.

The arriving Scraps had seen Prince Sol and watched what he tried to do.
Now they were following his lead and they were doing it, too.

Scrap Consciences were speaking to People. Scrap Consciences were the clue
that was causing folks to think twice about what they were trying do.
Special Clay was doing its job as it was meant to do.
But what would happen to Scraps, themselves? Right now, no one knew.

Each Scrap picked a person and whispered in that one's ear
the words of truth about today that each thought they should hear.
Scraps talked to their folks and told them what came into each Scrap's mind.
The words they spoke were not magic, but a very simple kind.

Such as:
"Sure, Grin and Brood were telling lies but you all went along."

"You loved their lies. You ate 'em up, so you were just as wrong!"

"You loved the stories, didn't you? Loved tales told to deceive."

"You lost your faith in your own, good King, chose liars to believe."

"Maybe you should stop and think before you beat these guys.
Just who was right and wrong here? Try that thought on for size."

Now folks backed off and let Brood up. This was not an expected thing.
They decided that they should do this, but why was this happening?

People asked each other and themselves, "What are we fighting for?"
They were not nearly as angry as they had been before.

Scrap Consciences kept on talking. Scrap Consciences were brave.
This job was very new to them. How should they behave?
They perched on People's shoulders as they had watched Sol do.
But what about their Special Clay?

...There was magic no one knew.
The Special Clay of each Conscience soon drifted down inside
the hearts of each of their People as its thoughtfulness was applied.
From the Clay inside each person, a Scrap arose, unbidden,
to deliver the thoughts of their Special Clay from the hearts where it lay hidden.

The People looked at their neighbors. Their eyes now opened wide.
They saw their world in a kinder way that they had never tried.
They looked again at King Sol as he stood tall and proud,
the guardian of his Castle against a warring crowd.

"What has the King done to deserve this? "Why did we want to fight?"

"Why does this battle we wanted before, now not seem quite right?"

Consciences—and the Legends of The Big Game

Scraps reasoned some more with the town folk. They began to talk of peace.
The People smiled and nodded, feeling a strange release.
This was part of Prince Sol's Plan, the Plan he had requested.

Whether Scraps would stay on as 'Consciences' was truly being tested.

Town folk began to mill about. What should they do next?
Their anger had totally faded. Coach Fighter was perplexed.

No...
more than perplexed, he was furious! What had happened here?
His Scoring Drive was stopped dead. There was nothing left to cheer.
The Game was in final seconds. All violence had stalled out.
With an Arctic blast down the sidelines, Fighter stalked about.

He slammed the land with stinging blasts meant to topple and destroy.
Some 'thing' in these final seconds was canceling his joy.

He roared against People's axes and shoved against each shield,
hurling their weapons into the mud and soaking the battle field.

But, although rain lashed the faces of each person in the troop,
the energy for blood and gore seemed to have left the group.

Fighter coached his team with fury but folks just held their ground
in favor of new more thoughtful thoughts (though their source could not
be found.)

Fighter tried taunts and ridicule. These had always worked before,
but the People sighed and shook their heads. Their anger was no more.

Brood was brushing off some dirt. He looked around to see
if he was still going to be beaten. Maybe this was time to flee.
But no one was paying attention. He decided then that he
had been right, indeed, to confess his deeds. Left agreed, silently.

Spirit sighed in deep relief. At last he finally knew
his People were listening to their hearts as he hoped they would do.
The Special Clay that he had dropped was now back in its place
to deliver thoughts of right and wrong to all his human race.

Prince Sol hopped from head to head of the town folk huddled around.
He looked for his Scraps with each person and was most proud when he found
they were still there with each person, where only Sol could see,
tiny folks speaking as Consciences, 'on the job' as they wanted to be.

Scraps seemed to know now naturally what they'd only guessed before.
Their future was to be Consciences for these folks...and many more.
Their new home was the hearts of Man, there snuggled deep inside
and ready to deliver thoughts of truth, with Special Clay their guide.

Scraps were now the messengers of the Goodness of the Clay,
free to come and go at will. But attentive in every way
to every choice that Man would make, each meaningful decision.
They would now help humans willingly. This was now their mission.

The Handshake

Then somebody started to chuckle. "I guess things ain't that bad."
People turned and asked each other. "So why were we so mad?"

"Yeah, them boys didn't really hurt nothin'." "They jest stirred us up a bit."

"Yep. They jest got us excited. Then *we* all throwed a fit."

"*We're* the ones that believed 'em. King Sol has been pretty good."

"Us River People, should be ashamed more than Storytellers should."

Slowly the People came forward, shuffling and bowing their heads,
showing the King they regretted what they had done and said.

Prince Sol skittered back toward the Castle, to relieve his parent's dread.
In a manner borne of inborn skill, he jumped from head to head,
landing on his father, where he very simply said,
"It looks like the battle is through for today. The People seem happier now.
They no longer believe the stories that started this crazy row.

They've listened to their Consciences so they're much smarter now.

"I think they would like forgiveness for the riot that they planned.
Just listen to what they say to you. I think you'll understand."

More town folk began to get verbal and spoke up without fear,
consulting with each other, about what their King should hear.

A spokesman now edged forward, urged by those behind.
"We're really sorry, Majesty. We've all been dumb and blind.
We took the word of them strangers before we talked to you.
We've got no explanation fer what we tried to do.
We should 'a knowed, if we asked ya, that you'd take care of us all
but we've thought it over more now and we're sorry, Good King Sol."

"We should never have done what we done. We all just went along
and joined the fight without thinking first. We know now that was wrong."

The spokesman hesitated and, in a way unplanned,
he smiled a sheepish little smile and held out a timid hand.

King Sol took the hand and shook it. Though he didn't understand, he smiled and nodded at the man as though he understood.
The man smiled more and tipped his hat. Was this something good?
"Do you know why that man is shaking your hand?" Luna whispered in Sol's ear.
"I'm not sure," King Sol whispered, "His motive isn't clear."

"Maybe his Conscience suggested it," said Prince Sol with a smile.
"Scraps seem to be friendly and helpful. That is just their style.
I think the People are sorry. They regret what they have done."
"I hear what you say," King Sol replied. "But what is a 'Conscience,' son?"

"They're just Scraps who speak up for Goodness when they talk to anyone."

"Okay, I hear what you say. Please, tell me more. Perhaps,
if Consciences are only Scraps, then, what in the heck are 'Scraps'?"

"They're little people just like me who scattered today in the crowd,
speaking softly of peace to humans, though they never speak out loud.
Scrap Consciences have a mission, to explain what's wrong and right
whenever folks get confused or mad... or want to pick a fight.
Scraps can't solve every problem. That, I'm sure is true,
but with messages from their Special Clay, that's what they'll try to do.

"Every fight will not be fixed because Consciences are near,
but they can help folks think better. That seems pretty clear.
When Consciences speak, their Special Clay instructs from within their heart
to help humans learn about Goodness as intended from the start.

"The goal is 'better humans' and a world with much less war
in exchange for thoughtful Goodness. That's what Consciences are for."

King Sol shook his head a bit and tried to look quite wise.
All he heard was new and strange and such a big surprise.
His son was still his son, that's true, but the change in him was large.
Yesterday, he was a tiny man. Today, he was "in charge".

The King smiled and forgave his people. "Everyone makes mistakes.
We must try to learn from all of them. Forgiveness is what it takes.
Isn't that what you say, Son? I think my son is right.
That's something that I've tried today, and it helped to avoid a fight."

The town folk looked at each other and smiled as if to say,
"We know our King is still crazy, but crazy in just one way."

"He's still talkin' to his son, a son that isn't here.
But now that don't matter none to us 'cause he don't know no fear
and we're all well protected by him. That fact's pretty clear."

And so they wandered off toward town. It was time to disappear
and their Consciences went with them. They always would be near.

Yes, the Consciences stayed with their humans. Hearts had now been mended.
Special Clay was back in their hearts as Spirit first intended.

That had always been Scraps' mission, where they were meant to be
...as Consciences, living in human hearts for all eternity.

Now Goodness survives in the universe. Now Goodness can be defended.
The Big Game was won by Spirit. That's the way The Big Game ended.

The earth is Spirit's trophy. He cherishes it still today,
displayed in its place of honor...as the 'star' of the milky way.

Was The Big Game worth the trouble and thousands of years of strife?
Of course! We got our Consciences. Now our Big Game is *life*.

- respectfully recorded by Maximilian Mouse

www.ingramcontent.com/pod-product-compliance
Lightning Source LLC
LaVergne TN
LVHW091657070526
838199LV00050B/2184